Remember This

A Family in America

D. E. Mungello

Hamilton Books

An Imprint of
Rowman & Littlefield
Lanham • Boulder • New York • Toronto • Plymouth, UK

Copyright © 2016 by Hamilton Books
4501 Forbes Boulevard, Suite 200, Lanham, Maryland 20706
Hamilton Books Acquisitions Department (301) 459-3366

Unit A, Whitacre Mews, 26-34 Stannary Street,
London SE11 4AB, United Kingdom

Library of Congress Control Number: 2016932466
ISBN: 978-0-7618-6745-6 (pbk : alk. paper)—ISBN: 978-0-7618-6746-3 (electronic)

Cover image: Napoli (Naples) and Vesuvio (Mount Vesuvius), Italy. Between ca. 1890 and ca. 1900. Detroit Publishing Company, 1905. Library of Congress Prints and Photographs Division, Washington, DC.

∞™ The paper used in this publication meets the minimum requirements of American National Standard for Information Sciences Permanence of Paper for Printed Library Materials, ANSI/NISO Z39.48-1992.

In memory of my aunt

Jeanette (née Mungello) Boake (1919–2006)

Twenty images can be found in a photospread following page 118.

Contents

Acknowledgments

The one person to whom I am most deeply indebted in writing this book is my late aunt, Jeanette (née Mungello; pronounced with a soft "g" as in Munjello) Boake (originally Bocchicchio) (1919–2006). In countless replies to my queries, she responded with endless patience, enthusiasm, and packages of homemade biscotti. As the last remaining sibling of six children, she was my main living link to the past. Although some of her dates and locations were faulty, most of her testimony about the past was repeatedly confirmed.

Additional information about my family was provided by my brother, Mark Donald Mungello, Esq., and by my cousins Cheryl (née Boake) Bidlack (1944–2010), Beverly (née Burns) Portillo, Donna Marianna Punaro, and Claudia (née Boake) Stough. However, I eventually realized that several of my cousins were at times reluctant sources. Crucial information about the murder of my granduncle Filippo Russo was provided by my second cousin Karen Panella and her nephew, Michael De Riso, Esq.

Gina Filipponi, Jeannette (née Capozolli) Matesic, and Theresa Anzlovar provided me with information about our family's home town of Slovan. Mary E. Westlake of the Fort Vance Historical Society helped me to find information about Burgettstown. John Michael Gabrielli kindly shared a copy of his Princeton University undergraduate thesis on Burgettstown. Steven Russo kindly responded to my queries about various sites I refer to in Pittsburgh. Dr. Marina Miranda of Rome helped me with information about dialectal expressions in the Neapolitan dialect. Information about my wife's family was provided by my late father-in-law R. H. McKegg. My second cousin Lothar Böttger of Lübeck, Germany, provided copies of numerous family letters and documents in German dating from around 1900. In addition, he transcribed several letters, which made the task of translating them much easier.

For information about Carl Wittman and his relationship to Students for a Democratic Society (SDS), I am deeply indebted to Helen Garvy. Although she disagrees with some of my interpretations, her information about Wittman's years in SDS and ERAP was invaluable. When I began gathering information on Wittman in 2001, I first corresponded by mail and then through telephone interviews. I attempted to follow up telephone interviews by sending a synopsis of the call to the person being interviewed in order to check for accuracy, eventually switching to email.

I obtained additional information about Wittman through telephone interviews with Amy Beller, Corinna Fales, Oliver Fein, M.D., David Gelber, Jill Hamberg, Michael Lesser, Frank Nelson, Charlotte Phillips, M.D., Walter Popper, Allan Troxler, Marya Warshaw, and Elaine B. Weiss. I am grateful for the correspondence and email exchanges with Paul Booth, Jeremy Brecher, Marsha Emerman, Prof. Todd Gitlin, William Hartzog, Tom Hayden, C. Clark Kissinger, Gerry Tenney, and Cathlyn (Cathy) Wilkerson.

Photographs were kindly contributed by Prof. Paul Bailey, Jason Bishop, Marsha Emerman, Gina Filipponi, Jeffrey Howard, Carol Karasik, Karen Panella, and Elaine B. Weiss. In addition, Ms. Weiss supplied me with a tape of Carl Wittman made by her sister, Marsha Emerman. Additional information was contributed by Dr. Jocelyn M. N. Marinescu. Ian K. Lekus, who was completing a doctorate in queer history at Duke University, was very generous in sharing his knowledge and support. I am grateful to the author Felice Picano who read the manuscript and offered helpful suggestions for improving it. I am grateful to Lynn Weber for her professional services in copyediting the manuscript. I am grateful to the editors of Hamilton Books for their assistance in producing this book. Excerpts from this work have appeared in *VIA (Voices in Italian Americana)* and *The Gay and Lesbian Review Worldwide*.

As a historian who has gone through the process of doing research for several books, I have learned that living people are the most difficult witnesses of the past. While the accounts of the dead are frozen in the past, the accounts of the living are often defensive in an ongoing way. Typically, we invest ourselves in the past and it becomes part of our personal narrative, even part of our psyche. Inevitably different people have conflicting views of the past, and my task as a historian has been to integrate these individual narratives into a meaningful master narrative.

Not everyone believed that this book was a good idea. A number of people either did not respond to my queries or declined to help. Wittman's sister Jane Van De Bogart answered only a few questions and then stopped communication because she was opposed to me publishing a book that dealt with her brother. She feared my book would hurt Wittman's last partner,

Allan Troxler. Mr. Troxler himself had reservations about the kind of book I was writing about his long-time partner, and he too limited his contributions. I regret not having been able to contact Wittman's former wife, Miriam Feingold (now Real), who declined through an intermediary to speak with me. Even now, forty-six years after their break-up, I am struck by the pain she must have endured. I believe she has an important perspective and I have tried to portray it.

When my sister Marianne (née Mungello) Rohrer learned that I was writing about her marriage and her murder trial, she broke off all contact, not only with me but with anyone connected to me. In so doing, she perpetuates a well-known Mungello family trait. I am dead to her. Each of us has our own narrative of the past. In writing this book I have learned how upset some people become when they cannot control the narrative. Who owns the past? We all do, but as the past recedes, our personal ownership of it diminishes. In this book, I have tried to convey both the fascination and the regret we feel for what has gone by.

Prologue

This is the story of my Italian family and its turbulent struggles in America. Some of us attained success while others acquired notoriety. Most of us were obscure and few of us were saintly. It is a story of the people we befriended, loved, hated, and banished from our lives. It is a drama of our dreams and animosities and affections.

There is a tradition in my family of resolving disputes by breaking off all contact with the other person with the words "he [or she] is dead to me." The intensity of the break lasts until death. This is a practice shared by many Italians. But while some destroy bridges of contact between family members, others struggle to maintain them by continuing to talk to both sides. This can create awkward situations and raise questions of loyalty. Nevertheless, it is the way we have lived and continue to live. Some of this seems to be passed down through the blood rather than learned.

For my family, it's through our loves and our feuds that we have most deeply defined ourselves. Some members of my family would prefer that these stories be kept secret. In their minds, revealing these stories is a betrayal of family loyalty. The Italian term for this silence is *omertà*, which is famously applied to the oath of silence demanded of Italian gang members. But it also applies to family secrets, and because, in the eyes of some members of my family, I have violated this code of secrecy, I am dead to them.

Why did I do this? To me the reason is simple: The story of my family is so beautiful and disturbing that I must tell it. Mine is a family in which the women are more striking than the men. They are passionate in a way that makes even their tragedies beautiful. I am their storyteller. I tell their stories and how they are intertwined with my story. The Italian word for history—*storia*—fits perfectly.

The mob and murder and spaghetti marinara are all part of the Italian-American fantasy. They are striking images, but only skin deep. For me, the reality is deeper. For me, deeper means the lies that my great-uncle told (before he was killed in a gang murder), the lies that my father told, that I continue to tell, and that my son never stops telling. It is as though lying runs in our blood, and maybe it does. The women in my family are more like intense songs than beautiful flowers. Their passionate bonds to lovers, husbands, and children are so powerful that they threatened to destroy them. We have passed these lies and passions on from generation to generation like family heirlooms.

The people we hate the most are those we loved the most and who we feel have betrayed us. My aunts Mae, Helen, Jeanette, and Evelyn shunned my Aunt Jessie. My cousin Cheryl shunned everyone in the family until just before she suffered an early death from cancer. Her parents, my Uncle Lou and Aunt Jeanette, shunned her. My cousin Bert shuns much of the family. My cousins Beverly and Jim shun their brother Bill, and Bill shuns them. My Uncle Tony shunned my father. His son, Anthony, shuns my father's children. My sister Marianne shuns me.

We are part of a pattern as old as our Italian ancestors and their surroundings. Twelve miles south of our ancestral village, Mount Vesuvius rises in majestic splendor. For my family (and for me), Vesuvius is a metaphor for the explosive and destructive behavior that runs through my family. In our women, the passion is physical and emotional. In our men, it is sexual and labor intensive. Loyalty is the greatest virtue and disloyalty is the greatest sin. These traits have been the driving force in my family, and in me. Like Vesuvius, the passions and hatreds lie smoldering just below the surface until they suddenly erupt, causing damage that almost destroys us. I share these traits with my family, and that is why my story and the story of my family are inseparable.

Chapter One

Uncle Filippo's Murder, 1919

For many families from southern Italy, organized crime was a reality that followed us to America like a shadow. And many of us, like my family, had to struggle for years to shake it loose. The most prominent of the gangs were the *camorristi* of the Neapolitan Camorra, the *mafiosi* of the Sicilian Mafia, and the *picciotti* (pronounced pee-*chaw*-tee) of the Calabrian 'Ndrangheta (pronounced an-*drang*-het-a). These secret brotherhoods fabricated their respective mythologies and created initiation rituals. According to one fanciful myth, the three brotherhoods were founded by three Spanish knights named Osso, Mastrosso, and Carcagnosso who fled to Italy after an honor killing in which they avenged the rape of their sister.[1] Each brother chose a patron saint and founded a society of honor: Osso with Saint George as his sponsor founded the Mafia in Sicily, Mastrosso with the Madonna as his sponsor founded the Camorra in Naples, and Carcagnosso with the Archangel Michael as his sponsor founded the 'Ndrangheta in Calabria.

The reality is less inspiring than the mythology. These brotherhoods were not founded until the unification of Italy in 1860. The arrival of Giuseppe Garibaldi at Sicily in May with his thousand red-shirted northern Italians was the precipitating event. As Garibaldi moved from Sicily to the Italian mainland, the criminal *camorristi* joined the Italian patriots in the streets of Naples to oust the Bourbon monarch, King Francesco II of the Kingdom of the Two Sicilies. The king abdicated in June of 1860, and the *camorristi* became partners with the new Italian government in ruling the Campania region around Naples.[2] It is a partnership that has plagued Naples to this day.

This Neapolitan brotherhood of criminals, which referred to itself formally as the Honored Society, borrowed many of its rules and rituals from the Freemasons.[3] However the rules were flexible in application. They excluded any man whose sister or wife was a prostitute or any man who was a pene-

1

trated or passive homosexual partner (*arruso* or *ricchione*). Knives played an important role in the Camorra. Initiates had to swear an oath over crossed knives and fight a dagger duel with another *camorrista* chosen by lot.[4] *Camorristi* were quick to use their knives to slash faces as a form of punishment. Consequently, the *sfregio* (facial scar) became a unique sign of Camorra power, even on the faces of prostitutes for whom they pimped. My Italian grandfather told his children that their mother's sister had cheated on her boyfriend and had her face scarred with a knife.[5]

The crystalizing event for the decline of the original Camorra was the murder of Gennaro Cuocolo and his wife Maria Cutinelli on June 6, 1906.[6] When the *camorrista* Gennaro Abbatemaggio broke the code of *omertà* on the witness stand, revealing gang secrets, a murder trial was expanded into an attack on the whole Camorra. The leading *camorrista* under indictment in the trial was Enrico Alfano, known by his nickname of Erricone (Big 'Enry) and the last boss of the Honored Society in Naples. The trial began in March 1911 in the small city of Viterbo, a city far to the north chosen to obtain a more neutral jury.[7] Over the course of sixteen months, 779 witnesses testified and brought worldwide attention to the Camorra. The accused *camorristi* were found guilty and sent to jail, even though the star witness, Abbatemaggio, later recanted his testimony in 1927. During the course of his testimony, Erricone told the jury: "We are Neapolitans. We are sons of Vesuvius. There is a strange violent tendency in our blood that comes from the climate."[8] This tendency is present in the emotional temperament of my family even though, unlike the *camorristi*, we have rarely used weapons or killed people.

The Honored Society went into steep decline after this trial, but it revived after 1945, during the post-World War II years, as in 1860, when the mob collaborated with the politicians of Italy.[9] The Camorra was revived in the form of separate gangs that formed unstable alliances. These alliances were subject to repeated bloody feuds. The Camorra was more violent than the Mafia or 'Ndrangheta, and most *camorristi* of the higher ranks were murdered by the time they reached middle age.

We can see what our emigrating ancestors left when we look back at the Campania region around Naples today. There are now five times as many *camorristi* as *mafiosi*.[10] The Camorra's network extends from the drug trade into high fashion, from construction to toxic waste disposal. The international distribution and sales of fake couturier brand name clothing has become as profitable as selling drugs. Gang wars have given the city's surrounding province of Campania the highest murder rate in Europe. Between 1979 and 2005, 3,600 people died in gang-related conflicts. For nearly two centuries, Neapolitans have fled their home region, but the gangs were not so easy to leave behind.

There is a famous scene in both the novel and movie *The Godfather* where Michael Corleone comes out of the men's room in a Bronx restaurant with a gun and kills a rival gang leader and a corrupt police captain.[11] He flees for his life, finding temporary refuge in his ancestral homeland in Sicily. This scene has always struck a chord with me because of my own family history. In 1914 my grandfather Raffaele Mungiello fled because of threats from the Black Hand in Pittsburgh. He eventually escaped with his family to build a new life in a small town outside of Pittsburgh. My granduncle Filippo Russo was not so fortunate.

Filippo Russo (1889–1919) was the youngest brother of my grandmother. He had arrived in America on February 11, 1909, at nineteen years of age. The ship's manifest listed him as illiterate and recorded his occupation as "tailor."[12] Two years after arriving in America he married Maria Maietta (1890–1978), a girl from his hometown of Roccarainola, just north of Naples. Maria had been traumatized by the 1906 eruption of Vesuvius when she was just sixteen years old. She had been so terrified by the explosion of thunder and cinders that she ran hysterically until her father pulled her to the ground. Her terror of living in the shadow of Vesuvius remained and unlike her two sisters, she agreed to emigrate to America and marry Filippo. She escaped the violence of the volcano, but she could not escape the violence that was in her husband.

In southern Italian culture at that time a betrothal involved a formal commitment that severely restricted a woman's contact with members of the opposite sex. Inappropriate behavior could lead to a cancellation of the betrothal agreement, but such behavior rarely occurred.[13] Maria's betrothal ceremony took place in August of 1911 in Roccarainola with her father standing in for Filippo, who was already in the US. The date "8/11" was inscribed into her wedding ring.

Maria was five feet, four inches tall with a fair complexion, black hair and chestnut eyes. She sailed from Naples and arrived at Ellis Island in November of 1911. Ellis Island tended to be a traumatic experience for unmarried women traveling on their own. Immigration inspectors subjected them to additional scrutiny in order to prevent the entry of women who might become dependent upon welfare services or become prostitutes.[14] Women lacking the calluses from hard labor on their hands were particularly suspect and were detained at Ellis Island until the authenticity of their sponsors was checked. Filippo himself probably met Maria in New York and together they made the onward journey by train 300 miles west to Pittsburgh, Pennsylvania. He established a tailor shop at 634 Corey Avenue in Braddock where Maria joined him as a wife and seamstress. Early in 1919 he moved his shop to 801 South Evans Avenue, next to the No. 3 fire station, in nearby East McKeesport.

By 1919, the couple had moved to nearby East McKeesport and he and Maria lived on the second floor, above the shop with their four children. He was thirty years old when the phone rang on the night of his murder. Shortly after 8:00 p.m. on Thursday evening, December 4, 1919, Filippo received a phone call at his apartment above his shop.[15] The call was brief, but after hanging up, Filippo put a revolver in his pocket and told Maria that he had to go out. Maria worried because Filippo rarely went out at night and he hadn't told her what it was about. He left their apartment almost immediately.

At around midnight Filippo bought five gallons of gasoline at the garage at Fifth Avenue and Huey Street where he kept his 1914 model Overland.[16] While driving along the streetcar tracks from East McKeesport to Wilmerding, two or more men intercepted his car. Perhaps one climbed on the running board and another got into the car. As they approached a steep ravine along the road leading from East McKeesport to Wilmerding, they fired eight bullets into his body. (Residents nearby heard ten shots fired at 12:40 a.m.) They fired the 38-calibre bullets from two different guns at a range close enough to blacken one of his ears. Five of the bullets entered Filippo's head, two passed through his heart, and one entered his shoulder. Then the killers pushed his car off the road and over a ledge. His body fell out half-way down the 350-foot ravine and smashed against the rocks on the hillside while the car crashed to the bottom.

Around 8:00 the next morning a railroad worker crossing the South Wilmerding Bridge saw the body.[17] It was frozen and covered with a light dusting of snow. Filippo's bullet-ridden hat was found at the top of the ravine. When he had not returned to their apartment by morning, Maria had become frightened and called the police. After hearing that a man had been murdered, she sent two male friends to the morgue and they identified the body. His revolver, his watch, and his money were still in his pockets.

Police authorities believed that Filippo was killed by "agents of the Black Hand."[18] The Black Hand (*La Mano Nera*) was the collective term for Italian immigrants who practiced extortion using intimidating symbols like a black hand as a warning. It was not an organized criminal brotherhood but rather consisted of individuals, young thugs who preyed on their fellow Italian-Americans in large American cities between 1890 and 1920.[19] Their method of extortion became well known. An anonymous letter would be sent to an Italian business or wealthy local Italian-American. The letter would demand that an envelope filled with a specified amount of cash be left in a certain location. Failure to comply would lead to the torching or bombing of the business or even to the murder of the victim or one of his family members. These murders received a great deal of publicity in the press and the crimes of the Black Hand became well known. In 1910 in New York the famous

Italian tenor Enrico Caruso received a Black Hand letter of extortion demanding $15,000 and threatening to kill him if the demand was not met. Caruso went to the police and they trapped the extortionists, but at other times, Caruso seems to have given in to Black Hand threats. [20]

In 1919 no one family or gang dominated the crime apparatus in Pittsburgh and western Pennsylvania, so it's difficult to identify which specific organization might have been responsible for Filippo's murder. Filippo shared a hometown (Roccarainola, in Campania) with Vito Genovese, who was born there eight years before Filippo and emigrated to American just three years after Filippo. [21] But the Genovese family was headquartered in New York City, where Vito had befriended the Sicilian mob leader Charles "Lucky" Luciano and eventually become the *capo di tutti i capi* (boss of all bosses). [22] A crime figure closer to home for Filippo was Frank Amato Sr. He also was born in Roccarainola, just four years after Filippo, on February 15, 1893. [23] When he immigrated to the US, Amato moved to Braddock, where Filippo and Maria lived from 1911 to early 1919, and was a member of a local criminal gang.

According to some accounts, such a local gang had an agreement with Filippo to provide "protection" in return for a regular payment, and refusing to pay protection money would provide a simple explanation for Filippo's murder. However, the evidence suggests a more complicated scenario. After his murder, *The Pittsburgh Post* suggested that Filippo had "figured in a blackhand plot some time ago," [24] making him an accomplice to Black Hand activities rather than simply a victim. And Filippo's relative prosperity was suspicious as well. For a thirty-year-old illiterate immigrant who had arrived in the United States less than eleven years before with $11 in his pocket, he had achieved a surprising degree of affluence. He owned a tailor's shop and supported a family of four small children. Unlike most people in 1919, he owned both a car and a revolver. The photograph on his gravestone indicates a dapper dresser. [25]

A clue might be found in the turf wars that broke out in cities all over the United States when Prohibition was ratified in 1919. The Black Hand was confronted with new opportunities for profit in the manufacture, transport, and sale of alcohol, and previously independent individuals or small groups of extortionists joined forces with larger crime organizations. In Pittsburgh, Italian gangs were dividing the city between the Sicilian Mafia, which controlled the north and the south, and the Neapolitan Camorra, which controlled the East End, with the central district subject to dispute.

One of the most important crime families at the time was the Volpe Eight, a colorful Neapolitan gangster family of eight brothers who claimed royal Italian blood. [26] They were based in the Turtle Creek Valley near Pittsburgh. Through a combination of bribes and threats, they controlled the police and politicians of Wilmerding and Pitcairn, which were approximately ten miles southeast of downtown Pittsburgh. One of the Volpe brothers, James, even served on the Wilmerding town council. The Volpes made an ostentatious display of their power. One of the brothers drove a sixteen-cylinder Cadillac with bulletproof windows and a license plate engraved "J.V.8" meaning "John Volpe of the Eight Volpe brothers."

The Volpes' dominance during this time period makes them a likely factor in Filippo's murder. In 1919 the Volpes had attempted to extend their control westward into East McKeesport, and family lore is that Filippo resisted pressure to shift his allegiance to them. After his murder, a famous gang war with the Volpes erupted. On December 14, nine days after Filippo's murder, a gun battle involving three Italians took place in broad daylight on Wylie Avenue in downtown Pittsburgh.[27] The wife of a clothing store owner barely escaped injury when a bullet smashed through a plate glass window in their store. One of the gunmen was wounded, but all of them escaped before the police arrived. Given the evidence of Filippo's prosperity and rumored Black Hand activities, a turf war with the Volpes is a more plausible explanation for his murder rather than a simple refusal of protection payment.

The evolution from unorganized Black Hand criminals to Mafia/Camorra crime families continued in the period after Filippo's death in 1919. In 1932 the Sicilian John Bazzano Sr. cultivated the Volpes by entering into a partnership on the numbers and sugar rackets with them. Bazzano's Roma Coffee Shop at 704 Wylie Avenue became their headquarters. After disarming the Volpes' suspicion through this partnership, Bazzano put out a contract for their murder. On the evening of July 29, 1932, three gunmen, including a former Volpe bodyguard, pulled up at the curb outside this coffee shop and opened fire with automatic pistols. They killed the eldest brother John Volpe on the sidewalk in front of the Roma and then entered the coffee shop to kill Arthur and James Volpe who were eating Corn Flakes in a rear room.[28] If these brothers had been the murderers of my granduncle, then fate had revenged him. That weekend 50,000 people—including police, politicians, prosecutors, and judges—trooped through the Volpe home to pay their respects.

The remaining Volpe brothers turned to the New York crime family for assistance in getting revenge. Bazzano was called to New York for a gang meeting where he was murdered. His body was found sewn into a sack on a Brooklyn street on the morning of August 8, 1932.[29] He had been garroted and stabbed twenty-two times in the chest with an ice pick—obvious signs of a revenge murder.

With the end of Prohibition in 1933 and the loss of revenue from bootleg-ging, this era of intense violence declined. With the demise of the Volpes, power in Pittsburgh was consolidated in the Amato family. In 1937 Frank Amato Jr. became head of the Pittsburgh crime family and presided over a long period of stability, succeeded by his son Frank D. Amato Jr. The Amato family had close ties to the Genovese family in New York, probably rooted in their mutual hometown of Roccarainola and a shared sense of *campanilis-mo* (intense attachment to the customs and traditions of one's native village).

A murder indictment forced Vito Genovese to flee from the United States to the Campanian town of Nola in 1934. A 1908 Baedeker's guidebook map indicates a fairly direct road linking the four miles between Nola and Rocca-rainola to the north.[30] Roccarainola lay at the end of a road, on the side of a ridge that rose to 1,500 meters. Nola was a cattle-market town and a historic base of organized crime in the Campania.[31] The census of 1901 recorded that the population of Nola was 12,000, but Roccarainola was much smaller.[32]

Back in Campania, Genovese became a prominent supporter of the Fas-cists. Using wealth, possibly generated from shipping narcotics to the United States, he made generous donations to the Fascist Party. Genovese contrib-uted 5,000 lire to the Roccarainola branch of the Fascist Party to buy the land for the local party headquarters and an even larger sum ($25,000 in US dollars of that time) to build a Fascist party headquarters in Nola. This building survives in the Piazza Giordano Bruno today where a branch of the Faculty of Law of the University of Naples is now housed. In Nola, Geno-vese entertained both Mussolini and his son-in-law, Count Galeazzo Ciano, who was Italy's foreign minister.

When the Allied army liberated Naples on October 1, 1943, Genovese shifted his affiliation from Mussolini to the US Army, acting as a translator and guide.[33] He served the Americans at no charge while using his position to make a fortune from the black market sale of Allied army supplies. In 1944 he was arrested for black market activities and sent back to New York to stand trial for the 1934 murder. He was released due to the deaths of every one of the prosecution's witnesses. In 1946 he rejoined the Luciano crime family in New York and in 1957 became the boss of what now became known as the Genovese family. He was indicted in 1958 and sentenced to fifteen years in the federal penitentiary in Atlanta. He continued to control his crime family from jail. He died of a heart attack while still in prison in 1969.

Family legend tells that, as a reward for Filippo's loyalty, the Genovese family provided his widow Maria and four orphaned children a brick house in the working-class Italian section of Pittsburgh called East Liberty.[34]

The Genovese are also said to have served as matchmaker in finding Maria another husband. Pietrangelo (Peter) De Luco had a reputation for playing pool and drinking too much, but the Genoveses told Maria that he was wealthy (although they also told him the same thing about Maria). It was difficult being a widow with four children, and Maria decided to marry him. They had two children together.

Demands for protection money are said to have continued on and off into the 1950s. My Italian-born Uncle Dominic Punaro (1900–1999), a successful Los Angeles tailor who married my father's eldest sister Mae, knew something about Uncle Filippo's murder. However, even seventy years after the event, he refused to say much about it.[35] United by fear of the ongoing threat of the gang, the family's lips were sealed by the ancient southern Italian code of silence (*omertà*) and distrust of outsiders and particularly of the authorities. My father's generation was suspiciously silent about this murder. That's why it was not until over eighty years after the event that I learned what had happened and how much it had affected my own life.

When I first heard about the murder of my granduncle, I was interested but did not feel any personal connection to him. It was only after I began to recognize the similar traits that kept emerging in each generation that I saw the connection. First I saw the link between my son and my father, then between my father and my granduncle, and finally between my granduncle and me. After a century of silence, I discovered the truth about my family and myself.

NOTES

1. John Dickie, *Blood Brotherhoods: A History of Italy's Three Mafias* (New York: Public Affairs, 2014), xxv–xxvi.
2. Dickie, 21–30.
3. Dickie, 41.
4. Dickie, 38–39, 207.
5. Letter from Jeanette Boake to the author, February 22, 2003.
6. Dickie, 189–196.
7. Dickie, 202–220.
8. Dickie, 205.
9. Dickie, 284.
10. Roberto Saviano, *Gomorrah*, trans. Virginia Jewiss (New York: Farrar, Straus & Giroux, 2007), 40–45, 120.
11. Mario Puzo, *The Godfather* (Greenwich, CT: Fawcett, 1969), 151–153; *The Godfather* (film) (Paramount Pictures, 1972).
12. The Statue of Liberty–Ellis Island Foundation (SOLEIF), www.ellisislandrecords.org, #0251–0252.
13. Anthony H. Galt, "Marital Property in an Apulian Town during the Eighteenth and Early Nineteenth Centuries," in *The Family in Italy: From Antiquity to the Present,* ed. David I. Kertzer and Richard P. Saller (New Haven, CT: Yale University Press, 1991), 313.
14. Jerre Mangione and Ben Morreale, *La Storia: Five Centuries of the Italian American Experience* (New York: HarperCollins, 1991), 167.

15. "Police Fail to Find Russo Murder Clue," *Pittsburgh Sunday Post*, December 7, 1919, sec. 1, 7.

16. "Much Mystery in Murder of Local Tailor in an Auto," *McKeesport Daily News*, December 5, 1919, 1; "Russo Murder Unsolved by Authorities," *McKeesport Daily News*, December 6, 1919, 1.

17. "McKeesport Tailor Murdered in Auto," *Pittsburgh Post*, December 6, 1919, 12.

18. "Russo Murder Unsolved by Authorities," 1.

19. In the mid-twentieth century, a tremendous defensiveness developed among many Italian-Americans over terms like the Black Hand and Mafia because they fed a stereotype of Italians as ethnically prone to criminal activity. This defensiveness dominates a study of the Black Hand by Thomas Monroe Pitkin and Francesco Cordasco entitled *The Black Hand: A Chapter in Ethnic Crime* (Totowa, NJ: Littlefield, Adams, 1977).

20. Howard Greenfield, *Caruso* (New York: Putnam's, 1983) 153–154, 238.

21. Bureau of Narcotics (US Treasury Department), *Mafia: The Government's Secret File on Organized Crime* (New York: HarperCollins, 2007), 307.

22. Dickie, 255–256.

23. Bureau of Narcotics, *Mafia*, 701.

24. "McKeesport Tailor Murdered in Auto," 12.

25. Filippo Russo is buried in a cemetery in McKeesport, Pennsylvania.

26. Thorston Ove, "Mafia Has a Long History Here, Growing from Bootlegging Days—Second of Two Parts," *Pittsburgh Post-Gazette*, November 6, 2000, www.post-gazette.com/regionstate/20001105greenbank1.asp., pp. 4–5 of 9.

27. "Why Go to the Movies? Try Wylie Avenue—Three Italians Stage a Lively Gun Battle in Street," *Pittsburgh Post*, December 15, 1919, 8.

28. "Washington Voices Satisfaction," *New York Times,* November 4, 1933, 34.

29. "Arrest of 14 Foils Murder Fete Plan," *New York Times*, August 18, 1932, 20; "Sack Murder Clues Sought in 2 States," *New York Times*, August 23, 1932, 4. Giuseppe "Big Mike" Spinelli was indicted as the killer of the Volpe brothers, but he fled to his native town of Agropoli in Italy where a prolonged extradition struggle ensued ("Extradition Fight Is Lost by Spinelli," *New York Times*, November 4, 1933, 34). Although courts in Naples and Rome ruled that Spinelli was no longer an Italian citizen and should be deported to Pittsburgh, the Italian Minister of Justice overruled them. An Italian court tried Spinelli, found him guilty, and sentenced him to thirty years in jail ("Italian Court Will Try Pittsburgh Murder Case," *New York Times*, April 8, 1934, E1; "Sentenced in Italy for Crime in U.S.," *New York Times*, December 17, 1935, 16).

30. Karl Baedeker, *Italien von den Alpen bis Neapel: Kurzes Reisehandbuch,* 6th ed. (Leipzig: Baedeker, 1908), map between pages 364 and 365.

31. Dickie, 544.

32. Italy: Historical Demographical Data of the Urban Centers. Population Statistics. http://www.populstat.info/Europe/italyt.htm.

33. Dickie, 278–280.

34. There were several Genoveses involved with the Pittsburgh gang, including the *capo* Francesco Genovese (1877–1965). Michael James Genovese (1919–2006) is said to have been a fourth cousin to Vito Genovese and was trained by him. He was born and raised in East Liberty. By the 1960s he became a co-boss with Sebastian John LaRocca of the Pittsburgh crime family and sole boss by 1985 until his death in 2006.

35. Jeanette Boake to the author, June 6, 1997.

Chapter Two

Roots, 1884–1914

I was born on November 20, 1943. Four months later on March 19, 1944, in war-ravaged Italy and within sight of my ancestral home, Mount Vesuvius erupted.[1] The smoke from the crater swelled slowly in a cloud rising in the sky to 30,000 or 40,000 feet and several miles in diameter. The volcanic cloud took the same shape as when Vesuvius had erupted in 79 CE, wiping out Pompeii. The Roman writer Pliny the Younger had written that the cloud looked like a pine tree, utterly still, as if painted on the sky until the day was plunged into darkness by the thick cloud of volcanic ash. That night in 1944 the lava streams began to slide slowly down Vesuvius's slopes. By the next day the sky was fogged over and ash fell like snow, accumulating to several inches in depth on the ground. Over the next few days the thundering noise and violence of the eruption increased as the earth shook violently. Cinders and showers of small stones (*lapilli*) fell sporadically and the lava flow crept down the mountain into nearby fields and towns, consuming entire buildings. Crowds of people knelt before the slowly moving lava, praying and holding up the image of the local saint San Sebastiano or the Neapolitan saint, San Gennaro.

San Sebastiano (d. 268) is one of the most famous Christian saints and martyrs and is still revered today as the patron saint of soldiers and athletes. Legend claims that he was appointed a captain in the Pretorian Guards by the Roman emperor Diocletian, who later martyred him after learning that he was a Christian. His image was invoked to protect against the 1944 volcanic eruption of Vesuvius because of the belief that in the seventh century his invocation had stopped a plague. His martyrdom has been immortalized in numerous paintings, the most famous being the oil painting by Il Sodoma (Giovanni Antonio Bazzi), ca. 1525, which depicts his near-naked body tied to a tree and pierced by arrows. The idealized image of Sebastian's martyred body became a homoerotic icon, fostered by a rumor that he had once been one of Diocletian's male lovers.[2]

By March 24, 1944, the lava flow from Vesuvius had ebbed and the eruption was over. This cataclysm occurred seventy-two years ago and Vesuvius has not erupted again in my lifetime. Perhaps for some, this volcanic eruption is just a coincidence, but for me it has meaning. For my family (and for me), the explosive and destructive force of Vesuvius runs in our blood. In my family and its history, this destructive pattern has erupted, again and again. This is what links me to my family and it makes it impossible to tell my story without the story of my family.

There had been a dearth of boys in my mother's family Her one brother Jesse died in infancy, causing my grandmother lasting grief. Perhaps as a result, my mother asked my grandmother to name me. She chose David Emil, taking David from the Bible and Emil from my grandfather, Gustav Emil Dittmar. As I grew up, they made sure that I knew the story of my namesake, the famous warrior-king in the Old Testament book of Samuel. It was a perceptive choice because I share much with the young David.

In terms of size, my five feet eight inches in height and slight body put me on the smaller end of the spectrum for American men. Although I have never been physically aggressive, I have surprised myself by my fearlessness. When a rat came out of the air ducts in my ninth-grade English class and caused such a commotion, frightening the teacher, Mrs. Zollars, into screaming, I picked up the metal trash basket, went over to where the frantic rat was desperately trying to escape through the grillwork back into the air ducts, and beat it to death.[3] In 1975 when my family and I were spending the summer in a New Age religious commune outside Baltimore, my children saw a fire in the ceramics shop. Immediately I went into the shop, picked up the pan of flaming paraffin, and carried it outside. It probably would have been smarter to use a fire extinguisher, but I acted instinctively.

For the first eighteen years of my life, I lived in the small town of Burgettstown in southwestern Pennsylvania. The countryside there consisted of beautiful rolling hills, mutilated by coal mines and strip-mining, which destroyed the original contours of the landscape. Abandoned buildings of long-departed industries dotted the countryside. I had a typical small-town upbringing experienced by millions of Americans in the late 1940s and 1950s. Ironically, it was to the Black Hand that I owe my small-town upbringing. Black Handers preyed exclusively on their fellow Italian-Americans, sending their extortion messages through the mail.[4] The messages contained the symbol of an open hand pressed with black ink against a sheet of paper. The Black Handers were active in the years 1895–1919 wherever there were large Italian-American communities (500,000 in New York, 100,000 in both Boston and Philadelphia, 70,000 in both New Orleans and San Francisco, 60,000 in Chicago, and 25,000 in Denver and Pittsburgh).[5] Because my grandparents refused to meet the Black Hand's demands, they moved to a town founded shortly before the Revolutionary War by Scotch-Irish Presbyterians. As a result, I grew up in a multi-ethnic small town rather than in an urban Italian-American neighborhood in Pittsburgh.

My family was recently arrived in the United States and our ties to Europe were still strong. The German side of my family left a weaker imprint on my personality. Family members on that side were less volatile, more disciplined, and less creative and had a stronger intellectual strain than on the Italian side. Only my maternal grandmother, Bertha (née Ries) Dittmar (1882–1957), was born in the United States and her family had only just emigrated from Saarbrucken, Germany, when she was born. All the others were classic immigrants who passed through Ellis Island, wide-eyed into this land of promise. My maternal grandfather, Gustav Emil Dittmar (1881–1953), was the only one of my grandparents who could claim (barely) middle-class status. The others were all poor; that's why they came to the Land of Opportunity.

My paternal ancestors lived in the village of Roccarainola, eighteen miles northeast of the Bay of Naples, where the land rises gradually from the sea. Roccarainola sits on a broad and sweeping hillside. Since antiquity, the villages in the Mezzogiorno (Italian region south of Rome) have been built on hillsides to protect against thieves or invaders and to provide distance from the valleys, which were filled with malaria-breeding mosquitoes.[6] Peasants lived in the villages and walked to their fields. From March to November, there was just enough rain to sustain food crops. To this day, Roccarainola lies at the end of a road beyond which are empty hills to the north. To the east lie the Apennine Mountains whose caps are snow-covered in the winter. But most prominent of all is Mount Vesuvius, visible to the south. Its massive form rises over 4,000 feet from the surrounding sea level to dominate the entire Bay of Naples.

I do not know how far back in time my ancestors have lived in this village. Naples (in Italian *Napoli*, from the Greek *Neapolis* meaning "new city") was founded by the Greeks in the eighth century BCE.[7] It was first called Parthenope, after the mythical siren, half-virgin and half-bird, who drew men to destruction by the irresistible power of her singing. The Greek poet Homer said that Odysseus resisted the sirens by plugging his ears with wax and tying himself to the mast of his ship. The siren Parthenope was so distraught by her failure to entice Odysseus that she threw herself from a cliff into the water and drowned.

Later the Romans came, conquering the region of Campania and building the estates and villas at Pompeii that were destroyed when Vesuvius erupted in 79 CE. In the fifth century the Goths arrived, followed by the Lombards, and in the eleventh century the Normans whose genes mingled with the native populace to produce the oddity of blue-eyed southern Italians. (My grandfather had blue-grey eyes and my grandmother had red hair, traits that have been passed down to my grandchildren.)

The Middle Ages produced a series of wars that caused a decline in the former stability and prosperity of the region. The periodic eruptions of Vesuvius, earthquakes, and the Black Death in 1348 killed thousands of people, the latter decimating over one-third of the populace in a two-month period. The shrine of Santa Maria in Moiano, just a few miles north of Roccarainola, attracted many pilgrims.[8] The local populace believed that prayers to Our Lady of Moiano empowered the defeat of the Muslim Ottoman Turks who invaded around 1571. By the fifteenth century Naples was a wealthy and powerful city. Along with Bologna, Padua, and Pavia to the north, it had a distinguished university that attracted foreign students. Two centuries of Spanish misrule caused an economic collapse in the seventeenth century. Abusive feudal barons and marauding bandits and beggars made life so miserable for people in countryside villages like Roccarainola that many fled to Naples for safety.

After Campania passed to the control of the French Bourbons, Charles de Bourbon, King of the Two Sicilies, began building in 1752 a magnificent *Palazzo Reale* or royal palace and gardens at Caserta, only a few miles northwest of Roccarainola.[9] It was a palace whose size and grandeur were built to surpass the famous palace of his great-grandfather Louis XIV at Versailles. Set in the forest and fields where Charles liked to hunt, the 1,200-room palace was constructed along a two-mile vista of a water staircase filled with statues of classical gods and goddesses. The royal court fled the stifling heat of Naples to summer there. The grandeur of this palace made a striking contrast with the poverty of my ancestors in Roccarainola.

When Giuseppe Garibaldi led his red-shirted army south to drive out the Bourbons, a constitutional monarchy was established that united Italy in 1861, but the plight of the Mezzogiorno did not improve. It was known as "the land that time forgot." In the late nineteenth century, the people of the Mezzogiorno suffered a rash of disasters, including an agricultural depression in the 1880s and a cholera epidemic in 1884.[10] Because the land had become deforested over the centuries, rain washed down the hillsides, creating swamps where mosquitoes bred, causing a plague of malaria that continued from 1860 until 1925. And yet the population continued to expand.[11]

The ownership of farm land increasingly flowed from the *contadini* (peasants) into the hands of the *latifondisti* (large landowners), so that by 1910 most of the land of the Mezzogiorno was controlled by a few hundred of these landed-gentry families.[12] The peasants were squeezed from two sides. The mostly absentee landlords raised the rent on tenant farmers while the new government in Rome increased taxes on grain and raised the government-monopoly price of salt, making it difficult for the peasants to preserve meat and fish. The taxes were structured such that large landowners could evade payment while the burden fell on the peasantry. Official documents indicate that in 1881, two-thirds of the population of Naples were either unemployed or hungry.[13] Out of desperation many peasants in the south began packing their bags and immigrating to the Americas. Between 1880 and 1914, two-and-a-half-million Italians crossed the Atlantic.[14] My grandparents were among them.

My paternal grandfather, Raffaele Mungiello, was born on August 13, 1884. The name of his father was Antonio and his mother was Anna. The name Mungiello may reflect his family's humble livelihood. In contemporary Italian, *mungiere* means to milk an animal and *mungitore* refers to a milker. The animals milked in this stark region would have been goats rather than cows. My grandfather was an only child, but he had many cousins. He was a good-looking man with thick dark hair that he never lost. He was a bit vain and dyed his hair as he aged. His name was a favorite one in the family, and even today there are three Raffaele Mungiellos listed in the telephone book of Roccarainola. A paternal uncle of my grandfather with the same name, Raffaele Mungiello, but born in 1866, immigrated to the United States at approximately the same time but settled in Hoboken, New Jersey, and retained the original spelling of the name.[15]

My grandfather was poor, unskilled, and illiterate, and he faced a hopeless future in his village. But he had a dream. And so at the age of eighteen, he said goodbye to his village, although not to his family because some of his cousins had already preceded him to America. Prior to 1915, steamship companies offered low-cost passage to America for $30 and competition sometimes reduced the cost to $16 or even $15.[16] My grandfather boarded the *S.S. Neckar* at Naples and traveled in third-class or steerage (so named because the compartments were located below the waterline and next to the enormous steering mechanism). Each compartment held 300 or more passengers. The *Neckar's* cruising speed was fourteen knots, and passage across the Atlantic took two weeks.

My grandfather arrived in America on March 27, 1903, declaring on his customs form that he had $11. Typically, the sighting of the New York skyline generated a lot of excitement among the passengers. Perhaps my grandfather was one of the young Italians who shouted "Viva LaMerica!" as the passengers crowded the ship's railing for a better look at their new home.[17] The Statue of Liberty, dedicated in 1886, was only a half-mile from Ellis Island, but since Ellis Island could not dock large vessels, the ship sailed to the Lower Bay of New York Harbor. Here the first- and second-class passengers disembarked while the steerage passengers were quarantined. Eventually they boarded barges that took them to Ellis Island for processing.

Their medical examinations took place in an enormous high-ceilinged hall. My grandfather arrived just as the immigration numbers were beginning to peak. By 1912, 600 staff members were processing an average of 5,000 immigrants each day. During their confinement on Ellis Island, the immigrants were jammed together so closely in overcrowded rooms that vermin spread from the infected to the uninfected. One can imagine the relief that my grandfather must have felt when he was finally allowed to enter America. Perhaps he kissed the ground.

The ship's manifest lists his occupation as "farmer." It records that he had an ongoing train ticket to his final destination in East Liberty, Pennsylvania, a neighborhood of Pittsburgh, and that his passage was paid for by "his brother Carmino in East Liberty, Pennsylvania."[18] However my grandfather was the only son in his family. The frequent appearance of the terms "brother" and "brother-in-law" in the immigration records probably reflects the close affinity of cousins and intermarriage between families that was typical of small Italian villages.

When people from the Mezzogiorno immigrated to the United States at that time, their ethnic group was listed by US immigration officials as "Southern Italian" rather than Italian. However, their prime identity was not with Italy at all but rather with their native village. So it is not surprising that my grandfather would have initially settled among his cousins, in-laws, and other *paesani* from Roccarainola in the American towns of East Liberty and Braddock.[19] A strong distrust of outsiders and an affinity for one's own people (*campanilismo*) led Italian immigrants to cluster together.

Soon after arriving in America in March, my grandfather returned to Naples, and in July entered the United States for a second time. He changed his destination from East Liberty to Braddock, Pennsylvania.[20] The Immigration Acts of 1921 and 1924 established quotas that severely limited immigration of southern and eastern Europeans, as well as Jews, East Asians, and others. This limited the free passage of many Italian men as "birds of passage" who travelled back and forth between Italy and the United States on a temporary or seasonal basis.[21] They worked on construction projects in the United States during the summer and returned to Italy during the winter. Because their savings were frequently insufficient to get them through the winter months, they borrowed money at usurious rates or else extorted money as Black Handers from fellow immigrants.[22]

In 1906 and in the typical custom of the time, my grandfather returned to his native village to find a wife. Using a handful of silver dollars that he spread out on the bed to show the riches that awaited them in America, he beguiled my grandmother, Marianna Russo (b. 1885), into marrying him and following him to America. Some beguiling was probably necessary because the Russo family owned a winery and was better off than the Mungiellos. However, their vineyard may have suffered from the disease called phylloxera that spread from France, decimating the vineyards of Italy in the 1870s. In any case, with three brothers, my grandmother would not have inherited much, if any, family property. For a time, my grandfather served (perhaps was conscripted into) the Italian army and worked as a cook.

It is likely that some prenuptial arrangements had already been made through my grandmother's brother in Pittsburgh, Aniello. Aniello Russo was born in 1876 and was the first of his siblings to immigrate to America, arriving in Pittsburgh in 1902 at the age of twenty-six.[23] Italian families tended to name children after their parents and the recurrence of names like Aniello, Antonio, Carmino, Domenico, Michael, and Raffaele in both the Mungiello and Russo families probably reflects a number of marriages between the two families over the years. There are no Davids because in Italy, Davide was a name used mainly by Jews. Of my grandmother's three brothers—Antonio, Aniello, and Filippo—only Antonio remained in Roccarainola. He was probably the eldest son, the one who inherited the winery from his father Domenico.

My newlywed grandparents departed from Naples on the *S.S. Perugia* and crossed the Atlantic through stormy winter seas. They were accompanied by my grandmother's younger brother Filippo. My grandmother was already pregnant and was very sick on the journey. She was apparently suffering from morning sickness but it must have been during the early stage of pregnancy because visibly pregnant women were restricted in entering the country. They arrived at Ellis Island on February 21, 1909. My grandfather was twenty-five and five-foot-five while she was twenty-four and five-foot-three.[24] Unlike her husband, my grandmother never returned to Italy.

In 1910 Michael Mungiello, apparently a cousin of my grandfather, also arrived in the United States. He is listed in the 1910 census as a twenty-four-year-old laborer, boarding in the home of a Raffaele Mungiello, forty-four, living in Hoboken. This may have been the Michael who came to Slovan and lived with my grandparents for a short time in the 1920s.[25] My Aunt Jeanette said his home was in Mt. Pleasant, Pennsylvania.

In Braddock (near Pittsburgh), my grandparents lived at 522 Braddock Avenue where their first children—a boy and a girl—were born and died.[26] Finally, my Uncle Tony was born on April 28, 1912, and my father Domenico was born on August 7, 1913. They ran a grocery store where profits were diminished by the need to extend credit to customers. As immigrant shop owners, they became targets for extortion demands from the Black Hand.[27] Unlike my granduncle Filippo, my grandparents refused to work with the Black Hand. When my grandparents resisted the Black Hand's demand for protection money, Filippo warned his sister that her husband Raffaele was in danger and they fled.[28]

My grandfather disappeared and it is unclear where he went. My Aunt Jeanette claimed that he disappeared for six months in Italy, presumably to return to the safety of his native village Roccarainola.[29] He supposedly left soon after my Aunt Mae was conceived in January of 1915 and returned shortly before World War I broke out in August. However, there is no documentation in the immigration records of anyone with his name entering the country during that time, although he might have used an alias to avoid alerting his pursuers. It is also possible that he never left the country and took refuge among relatives in New York or elsewhere, spreading the rumor of his return to Italy to throw the Black Hand off his track. Jeanette said the matter was never discussed at home. The rest of the family fled initially to Albion, near Erie, over a hundred miles north of Pittsburgh where they probably had help from friends. After my Aunt Mae was born there on October 14, 1915, the entire family returned south with the Filiponi family and settled in Slovan, Pennsylvania. Helen was born on September 28, 1917, Giovannina (Jeanette) on January 11, 1919, and Evelyn on November 25, 1920.[30]

My grandparents' resistance to cooperating with the Black Hand was dangerous. Refusing to submit to their demands, my grandparents, in the typical American pattern, pulled up their roots and made a new life in another town. Pap was still a target, so he altered their surname, dropping the letter 'i' from Mungiello to make it Mungello.[31] But it seems that even in their new home, they were unable to completely escape the mob, which for many years kept a grip on Italian-American life.

NOTES

1. Norman Lewis, *Naples '44: An Intelligence Officer in the Italian Labyrinth* (New York: Holt, 1978), p. 101–106.

2. Michael Goodrich, "St. Sebastian," in *Who's Who in Gay and Lesbian History: From Antiquity to World War II*, ed. Robert Aldrich and Garry Wotherspoon (London: Routledge, 2001), 74–75; James M. Saslow, *Pictures and Passions: A History of Homosexuality in the Visual Arts* (New York: Viking Penguin, 1999), 98–99.

3. Many years later, Ms. Zollars in correspondence confirmed that this incident with the rat had actually happened.

4. On the Black Hand, see Richard Gambino, *Blood of My Blood: The Dilemma of the Italian-Americans* (New York: Anchor Books, 1975), 294. In the late nineteenth and early twentieth centuries, anti-Italian feeling in the US grew with the large numbers of poor immigrants arriving from southern Italy, and this fostered the erroneous belief that the Black Hand was a highly organized criminal organization. This belief strengthened when a well-known New York City detective named Joseph Petrosino (b. 1860 in Padula near Naples) was murdered in Palermo in 1909 while investigating Italian links to crime in the United States. See Anthony R. Cannella, "Detective Petrosino and the Black Hand," *Connecticut Review* 17, no. 2 (fall 1995): 1–16.

5. Gaetano D'Amato, "The 'Black Hand' Myth," *North American Review* (April 1908), reprinted in Wayne Moquin with Charles Van Doren, eds., *A Documentary History of the Italian Americans* (New York: Praeger, 1974), 176.

6. Gambino, *Blood of My Blood*, 13.

7. Ronald G. Musto, "An Introduction to Neapolitan History," in Enrico Bacco, *Naples: An Early Guide*, ed. and trans. Eileen Gardner (New York: Italica Press, 1991), xix–lxii. Also see Rolf Legler, *Der Golf von Neapel. Das Traumziel der klassichen Italienreise; Geschichte, Kunst, Geographie*, Dumont Kunst-Reiseführer (Cologne: Dumont Buchverlag, 1990), 72.

8. Italians in America, http://www.italiansinamerica.com/Madonna.htm.

9. Elisabeth Blair MacDougall, "Reggia at Caserta," in *Gardens of Naples*, photographs by Nicolas Sapieha (New York: M. T. Train/Scala Books, 1995), 13–28.

10. Gambino, *Blood of My Blood*, 64; Frank M. Snowden, *Naples in the Time of Cholera, 1884–1911* (Cambridge: Cambridge University Press, 1995).

11. Gambino, *Blood of My Blood*, 62.

12. Gambino, *Blood of My Blood*, 54.

13. Gladys Nadler Rips, *Coming to America: Immigrants from Southern Europe* (New York: Dell, 1981), 7.

14. Although the immigration records of the period of great Italian immigration into the United States, 1860–1920, list 4,182,067 Italians, this number includes many *ritorni* (immigrants who had previously entered the United States and returned to Italy). Consequently, this large number must be reduced in order to arrive at an accurate estimate of the total number of Italians who immigrated to the US during this time. See Roger Daniels, *Coming to America: A History of Immigration and Ethnicity in American Life*, 2nd ed. (New York: HarperCollins, 2002), 188–189.

15. This branch of the Mungiello family did not change the spelling of the name. Entries for this branch appear in the 1910 census in Hoboken, New Jersey. Descendants of this line live in New Jersey today and continue to use family names like Michael and Filomena.

16. Rips, *Coming to America*, 12.

17. Jerre Mangione and Ben Morreale, *La Storia: Five Centuries of the Italian American Experience* (New York: HarperCollins, 1991), 109–117.

18. Records of immigrant arrivals at Ellis Island, New York, 1892–1924, The Statue of Liberty-Ellis Island Foundation (SOLEIF), www.ellisislandrecords.org, #0432.

19. Richard D. Alba, *Italian Americans* (Englewood Cliffs, NJ: Prentice-Hall, 1985), 30.

20. The immigration manifest records that Raffaele Mungiello was going to live with "his brother-in-law Andreas Montratorios, 10th Street 303, Braddock, Pa."

21. Stefano Luconi, *From Paesani to White Ethnics: The Italian Experience in Philadelphia* (Albany: State University of New York Press, 2001), 49–50.

22. Mangione and Morreale, *La Storia*, 168.

23. See SOLEIF, www.ellisislandrecords.org, #0478. The ship's manifest lists Aniello Russo's destination as 79 Linden Street in the Homewood section of Pittsburgh.

24. My grandmother's name is listed on the ship's manifest directly under my grandfather's name as Marianna Moglie. The word *moglie* is Italian for "wife." See SOLEIF, www.ellisislandrecords.org, #0251–0252.

25. Jeanette Boake to the author, August 2002.

26. Jeanette Boake to the author, June 6, 1997.

27. Mangione and Morreale, *La Storia*, 167.

28. Jeanette Boake to the author, July 24, 2002, and September 23, 2002.

29. Jeanette Boake to the author, July 7, 2002.

30. The birthdates of the six Mungello siblings are given in the petition for naturalization of Raffaele Mungello, dated March 15, 1923.

31. Jeanette Boake to the author, August 24, 2004, and May 14, 2005.

Chapter Three

A Death in the Family, 1915–1949

In 1926 the summer heat lingered in western Pennsylvania. On the evening of September 10, my grandmother was sitting, drinking orange soda and laughing in the overheated ticket booth of the Lyric Theater in Langeloth. Suddenly she collapsed and died almost immediately. Her death provoked a crisis in the family and in the small town of Slovan. My Aunt Jeanette was seven years old at the time and learned of her mother's death while sitting in the nearby Penn Theater in Slovan. An announcement was made in the theater that there would be no vaudeville that night because Mrs. Mungello had died. She remembers my grandfather screaming when he heard.

My grandmother's early death at forty-one was tragic and surrounded by questions. It's possible that her heart had been weakened by rheumatic fever as a child, although this is just speculation. It's also possible that the onset of early menopause (her youngest child was five years old) might have contributed. However, the suddenness of her death, the lack of any prior warning symptoms, and perhaps, most of all, the silence that followed her death were indicators that her death may not have been from natural causes. The gang usually targeted men rather than women, but Marianna Mungello was known to oppose their extortion efforts and she might have become one of their targets. Given the lifelong reluctance of my grandfather to discuss either her or the gang, one wonders if there could be any plausibility to my Aunt Jeanette's suspicion that her mother might have been murdered by poisoning.[1] Twelve years after fleeing the extortion demands of the gang in Braddock, the gang may have caught up with them in Slovan and may have been seeking to extort funds from the Mungellos' prospering theaters. While this is merely speculation, the fear of such attacks was very real and plagued the family for years. A silence descended over the family and Marianna was rarely discussed by her children or her husband.

21

My grandmother's early death had a profound impact on her family. She was the emotional and entrepreneurial core of the family and without her, the emotional bonds of her husband and children frayed and the upward momentum of the family ebbed. They came together to survive, but afterward they were never at peace with one another. Unlike many Italians, they never learned how to touch one another and were physically unaffectionate, not only with one another but also with their children.

I have only one clear photograph of my grandmother Marianna. By today's tastes, it is a morbid photo of her in an open casket at the gravesite, just before burial and surrounded by people she knew. There is a mirror conspicuously placed in the casket, probably a custom carried from Italy. Behind the casket stand her husband and children. At her head stand the flower-bearers, three theater ticket-sellers wearing white make-up on their faces. At her feet are two movie projectionists and the piano player for the silent movies. Near the children stands Filippo's widow Maria, whom they called Aunt Mary. And behind them are the townspeople who had come to pay their last respects.

In 1984 I took my wife, daughter, and son to see my ancestral village of Roccarainola. At a cafe we met a man who took us to relatives of my grandmother. There I met a very old lady who grabbed my face in her hands and with tears in her eyes exclaimed "Marianna!" She was Pasqualiana Russo, a niece of my grandmother and daughter of my grandmother's brother Antonio Russo. Exactly seventy-five years after my grandmother had left her native village, a circle was closed. Anyone who knows the force of blood and *la mia famiglia* will understand what this moment meant.

When I was a boy in the 1950s, I spent many hours with my father on his property in Slovan. By then Slovan's glory days were past and I remember following him through the deserted Penn Theater and the empty apartments in the adjoining building. The apartments were cold and a sense of abandonment dominated these empty rooms. My father rarely offered an explanation of the building's history. It was not until many years later that I realized he had lived in these rooms, first as a youth with his family and later when he married my mother. Things had been different then.

When my grandparents moved there in 1915, Slovan was a small boomtown thirty miles west of Pittsburgh. It developed only two miles south of the older town of Burgettstown, which had been founded in 1773 by a native German named Sebastian Burgett.[2] Originally called West Boston, Burgettstown was an agricultural town dominated by Scotch-Irish Presbyterians. However, the construction of the railroad in the late nineteenth century stimulated the development of coal mining, and the area became one of the most prosperous coal-producing regions of the United States during the years 1910–1930. Its prosperity attracted large numbers of poor southern and eastern European immigrants who were predominantly Catholic.

The impetus for the development of Slovan came in the years 1913–1914 with rumors about the building of a new plant by the American Zinc and Chemical Company, a subsidiary of American Metal (now Amax).[3] This set off a flurry of real estate activity in which John S. Easton divided up his farm into lots that became the town of Eastonville.[4] Later, with the arrival of so many Slovenian immigrants, the name was changed to Slovan. The American Zinc plant was built on a big hill overlooking Slovan, and it used coal from a mine at the foot of the hill. The main trunk line of the Pennsylvania Railroad in nearby Burgettstown enabled the plant to ship in zinc ore from Missouri mines and ship out processed zinc to Pittsburgh mills, which was then used in galvanizing steel. The hilltop area near the plant became the company town of Langeloth while workers who wanted to buy or build houses lived in the hollow below in Slovan. Other mines opened in nearby Erie Mine and Atlasburg.

During this time, most of the residents of Slovan could not speak English. At one time the thousand men who worked in the American Zinc plant earned $3.78 a day ($88 in 2015 dollars) while the railroad workers earned $3.20 ($75 in 2015 dollars) a day. Slovan was like a frontier town. Taverns lined the street and stayed open all night. The main street (Route 18) was muddy and unpaved until 1921. Most workers in Slovan were required to buy their products at the company stores. These were typically hard-working, illiterate immigrants who struggled to give their children an education. In 1916 at the peak of Slovan's boom, 500 children were jammed into a four-room brick school building there. The area around Slovan soon acquired a bleak look as the eight large zinc plant smokestacks on the hill overlooking Slovan belched out toxins that killed most of the vegetation in the surrounding countryside. These smokestacks may also have dispersed carcinogens that my aunts' bodies absorbed, causing the cancers that later afflicted all of them. My Aunts Mae, Helen, and Jeanette would survive breast cancer, but my Aunt Evelyn and Aunt Mae succumbed to colon cancer.

Despite the zinc plant's dire consequences for the environment and residents' health, the plant did provide the prosperity that enabled workers and their families to go to the movies, and this became the source of my grandparents' livelihood. The idea of owning movie theaters had occurred to my grandmother one day when she passed a theater in Pittsburgh and was struck by the fact that people were paying cash rather than buying on credit as they did at their grocery store in Braddock.

My grandmother Marianna thus became the architect of the family's business. Born in 1885 as Marianna Russo, she never learned to read and had to sign checks with an "x." Nonetheless, she was a shrewd businesswoman. She traveled to Pittsburgh to exchange films for the theaters, a long trip involving a car ride to Burgettstown where she would board a train to Pittsburgh. Sometimes she carried a present of homemade red wine, a welcome gift in Prohibition times for the largely Jewish film distributors on Film Row. She would pay for the rental of only one set of films, concealing the fact that she would have workers "bicycle" the movie reels between towns, so that the film could be shared with the other four theatres. These films were on reels in heavy metal containers. Sometimes she took my father with her to read the English which she could not decipher. As an immigrant and a pioneering businesswoman in the 1920s, my grandmother was remarkable. She was enterprising, inventive and a problem-solver. When her youngest child Evelyn came down with a life-threatening fever, she heated bricks and piled them around the bed to keep her warm. My Aunt Evelyn's hand was badly burned by those bricks, and she lost a finger, but she survived. Marianna was a savvy marketer as well. She loved to run the movies of Rudolph Valentino. He had been born Rudolpho Guglielmi (1895–1926) in a region near her own home in Italy, and she regarded him with special affinity and gave away promotional photographs of him. Valentino's silent movies were played to the accompaniment of a piano player named Henry Gerrero, a Seventh Day Adventist who later married one of my grandparent's ticket-sellers, Anna Tucci.

My family never shirked from a fight, a trait that I (for better or worse) have inherited. My grandmother was a Catholic who bought a Saint Anthony statue for Our Lady of Lourdes, the first Catholic church in Burgettstown, built in 1918.[5] Irish priests sometimes clashed with Italian parishioners. When the local priest, the Irish Father William J. McCashin, condemned movie-going during Lent, my grandmother (and her entire family) stopped going to mass.[6] And although she was a somewhat distant mother, she was fiercely protective of her children. When my Aunt Jeanette broke some crayons in the first grade, she was beaten by the teacher so badly that there were marks on her buttocks.[7] The next day my grandmother accompanied her on the bus to school, carrying an umbrella, although the day was bright and clear. Jeanette pointed out the teacher, whom my grandmother chased down, screaming while beating her with the umbrella.

She could be tough with her children as well. When the movies stoked my Uncle Tony's dreams of going West with some buddies and becoming cowboys, he stole the needed money from the ticket-seller's till. My grandmother punished him by placing him in a boy's reform school. She was so busy running the business that she did not have much time for her children. At night the youngest daughters sometimes fell asleep on movie posters on the floor of the Penn Theater box office with the ticket-sellers as their babysitters.

Under Marianna's guidance, the family business thrived. With my grandfather doing the construction, my grandparents opened five silent movie theaters in Slovan, Burgettstown, Erie Mine, Langeloth, and Cherry Valley. My grandmother managed the theaters while my grandfather worked during the day as a foreman at the zinc plant. In the evenings he would work as a projectionist in one of the theaters. He taught young Tony to run the projection machines and change the reels when Tony was only twelve years of age.[8] Later, after my grandmother's death, my grandfather built the adjoining two-story office and apartment building next to the Penn Theater in Slovan, and the family occupied one of the apartments. These apartments had the luxury of running water and indoor toilets at a time when most of the other homes in Slovan had outhouses.

My grandmother Marianna married my grandfather, Raffaele Mungiello, in 1908. Raffaele became an American citizen in 1923 and soon started calling himself Ralph, though he was known to the family as Pap. Unlike many Italian families of that time, my grandfather did not speak Italian to his children.[9] I am sure it was because he wanted to Americanize them, especially after my grandmother's death.

My grandfather was a hard worker and good businessman. In addition to working at the zinc plant, he took care of the theaters (occasionally having to battle the rats who sometimes overran the theater and apartment). In the area behind the Penn Theater, he cultivated a large vegetable garden and built a *bocce* (lawn bowling) court where he and the men in the neighborhood played. Gina Filipponi (1920–1998) remembered him, during the Depression, giving out theater passes to children in exchange for sacks of coal that they had picked off the slate dumps. Some of the more enterprising children stole the coal from his pile and resold it to him for admission to the theater. After the death of her first two infants (a boy and a girl), my grandmother had six children at regular intervals of eighteen months from 1912 to 1920:[10] Antonio, Domenico (my father Donald), Filomena (Mae), Helen, Giovannina (Jeanette), and Evelyn. The children stand at the head of her coffin in the graveside picture, from Evelyn (5) to Jeanette (7) to Helen (9) to Dom (13) to Tony (14) to Mae (almost 12) who is standing beside her father, wearing an adult-looking black hat and beginning to play the role of little mother over this lively brood.

Although my father and uncle, as well as their first two children who died as infants, had been baptized in Braddock, the four later-born daughters were not baptized until 1931.[11] Pressure from local townspeople forced my grandfather finally to have them baptized, although he commented sourly at the time that the nuns were wearing long skirts to hide their pregnancies. Jeanette remembered getting a new dress for confirmation, although she denied that she was Catholic. [12]

Of the Mungello daughters, only Mae was devout, although she and Helen and Evelyn all sent their children to Catholic schools. Their brothers, Tony and my father Dom, became lapsed Catholics, although Dom quietly used his Catholic background to good advantage in his extensive business dealings with Catholic clerics. Jeanette became the most hostile to the Catholic Church, although her hostility seems to have developed later in life. She retained fond memories of her godmother, whose garden provided the yellow roses she carried at her high school graduation. [13] Moreover, she was married in Our Lady of Lourdes Catholic Church in Burgettstown in a ceremony on November 27, 1941, arranged by her two older sisters. [14]

In one of his rare references to his wife Marianna, Pap disparagingly claimed that none of his four daughters took after their mother. [15] However, Helen most resembled her mother in intelligence and financial ambition. Just as my father would encounter social prejudice because of his Italian background, so too did Helen. Unlike Jeanette, who married a pharmacist with a college degree, Helen married a steelworker who was a good husband but whose ambitions failed to match her dreams. She had a brutal encounter with class bias when she and her husband attempted to acquire status by buying an expensive house in the Mount Lebanon district of Pittsburgh. She gave a party and invited her neighbors, but no one came. [16] Undaunted, she made a new start by moving her family to California where she had some success investing in the stock market.

After Marianna's death, Pap's children opposed his remarrying, and his daughters were told by their older brothers to "act up" in front of his girlfriends to discourage any interest. [17] My Aunt Jeanette said, "We all did not want my father to marry all on account of greed." [18] He never did remarry, but he did have several attractive girlfriends. Like many poor people who attained a touch of affluence, he bought an extravagantly expensive car—a black Packard and for a time he employed a Russian immigrant named Harry Drazio to drive it. However, he suspected that Drazio was stealing money from the family business. Pap even got involved, briefly, in politics when he helped organize an independent ticket of candidates for the Citizen Party in Smith township elections in fall of 1929, just as the stock market was crashing. [19]

My father, Donald Domenico Mungello (1913–1983), inherited my grandmother's intelligence but not her drive. My Aunt Jeanette said, "Dom was my Mom's favorite; she spoiled him."[20] My father became the favored child in the family, in part, because he had his mother's mathematical ability that had proven so useful in counting the small change and bills that passed through the theater ticket office. I remember that he was always very quick with simple math, although he was never able to give me a clear explanation of the Italian finger game *Morra*. He received special attention from my grandmother. He was sickly as a child and when she learned that he was allergic to cow's milk, my grandmother bought a goat that provided milk just for him. My grandmother once dressed him in a stylish Buster Brown suit when she took him with her to visit my Uncle Tony in the boy's reform school at Oakdale. My father was such an object of ridicule by the other boys that my embarrassed uncle begged his mother not to bring him again.

My grandmother sent her sons to the grade school on the hill in Langeloth because it was regarded as better than the crowded school in Slovan. During their lunch breaks, Tony swept the floor of the Lyric Theater in Langeloth and Dom swept the theater in Burgettstown.[21] Tony showed far more interest in the theater business than in getting an education. After my grandmother died, Tony disregarded my grandfather's objections and quit school to go into the family business. He became the youngest film exhibitor on Film Row in Pittsburgh.[22] Pap had bigger things in mind for my father, who was sent to Union High School in Burgettstown.

At Union High School my father became well-known for playing baseball and especially football (left halfback), a sport with a large following in western Pennsylvania, famed for so many star NFL players. In Burgettstown nearly 7,000 people, far more people than lived in the town, attended a scoreless tie between Burgettstown and McDonald high schools on November 22, 1929.[23] Once during a memorable rainy game when my grandfather was holding an umbrella on the sidelines, my father accidentally ran off the field and into him, knocking him down.[24]

My grandmother had fostered a high sense of self-esteem in my father. Photographs from his youth reveal a handsome young man, barely average in height but with a strong body. He had a dramatic flair in his personality and liked being the center of attention. During that time in Burgettstown, the children of immigrants were rarely cast in high school plays.[25] However, my father attained a certain degree of youthful popularity and he was unusual in having one of the leading roles in a high school drama.

In September 1933 when my father left Slovan to enter Washington and Jefferson College (W&J), seventeen miles away in Washington, Pennsylvania, the other children who had grown up with him in the alley behind the Penn Theater looked up to him. My father was the one chosen by my grandfather to go to college, and the support he received from the family's meager resources during the Depression made it impossible for my Aunt Helen to continue at the State Teachers College in California, Pennsylvania.[26] My

Aunt Jeanette told me that the family "made sure Aunt Helen quit college; the extra money went to your father's college. It was depression."[27]

W&J was founded in 1781 and is the eleventh oldest institution of higher learning in the United States. The college was far beyond the means of most Slovan residents, and my father was able to go there only because of his football scholarship. Money was tight and he had many cheap dinners of liver and onions to survive. He loved to tell me the joke about the son in college writing home to his father: "No mon, no fun, your son" and the father replying "Too bad, so sad, your dad." Perhaps he had this exchange with his father.

My father arrived on campus a decade after W&J's glory days in football. In 1922 it had sent a team to the Rose Bowl where it battled the University of California to a scoreless tie. In his day, they still played against the power-house Pitt (and lost by large margins). In college he played on the line as a center. In spite of his financial situation, practicality did not dictate his major in college. He pursued his intellectual interests by majoring in history and minoring in English. I would later continue his interests by becoming a historian, although I didn't know that he had majored in history until after his death when I saw a copy of his college transcript.

In the 1930s W&J was a men's college whose student body divided on socio-economic lines. Coming from an immigrant home without even a mother, his manners at the time were unpolished. My father's college transcript lists him as "non-Frat." The friends he retained from college had almost all been poor boys who played football with him. My father was not a bitter man and he never talked much about his social relationships in college, but he was aware of the gulf that divided him from his more affluent class-mates. Among them, he felt ashamed of his Italian family. When his sisters Evelyn and Helen met W&J college men, the young men were surprised to learn that my father had sisters.[28]

It could not have been easy for my father, whose illiterate Italian parents spoke broken English, to have mingled with these WASP fraternity boys. The W&J yearbook during his senior year, *Pandora 1938*, is filled with descriptions of dances organized by the fraternities. Photographs of the third annual Quadrille, the pre-Christmas Greek Swingout, and the Pan-Hellenic Formal all show young men in tuxedos and young women in sleek evening gowns. My father is not among them, although he loved to dance and he and my mother did a lot of it when they were dating.

While at college my father met my mother, Lois Louise Dittmar (1914–1996), in an Isley's Ice Cream shop where she worked making sand-wiches.[29] She was a quiet wallflower and was attracted to my father, a vain and boastful jock. His loud Italian masculine style was completely unlike the understated ways of her own German family. My mother was an insecure young woman who was intimidated by my father's boisterous family. Her early visits to the Mungello family apartment in Slovan are remembered chiefly for her drinking coke with aspirin to nurse her headaches.[30] She once became very upset when she overheard the Mungello sisters talking about her, although they generally liked her and this was not a family that hid their feelings.

My father did not want to marry an Italian girl because he said they were too bossy (like his sisters). Instead he chose the daughter of a German family, who turned out to be even bossier. They married in 1939. My Aunt Jeanette claimed that her brothers "both married Mothers."[31] I think my father wanted to marry into a German family because, in the subtle class rankings of that time, it would make him more American; This type of ethnic miscegenation was a form of upward social mobility because in 1939 Germans, who were more Anglo-Saxon and had been in the US longer, ranked higher in social status than Italians. While English, Irish, and German immigrants were grouped with native English speakers, Italians were seen as one step below— and the newly arrived Slavic immigrants were regarded as alien.[32] For similar reasons, my father fulfilled a lifelong wish to become an Episcopalian in 1977. He never said this was the reason, but I think he felt that Episcopalians had a higher social standing than Catholics.

Much of this seems ironic now, particularly since his own Italian family was more successful than the German family of my mother. My mother's father, Gustav Dittmar, had left his German school at fourteen and was brought to America to work in his uncle's car painting shop. After trying to establish his own auto-painting shop, he had to give it up because of respiratory problems due to the inhalation of paint fumes. He was obliged to work until his death at seventy-two as a maintenance man at Washington Steel Company. Today things look very different than they did then and it is hard for me to know exactly how my father felt as he worked his way up the social ladder. Unlike my father, no one ever called me "hunky." Elderly residents recalled that in Slovan, the epithet "hunky" was applied to all immigrant working-class families, like the Mungellos.[33]

After my father graduated from college in June of 1937, he tried teaching in high school in Washington but hated it. My mother was happy in Washington being near her family, but my father told Jeanette that he would rather "take the hose" (i.e., commit suicide) than continue teaching.[34] So he went back to Slovan to help tend the family business and became the manager of the newly built Mary Ann Theater in Burgettstown. After college, his manners improved, but he always retained certain coarse Italian peasant customs, such as blowing his nose onto the ground instead of using a handkerchief. But there was something more. Unlike his parents, who had crossed an ocean to seek out their dreams, my father lacked the drive to seek his fortune in the wider world. Instead, he returned to his hometown, savoring his college-educated status among the people he had grown up with and encouraging his children to do more.

My mother hated the unpredictable nature of the movie business, but she was infatuated with my father and naively believed she could change him. So despite his return to Slovan, they were married in July 1939. They went to Ligionier with a couple who were friends of my mother and were married by a justice of the peace. My Aunt Jeanette was surprised that none of the Mungellos were invited.[35] It was not an auspicious way to begin their marriage because as dysfunctional as my father's family was, he was bound to them in a way that (unlike his tie to my mother) could never be severed. The newlyweds set up housekeeping in one of the second-floor apartments next to the Penn Theater in Slovan. My father's family lived in the other second-floor apartment. It was the beginning of a stormy and troubled marriage that would last for forty years.

Jeanette shared my mother's dislike for the unpredictable motion theater business because "life must be planned for us." Movie theaters thrived until around 1950 when television appeared and thereafter they went into gradual decline. Along with this downward spiral, the marriage of my mother and father disintegrated.

The coal-mining economy of the Slovan-Burgettstown area was hit hard by the Great Depression. Between 1929 and 1933, the bituminous coal production in the local mines fell by almost half.[36] Things became so desperate that my grandfather and Uncle Tony went to work for a while for the WPA (Works Progress Administration), a Depression-era public works project established in 1935 that offered paying jobs to people on relief. Few people had extra money for the movies, and all but the Penn Theater closed. My grandfather went bankrupt spending over $30,000 (a half-million in 2015 dollars) to build a deluxe theater in nearby Burgettstown, a striking structure built through a family effort. Pap and Tony constructed the theater with the help of hired workers. (My dad was in college and avoided manual labor.) Jeanette shopped and Helen made the bread and together they made sandwiches for the worker's lunch. The theater was built in the art deco style typical of the thirties. It opened on April 24, 1937, and the local newspaper described the theater as "one of the finest in this part of the state."[37] My grandfather named it after his late wife Marianna (Americanized to Mary Ann), but the theater suffered from several disasters. Pap knew how to build buildings, but it was my grandmother who had the business acumen.

The troubles began only a few months after its opening. Fires struck the Mary Ann Theater in its opening year. On the evening of November 2, 1937, an usher discovered a fire in the rear of the theatre.[38] He informed my father and uncle who rushed to the front of the theatre and had the 300 people evacuate the building while flames swept through the second floor. Firemen gained control of the fire after an hour and a half.[39] This first fire destroyed the roof and the front of the auditorium, including the screen and sound equipment, causing over $10,000 ($164,000 in 2015 dollars) in damage. My grandfather repaired and reopened the theater in January of 1938 and installed air conditioning that summer. But a few months later in October 1938 a second fire completely destroyed the theater.[40] A newspaper article reported that the owners, the Mungello family, believed the second fire was caused by arson. Several nearby residents reported hearing two distinct explosions five minutes before the fire was discovered around 3:40 am, and state fire marshals investigated.

It seems that twenty-two years after my family fled the mob in Braddock, the mob had once again caught up with them in Burgettstown. The statistical likelihood of two accidental fires occurring in one year at a new theater is quite improbable. There were other possible causes, of course. Some family members believed that the owners of the older, competing Keith Theater had something to do with the fires. My Aunt Jeanette suspected a labor union who had picketed the theater over the Mungellos' refusal to hire union projectionists. The International Association of Theater and Stage Employees, an AFL union, applied pressure to hire their members. A newspaper reported that when the projectionist Mike Matusik was fired, the Mungello brothers began operating the projection machines themselves. According to the newspaper account, Matusik claimed that the cause of his dismissal was union activity while the Mungellos maintained that it was his "misconduct."The union filed a complaint with the Pennsylvania State Labor Relations Board, which held a public hearing on Matusik's firing in Pittsburgh on March 19, 1940,[41] Witnesses on both sides were called to testify.

Arson by—or with the collusion of—the Mafia seems most likely, however. In the late 1930s, the East Coast Mafia was a powerful force in the movie industry. It operated through gang-controlled unions, extorting money from both the movie studios and the studio-controlled theater chains.[42] A few years before dying in 2004, a long-time resident of Burgettstown told me the names of long-dead Mafia-connected residents of Burgettstown. The labor strife at the Mary Ann Theater and the fact that a smaller fire was followed a few months later by a more destructive fire would fit the pattern of Mafia pressure. But it also reinforced the continuing flight of my grandfather from gangsters.

Also suspicious was the funding for the Mary Ann Theater. Just as some questioned how Uncle Filippo became prosperous in his own time, many questioned where a poor illiterate Southern Italian immigrant and manual laborer like my grandfather found $30,000 (a half-million in 2015 dollars) to build a state-of-the-art theatre. Jeanette claimed that her father's and brother's labor and income from the Penn Theater built the theater, but $30,000 seems much too large a sum to have been earned that way. There must have been credit extended, but Burgettstown was an old, largely WASP town, whose local bankers seem unlikely to have extended such credit to an illiterate Italian in the depths of the Depression. A more likely source of funding was one of the Pittsburgh mob families. Prohibition had ended in 1933 with the repeal of the Eighteenth Amendment, and the Pittsburgh mob was searching for new sources of profit. If mob lending were involved, my grandfather might have had difficulty repaying. The fires and labor union strife could have been one way in which the gang pressured my family to make payment on a loan in arrears.

Such tactics were common at the time. For example, Nicolas A. Stirone (1902–1984) was a member of the Pittsburgh crime family who organized labor unions. He became president of Local 1085 of the International Hod Carriers and Building Laborers' Union (later renamed the Laborers' International Union of North America) and used his position to extort money from employers in return for labor peace.[43] Union membership fell during the Depression, and it is possible that the projectionists at the Mary Ann Theater became a target for expanding union membership. Much later, in 1958, Strone was arrested in Pittsburgh for violating the Hobbs Anti-Racketeering Act and convicted of extortion.

After the second fire in 1938, only the walls of the theater were left standing and these were so dangerously buckled that they had to be razed. Although the loss was estimated at $30,000–35,000, a considerable sum in 1938 dollars, damages were said to be largely covered by insurance. The theater was rebuilt, though the marquee was never restored to its original glamour. Popular movie stars like Hopalong Cassidy and the Cisco Kid appeared on the stage of the Mary Ann Theater during the intermission to promote their films. In 1942 the character actor Chris-Pin Martin (1893–1953) made an appearance. Martin was a Yacqui Indian who had been born in Tucson, but became famous as the comical big-bellied, wall-eyed Mexican Pancho in the Cisco Kid movies, and he and my grandfather became friends.

At fifty-eight years of age, Pap was ready to move again. He wanted to remarry and had an attractive widow from Pittsburgh in mind, but he needed to escape the opposition of his family. He also wanted to get away from my father and possibly also the mob. My grandfather's lifelong silence on the Black Hand/Mafia betrayed an anxiety that was never laid to rest. He had escaped them in 1914 when he fled and again in 1915 when the family moved to Slovan. But his need to escape from them yet again may have been based on his inability to meet their financial demands. So when Martin urged him to go to Los Angeles, my grandfather agreed. Before he left, my grandfather told my Uncle Tony to watch out for his brother (my father) because he took after Uncle Filippo, the Black Hander.[44] Twenty-five years later, Tony would have cause to believe this warning when he felt my father had broken his word on the sale of the drive-in.

My grandfather left for California in 1942. He left his Packard behind because he had never learned to drive it. Instead, he went by train with his daughter Helen who was traveling to marry William J. Burns Jr., her handsome blond sailor stationed in California. When Helen and Bill married on August 4, 1942, Martin arranged a wedding dinner for the newlyweds at the Twentieth-Century Fox studio restaurant. There is a studio portrait with my grandfather standing proudly behind them.

Except for one visit back to Pennsylvania in 1944, my grandfather spent the rest of his life in Los Angeles. He felt comfortable in the sunny southern California climate, so like his homeland in Italy. His daughters Mae, Helen, and Evelyn kept house for him. Mae was the first daughter to move to California. The family did not want her to sell tickets at the Mary Ann Theater and so she went to beauty school and opened a beauty shop in Slovan, one block from the Penn Theater. She later moved the shop to Homewood in Pittsburgh. Mae married a "gem" in Dominic Punaro who had been trained as a tailor in New York.[45] The newly married couple moved to Los Angeles where Uncle Dom established a successful custom tailor's shop on Wilshire Boulevard as a tailor to Hollywood movie stars like Burt Lancaster, Ava Gardner, Red Skelton, and Ozzie and Harriet Nelson's two sons David and Ricky.[46] He also cared for his mother in a nursing home and put his brother through college.

With Chris-Pin Martin's connections in Hollywood, my grandfather worked as an extra in some movies, but money was still tight. Because of his personal bankruptcy, his property was transferred, in part, to Mae as co-owner. Mae's brother-in-law was an accountant who did the book work on the transfer. Helen helped her father hire an attorney who obtained a court order forcing his sons to send him $25 each week from the family business for the rest of his life.[47] Always moved by the urge to build, my grandfather constructed a small apartment building at 1437 Lucile Avenue in Los Angeles. Mae asked her sisters to invest in the apartment.[48] It seems that Jeanette and Helen did not invest, while Mae and Evelyn did. The structure consisted of four attractive four-room apartments, with a basement, 3,577 total square feet.[49] It still stands today in Silver Lake, near the Sunset Junction, distinctly east or central, and a very hip part of town today.

My grandfather had "many girl friends" and according to Jeanette, he was good-looking ("better looking than his sons").[50] She remembered that "a good looking woman followed him to California."[51] She heard that he had lived with a woman for a while, but their relationship broke up.[52] Later he had another relationship with a younger woman who wanted to marry him.

According to Jeanette, Pap wanted Mae to remove her name as co-owner from the Lucille Avenue apartment property deed so that he could remarry.[53]

However, time ran out before any changes in the deed were made. On the evening of March 13, 1949 he asked his daughter Evelyn for a drink of water, suffered a heart attack, and died. His death certificate listed a coronary thrombosis due to arteriosclerosis. He was buried in Forest Lawn Cemetery in Glendale. I remember my father flying from Pittsburgh to Los Angeles for the funeral, a long journey by small twin-engine planes at that time.

My father apparently had additional reasons to fly to his father's funeral other than mourning for his father. The settlement of Pap's estate has remained murky. There were rumors about a will disappearing. Jeanette said Pap's attorney wanted to go to California after Pap died, but did not. Jeanette and Helen complained that they did not receive a share of the sale of the apartment house on Lucille Avenue.[54] However, they had not accepted Mae's invitation to invest in the property. The estate sale of Pap's apartment building on Lucille Avenue was handled by Mae who reimbursed Evelyn for her investment. After Mae's death, Jeanette complained to Donna that her mother bought a "nice Spanish home" in Beverly Hills for $60,000 and "gave us nothing from [Pap's] apt home."[55]

NOTES

1. Jeanette Boake to the author, August 24, 2004, and May 14, 2005.

2. John Michael Gabrielli, "The Economic and Social Development of an American Small Town: Burgettstown, Pennsylvania: 1773–1991," Bachelor of Arts thesis in history, Princeton University, Princeton, New Jersey, 1991, 13–14.

3. David Demarest and Eugene Levy, "Remnants of an Industrial Landscape," *Pittsburgh History* 72, no. 3 (Fall 1989): 130–131.

4. A. D. White, "Slovan," *Burgettstown Enterprise* (1946).

5. Jeanette Boake to the author, March 12, 2002.

6. Jeanette Boake to the author, May 12, 1999.

7. Jeanette Boake to the author, June 28, 2000.

8. Jeanette Boake to the author, May 12, 1999.

9. See Jerre Mangione, *An Ethnic at Large: A Memoir of America in the Thirties and Forties* (New York: Putnam's, 1978; reprinted 1983), 13.

10. Jeanette Boake to the author, June 6, 1997.

11. Jeanette Boake to the author, June 15, 2001.

12. Jeanette Boake to the author, July 7, 2002.

13. Jeanette Boake to the author, February 23, 2005.

14. Cheryl Bidlack to the author, April 21, 2009.

15. Jeanette Boake to the author, July 7, 2002.

16. Jeanette Boake to the author, March 2, 2006.

17. Jeanette Boake to the author, May 12, 1999.

18. Jeanette Boake to the author, July 2, 2004.

19. "Thirteen Independent Tickets in the County," *The Daily Notes* (Canonsburg, Pennsylvania), October 9, 1929, 3.

20. Jeanette Boake to the author, July 11, 2003.

21. Jeanette Boake to the author, May 12, 1998, and February 23, 2005.

22. Jeanette Boake to the author, January 13, 2006.

23. "McDonald Hi Held Scoreless by Union Hi," *The Daily Notes* (Canonsburg, Pennsylvania), November 23, 1929, 8.

24. Jeanette Boake to the author, June 26, 2002.

25. Gabrielli, "Economic and Social Development of an American Small Town," 84.

26. Jeanette Boake to the author, May 12, 1999.

27. Jeanette Boake to the author, December 27, 2005.

28. Jeanette Boake to the author, May 1, 2006.

29. Jeanette Boake to the author, August 2, 2004.

30. Jeanette Boake to the author, spring 2002.

31. Jeanette Boake to the author, May 12, 1999.

32. David Brody, *Steelworkers in America; The Nonunion Era* (New York: Harper and Row, 1960), 119–121.

33. Gabrielli, "Economic and Social Development of an American Small Town," 49.

34. Jeanette Boake to the author, January 28, 2004.

35. Jeanette Boake to the author, spring 2002.

36. Gabrielli, "Economic and Social Development of an American Small Town," 69.

37. *Burgettstown Enterprise*, November 1, 1937, 1.

38. "Audience Leaves Burning Burgettstown Theater Safely," *New Castle News* (New Castle, Pennsylvania), November 2, 1937, 9.

39. "200 Persons Escape from Burning Theater," *Wilkes-Barre Record* (Wilkes-Barre, Pennsylvania), November 2, 1937, 1.

40. "Fire Destroys Burgettstown Theater; Probe Is Started," *The Washington Observer*, October 11, 1938, 1.

41. "State Labor Board Hears County Case," *The Daily Republican* (Monongahela, Pennsylvania), March 19, 1940, 1.

42. Thomas Repetto, *American Mafia: A History of Its Rise to Power* (New York: Holt, 2004), 205.

43. Bureau of Narcotics (US Treasury Department), *Mafia: The Government's Secret File on Organized Crime* (New York: HarperCollins, 2007), 722.

44. Jeanette Boake to the author, June 25, 2003.

45. Jeanette Boake to the author, September 19, 2003.

46. Jeanette Boake to the author, June 6, 1997.

47. Jeanette Boake to the author, September 15, 1999.

48. Jeanette Boake to the author, September 25, 1998.

49. The Zillow.com listing as of June 26, 2015, indicates that the apartment house at 1437 Lucile Avenue, Silver Lake, Los Angeles, California 90026 was built in 1949. It last sold on December 1990 for $280,000 and the current value is listed as $1,432,949.

50. Jeanette Boake to the author, March 11, 2004.

51. Jeanette Boake to the author, July 11, 2003.

52. Jeanette Boake to the author, September 23, 2002.

53. Jeanette Boake to the author, July 11, 2003.

54. Jeanette Boake to the author, September 23, 2002, January 24, 2003, March 2, 2004, and July 10, 2004.

55. Jeanette Boake to the author, March 2, 2006, and July 5, 2005.

Chapter Four

Dreams and Feuds, 1941–1989

My sister Marianne was born in 1941, five months before the Japanese attack on Pearl Harbor. My father used to joke and call her "a Pearl Harbor baby" because she saved him from an early military induction. The sons of Italian immigrants to the United States worked hard to demonstrate their loyalty as American soldiers and many lost their lives in the war, but my father's attitude was more complicated. He taught me that the most important thing in life is loyalty to my family. However, he was an imperfect messenger of that teaching and I would share his imperfection.

When Italy was united in 1861, the nationalistic impetus for the movement called the *Risorgimento* came from the north. Although the revolutionary leader Garibaldi had enlisted the support of thousands of peasants from the south, the southerners fought not for nationalism but rather to protect their families from the oppressive landlords and the burdensome government. The dreams of reviving the glories of ancient Rome that inflamed the northerners were irrelevant to the southern peasants who distrusted all political ideologies. Their primary concern was for *l'ordine della famiglia,* which, above all, meant paying honor and loyalty to the family rather than to anyone else.[1] In the late nineteenth and early twentieth centuries, many Italians had emigrated to the US to avoid being conscripted to fight other peoples' wars, and something of this old loyalty of family over state lingered in my father's mentality.

I was born late in 1943, but in the fall of that year the deferment for married fathers was being abolished and my father was finally inducted on June 29, 1945. This was after the war had ended in Europe, although fighting continued with no definite end in sight in the Pacific. But he was never shipped to the Pacific theater. Instead, he was sent to Wiesbaden in the American Occupied Zone of Germany where he served for six months in a

Special Services company as an administrative non-commissioned officer. Because of postwar demobilization and his dependents, my father was given an early discharge in May of 1946, less than eleven months after entering the army.

In spite of its brevity, that brief tour of duty in Germany gave my father a glimpse of a grander and more exciting life that he might have had. After he died, my brother sent me a box of his things. Among this assortment, I found four letters written between 1948 and 1954 with some photographs that he had carefully preserved for almost forty years. They were from a young and attractive German widow named Helga I. Steiner whom my father had met in Wiesbaden soon after her release from a concentration camp. The letters make no mention of the reason for her internment, which was probably a painful subject to discuss. Postwar Germany was filled with young women, including widows with children, who lived in desperation. Helga had two young sons, born shortly before her imprisonment.

In a letter from January 1950, Helga wrote that "the 'Cigarette and Candy-Days' passed away and the 'Fräuleins' are cooling off again. No more: *C'est la guerre.*" The cigarettes and candy made otherwise humble American soldiers rich and powerful in occupied Germany and attracted these desperate young women to them. American soldiers used cigarettes as currency and the women sold their youthful charm (and certainly sex) in exchange. But, in the process, affection and even love sometimes happened. Many German Fräuleins married GIs and escaped to new lives in America, but Helga's two boys were an obstacle to that.

My father was not a smoker, but he sold American cigarettes (and who knows what else) in the postwar German black market and he brought home enough money to build two small rental houses behind our home on Archer Lane in Burgettstown. The letters from Helga indicate that it was kindness rather than just cigarettes and candy that my father exchanged for her charms. The result was romantic feelings for one another and probably an affair. Helga was educated and articulate. She wrote in proficient (though imperfect) English and, after my father left, she worked for a few months as an interpreter for the American occupation forces. She had considered marrying an American GI and coming to live in the United States, but then she decided against it.

In one of her letters in 1948 she asked my father to send used clothing and shoes for herself and her sons, something she had never believed she would become desperate enough to request. I don't know if he sent them, although one of her letters refers to a package he had sent. Helga knew that my father was married and had two children, and I suspect they both sensed the limits of their wartime relationship had been reached when they'd said goodbye in 1946. My father was not the divorcing kind. But although the relationship was at an end, the feeling lingered in both of them. In a postscript to her last letter, Helga wrote, "Your picture has been framed and will last for the next fifty years." My father saved her letters and picture for almost that long, but he never left his family for her. It was from him that I absorbed this value and found myself reliving it twenty-three years later.

My father was always dreaming dreams. Most of them never came true. One of my most vivid memories of spending time with him was riding around in his car. He loved to drive around and he liked having me along, riding in the front passenger seat, as he visited all the places where a small and independent businessman went. He was restless and always looking for new business opportunities. When we drove to Film Row in Pittsburgh, he took me to a private screening room where new movies were previewed. He proudly introduced me to his business associates. We also went to odd places, like a fireworks factory to buy fireworks for the drive-in theatre or to property sites he was thinking of buying. We also visited people that my father had known from years before. When I grew up, I had a different occupation and never drove around like that with my son. Maybe I should have. Maybe it would have kept him from becoming a drug addict.

Some of my earliest childhood memories are images from the construction of an adjoining building at the side of the Mary Ann Theater in Burgettstown. In July 1949 Leonard Sasso, president of Penowa Coal Company, announced plans to move the company headquarters from Pittsburgh to a new office building in Burgettstown under construction by the Mungello brothers.[2] Pap's two sons—my father and Uncle Tony—were expanding the model he had used with the Penn Theater in Slovan. Instead of apartments, they built commercial rental spaces for the coal company, an attorney, dentist, florist, beautician, and a medical doctor. The physician, Dr. Angelo Spanogians, had originally rented office space from the Mungellos' building in Slovan, next to the Penn Theater. He was a kindly man who reset my arm when I broke it at the local swimming pool. My father and Uncle Tony both lived in houses nearby and managed the property together. The new building included a large hall on the ground-floor that began as a bowling alley and later evolved into a roller-skating rink and ballroom for dances as well as a banquet hall. As children of a landlord, my sister and I were given free access to most of the activities there, not all of which were in my view enjoyable. When the entertainers Salt and Peanuts began teaching dancing classes for children in the ballroom, I was (much to my humiliation) one of only three boys enrolled. I was already beginning to feel sensitive about my masculinity and this didn't help. However, I was less than ten at the time and too young to disobey my parents' wishes.

Salt and Peanuts were typical of the colorful, slightly over-the-hill people who filled my boyhood. They were a married radio and vaudeville team who sang comic songs and love ballads. Frank "Salt" Kurtz was born around 1900 in Kansas while Peanuts came from Joplin, Missouri. Peanuts was dancing in a Chicago revue when Salt spotted her. He recruited her into their song-and-dance team; he played the guitar, she danced, and together they sang duets.[3] They lived an itinerant theatrical life, performing in theaters and radio stations from New York to St. Louis.

Salt and Peanuts were already past their prime when they began teaching dance lessons in Burgettstown, but my sister adored them. Salt had put on some weight and he handled the business ends of things with style. The large roll of dollar bills that he carried around impressed me. Peanuts was trim and dark-haired, wore fishnet stockings, and had once been quite pretty. I didn't like these dance lessons any more than the piano lessons my mother forced me to take from Miss Taggert. By contrast, the roller skating operation was run by a sweet old guy we called "Pop Stewart" and was a lot more fun; I went twice a week without fail.

Although my father was a prominent businessman in Burgettstown, prominence in a town of only 2,383 people is a very relative term. The population of Burgettstown between 1940 and 1960 was stagnant while Slovan and the nearby towns declined. My father loved show business people and there were many others beside Salt and Peanuts who entered his life. Burgettstown is only forty miles from Wheeling, West Virginia, the home of the Saturday night *Wheeling Jamboree* that was broadcast from the Capitol Theater by WWVA radio station. WWVA's powerful 50,000-watt transmitter introduced country music to the northeastern part of the US.[4] My father and uncle brought a number of these country singers, such as Patsy Cline, to Burgettstown to perform on the Mary Ann Theater stage. One of these cowboy entertainers gave me a lifelike replica of a six-gun with revolving bullet chambers. Sometimes my father would bring these show biz characters home where my mother would always dutifully feed them, though she would have much preferred seeing people who held more 9–5 jobs and received regular paychecks.

One of the strangest of these people was an elderly gentleman named Jack Rose. (My mother called him a "Hungarian Jew," as if she were describing a runaway felon.) He was then selling cheap stone exteriors for homes and offices, and he had a crew of low-paid Puerto Ricans who would apply the stones and mortar. Mr. Rose always dressed in a suit and vest with an impressive pocket watch that announced the time with chimes. He also wore a prosthetic device where one of his legs had been amputated, perhaps because of diabetes. He had been a magician and would sometimes demonstrate card tricks and even acts of telepathy. These upset my mother because telepathy was too close to mesmerism (hypnotism), necromancy, and other forms of spiritism that her religion (Christian Science) roundly condemned. Anyway, Mr. Rose became a fixture in our home. I would come home from school and find him sleeping on the living room couch. When we had dinner, he would always join us. Finally, he made the mistake of interfering in the kitchen. My mother insisted that my father speak with him and Mr. Rose disappeared.

My father was not the only one who brought people into our home, but while my father loved show biz types and eccentrics, my mother favored members of her family. In 1953, my mother's family brought her widowed cousin and fifteen-year-old son from postwar Germany to live with us for almost a year. My Aunt Frieda was a war widow from Memel whose husband had died fighting in the German army in World War II. She and her son had to flee East Prussia when the Russian army made its brutal advance. She slept in my sister's room while my 16-year old cousin slept in my room. I enjoyed having him as a roommate partly because I was attracted to him on an adolescent sexual level. I dreamt of climbing into bed with him, but he was not very experimental and he had an unforgivable habit of telling my mother everything that happened.

One of the defining features of my Italian family has been our feuds. Our explosive and destructive behavior generated these bitter feuds, the kind of feuds people fight with the intensity of a tragic drama and carry to their graves. These feuds became so ingrained that the next generation was expected to continue them, as though inherited through the blood, without even knowing the reasons why the feuds began. One of the bitterest feuds involved my Aunt Jessie, the woman my Uncle Tony married. When I was in grade school, I wanted to join the Cub Scouts. There were two Cub Scout packs in Burgettstown. One met very close to my home and the other met on the other side of town. However, I was not allowed to join the closer one because the den mother was my Aunt Jessie, who had been shunned by the rest of the Mungellos. The poor woman lived almost like a recluse in a house only a block away from the Mary Ann Theater. She wore dark glasses and was almost never seen, although my Uncle Tony was constantly around the theater and everyone was on amicable terms with him. Because I could not join her Cub Scout pack, I had to walk three miles to the other side of town where Mary DiOrio's pack met.

Once when Mrs. DiOrio was ill, my Aunt Jessie had both Cub Scout packs meet together and I was surprised at how nice she was to me. Much later, I learned the reason why she had been shunned by my father's family. My Aunt Jeanette claimed that Tony and Jesse had been childhood sweethearts, but she had "left Tony and got married and came back when the show [theater] was making money."[5] After she returned, my Uncle Tony forgave her and married her, but my aunts saw her leaving Tony as a betrayal of him and my family. Their hostility was so great that late one night around 1940 after the Mary Ann Theater closed, a fight broke out. When my Uncle Tony was driving my aunts Helen and Evelyn home to Slovan, my Aunt Jesse refused to ride in the car with them. The three women had an argument that ended in a screaming, hair-pulling fight with Jessie on Main Street in front of the Mary Ann Theater. Violence between women was very rare and the incident solidified the hatred which then continued until all of the parties involved died. As far as my family was concerned, my Aunt Jessie was already dead to them a half-century before she died.

The women of the Mungello family felt intensely not only about their siblings, husbands, and lovers but also about their children. The relationships between mothers and daughters have been particularly intense and oftentimes acrimonious. My Aunt Jeanette was trained as a maternity nurse at St. Rosella Nursing School in Pittsburgh. She met a young pharmacist named Louis Bocchicchio, whose family came from Caserta, near my ancestral hometown. She married Lou two weeks after graduating from nursing school in 1941. At that time, Italian-sounding names were abandoned by many Italian-American immigrants. Their first-generation American children's greatest desire was to be accepted as full Americans. Jeanette believed that anti-Italian feeling about the very Italian-sounding name Bocchicchio had hurt her husband's career as a pharmacist. She wrote, "I did not want my girls with that name."[6] So, during her first pregnancy she had her father's attorney in Washington, Pennsylvania, change their name from Bocchicchio to Boake.[7]

Jeanette's acrimonious relationship with her first daughter, Cheryl Marie, began during her pregnancy. Her husband Lou was serving in the wartime Navy as a pharmacist and he visited only once in three and a half years.[8] Jeanette lived in the family apartments in Slovan and helped her sister Evelyn run the Penn Theater. When she was near the time of birth, she was swollen and suffering from toxemia (blood poisoning). Her physician said she was "walking around with a bag of dynamite."[9] She said she was "near death when Cheryl was born."[10] Cheryl weighed only four and a half pounds. Jeanette's near-fatal delivery of her daughter was a harbinger of their acrimonious relationship that would follow.

When Helen announced that she was going to California with her father in 1942, Jeanette said "it broke her heart" because she really wanted to go.[11] But she had married on November 27, 1941, and soon after became pregnant with Cheryl. She waited forty-three years to go to California. When she was in her eighties she voiced a poignant regret: "I wish I could live my life again, I would be a different person." And yet she also said, "I believe in fate."[12]

Cheryl was only eight months younger than me, and we spent a lot of time playing together as children at family gatherings. Cheryl was very sweet, but she had the kind of innocence that was a magnet for abuse. My Uncle Lou nursed a lot of inner grievances that led him to drink. I remembered seeing the Seven Roses Whiskey bottles at his house, something that was completely absent from my home. In family gatherings he controlled his drinking, but when at home, he drank and became abusive, particularly toward Cheryl. She had childhood insecurities and she had inherited a skin condition that afflicted certain women in the Mungello family. However, she also had inherited the trait of steely determination found among the Mungello women, and as she matured, she would lose her passive childhood personality.

Cheryl believed that her parents' verbal abuse of her intensified when their second child was born with spina bifida (an incompletely formed spinal cord). Jeanette refused to even hold the infant and he died thirteen days after birth. My Uncle Lou's bitterness over the death of his only son was turned toward his wife and his daughter. In short, my aunt and uncle shared a great sorrow, and they took it out on their oldest daughter.

My Aunt Jeanette's late-life view of Uncle Lou was colored by her loneliness and nostalgia. There was a family rumor that she had considered leaving him, and certainly he never shared her lifelong dream of moving to southern California. He eventually retired and reluctantly moved with her to San Diego. Lou had enhanced Jeanette's status, enabling her to move from a "coal mining town to marry a 'city boy'" who was a University of Pittsburgh graduate and a pharmacist. [13] Several times in her letters, she noted with pride that while her sister Helen had married a steelworker, she had married a professional.

Lou came from a hardscrabble, abusive Italian family. He was a hard worker, and for this quality Jeanette forgave him everything. Work was a solace for Lou's pain and insecurities. His hands would break out with an eczema and he drank whiskey excessively. [14] Eventually after moving to California, his condition caught up with him and he began losing weight. He had surgery for colon and liver cancer, and he knew he was dying but he never discussed it with Jeanette. Finally he asked her to call hospice and they came with a bed, oxygen tank, and medicines. [15] When Lou was in hospice care, dying of cancer in San Diego, Jeanette had such difficulty dealing with his demise that she refused to tell her younger daughter in New Jersey that he was near death. [16] My cousin Claudia needed to have a nurse call to convey news of her father's death.

Cheryl was a bright and a talented pianist of popular music, but she felt that she could do nothing right in her parents' eyes. One must emphasize "felt" here because her younger sister Claudia felt that their parents favored Cheryl over her. My Aunt Jeanette saw things differently: "Cheryl cost us a lot of money. We paid for piano lessons $45 each to get her in Carnegie Mellon." [17] "We gave her a Baldwin [piano]." [18] This sounds strange coming from middle-class parents, but Jeanette had spent a long time climbing out of the poverty of the Great Depression and they had a phobic fear of becoming poor again. But comparing their letters, it became clear that they struggled with an intense underlying mother-daughter dispute that they were never able to resolve. I think the dispute was based on Cheryl's feeling that her mother never really loved her.

After living with Aunt Evelyn in California for a few months in 1966, Cheryl moved out and attended San Fernando Valley State University for a while, but then returned to Pittsburgh. Carnegie Mellon University accepted her because of her musical talent and she went there for a while, mostly, she claimed, to please her parents. Later she transferred to Point Park College and majored in early childhood education. Unsupported by her parents, she lived in a room at the Salvation Army for two years. When she graduated, her mother pointedly went to the circus (which she hated) instead of attending her daughter's commencement ceremony.

After turning thirty, Cheryl met Duane Bidlack, who had a doctorate in engineering and a disintegrating marriage. They fell in love and had an affair. After he divorced his first wife, Cheryl married him at the age of thirty-four. It was Uncle Tony who drove Cheryl to the wedding. Her dad did walk her down the aisle, but he refused to pay for the wedding dinner because he and Jeanette both disapproved of Duane, a divorced man. Cheryl and Duane had two children—a girl named Belinda and a boy named Andrew. Andrew had inherited Cheryl's musical talent, and by 2007 he was singing as a tenor in several opera companies, including the San Francisco Opera Company. [19]

Meanwhile, when Cheryl underwent a hysterectomy in November 1988, her parents came to her home in Laramie, Wyoming, supposedly to help. However, a terrible argument ensued and they separated on bad terms. This is another trait of my family—running away at the height of an argument.

Cheryl wrote to me saying that her mother had become hysterical, but the problem between them went much deeper. [20] The Mungellos compensated for their lack of physical affection with an excess of inappropriate and destructive emotion. This family trait of explosive and self-destructive behavior once again surfaced and Cheryl complained, "I am most definitely a victim." But if so, she ended her victimhood by breaking off ties not only with her parents and her younger sister Claudia but also with the entire family. Her last letter to me was in February 1989 and my Christmas card of 1991 was returned with the postal notation that the forwarding period had expired. She and Duane had moved, but no one knew to where. For many years her family was dead to her.

For twenty years, all efforts to contact her failed. In a family whose highest value is loyalty, Cheryl's severing of all ties seemed to be the greatest disloyalty. My Aunt Jeanette and Uncle Lou refused to even speak her name. They disowned her both legally and emotionally. When I asked my Aunt Jeanette what year Cheryl was born in, she wrote, "I think Cheryl was born in 1943. We never think about her; I think she is dead." [21] In 2005 Jeanette rewrote her will to exclude Cheryl's children Andrew and Belinda. [22] Given the fact that the Mungello sisters never forgave my Aunt Jessie for what they felt was her betrayal of my Uncle Tony, it is not surprising that my Aunt

Jeanette died without ever being reconciled to Cheryl. Forgiveness is not highly rated with the Mungellos.

Finally in 2009, my cousin Beverly Portillo, my Aunt Helen's daughter, located Cheryl and spoke with her by phone. Finding her again was a happy event but mixed with sadness, as Cheryl had a terminal case of ovarian cancer. She had been my favorite cousin for years, and we both shared a deep vulnerability. In one of our last e-mail exchanges, she wrote: "As for me, I had to stop the chemo treatments because we were getting no results. It never helped in all these years, so I am in Hospice Care now. It makes me sad that I fought so hard and now it has come to this for us. What can I say?"[23] Like so many of the Mungello women, her life was more like an intense song than a beautiful flower. She died on July 25, 2010.

NOTES

1. Richard Gambino, *Blood of My Blood: The Dilemma of the Italian-Americans* (New York: Anchor Books, 1975), 3–4, 71.

2. "Coal Company," *The Daily Notes* (Canonsburg, Pennsylvania), July 20, 1949, 3.

3. Frank [Salt] Kurtz self-published a songbook entitled *Salt and Peanuts: Songs of the Shenandoah* (Staunton, Virginia, 1942), 16 pp. It contains the lyrics, melody lines, and guitar chords of twelve sentimental songs written by Kurtz and Richard Liller, including "Who'll Take the Place of Mother" and "Old Fashioned Family Prayers."

4. Bill C. Malone, *Country Music, U.S.A.*, rev. ed. (Austin: University of Texas Press, 1985), 98; Ivan M. Tribe, *Mountaineer Jamboree: Country Music in West Virginia* (Lexington: University of Kentucky Press, 1984), 42–72.

5. Jeanette Boake to the author, June 28, 2000.

6. Jeanette Boake to the author, December 20, 2003.

7. Jeanette Boake to the author, December 27, 2005.

8. Jeanette Boake to the author, December 20, 2003.

9. Jeanette Boake to the author, March 1, 2006.

10. Jeanette Boake to the author, March 11, 2004.

11. Jeanette Boake to the author, January 11, 2003.

12. Jeanette Boake to the author, November 15, 2004.

13. Jeanette Boake to the author, November 15, 2004.

14. Jeanette Boake to the author, August 2, 2004.

15. Jeanette Boake to the author, July 10, 2004.

16. Jeanette Boake to the author, April 18, 2005.

17. Jeanette Boake to the author, July 16, 2003.

18. Jeanette Boake to the author, April 14, 2004.

19. Andrew Bidlack (b. 1979) is a tenor who has sung with the Florida Grand Opera, San Francisco Opera, and Opera Omaha. He currently lives in Baltimore, Maryland.

20. Cheryl Bidlack to the author, January 29, 1989.

21. Jeanette Boake to the author, July 10, 2004.

22. Jeanette Boake to the author, February 23, 2005.

23. Cheryl Bidlack to the author, March 31, 2010.

Chapter Five

A Small Town in Pennsylvania, 1947–1955

Going back to my earliest memories, I have always felt an erotic attraction to other males. I first realized this in childhood and long before puberty. No one taught it to me, no one abused me sexually, and no one ever forced me to do anything that I did not want to do. I am not a passive personality. At the age of ten I would get crushes on older males, particularly lifeguards at pools, and I would follow them around. But from an early age, I knew that my attraction to males was something I should keep secret.

By the time I was a teenager, I knew of a young unmarried businessman in town who spent a lot of time with younger guys. He drove an expensive convertible, and one day in a neighboring town he picked up a hitchhiker and propositioned him. When word of this got out, he disappeared and I never saw him again. The shame over exposure of homosexuality among adult males was so intense in small towns in America of the 1950s that flight was usually the only option.

My childhood was naturally shaped by all the movies I saw at my father's theaters. The post–World War II male sex symbol was embodied in the hypermasculine movie heroes of the fifties—pretty boys with bland personalities and limited acting talent. Several of these movie icons were creations of a movie agent named Henry Willson (1911–1978), a closeted homosexual who easily secured sexual favors from both gay and straight clients. In the sexually repressed style of the fifties, none of this was known outside of Hollywood. Willson had a remarkable talent for spotting photogenic Adonises, and he was famous for renaming actors with catchy macho names like Guy, Tab, Troy, and Rock.

In the many movies I saw, I felt an erotic attraction to certain male movie stars; among them, James Dean, Tab Hunter, Anthony Perkins, Troy Dona-

47

hue, and Guy Madison (but not Rock Hudson) were particular favorites of mine. Even at that young age, my sensitivity to same-sex feelings in others ("gaydar") must have already been activated because several of these stars were, in fact, closeted gays or bisexuals. [1]

The Italian families who lived in my small town shared most of the homophobic attitudes of post–World War II America, and this misled me in my understanding of the native culture in Italy. Most of the Italians who immigrated to the United States in the early twentieth century were peasants whose rural values were centered on marriage and family. I didn't realize then that same-sex activity had flourished throughout history in the more urban areas of Italy. Not until I first visited Italy in 1974 at thirty years of age did I become aware of the amorphous sexuality of Italians. It helped me to realize that my same-sex feelings were part of who I was and where I came from.

In Italian Catholic culture, sexual sins were regarded more lightly than in American Protestant culture. The most famous depiction of hell ever written is by the Italian (actually Florentine) Dante Alighieri (1265–1321). He viewed sexual lust as one of the least serious of the seven deadly sins (pride, envy, anger, sloth, avarice, gluttony, and lust). [2] The third ring in Dante's seventh circle of hell has often been said to contain people guilty of "unnatural vice" (sodomy). However their sexual sinfulness seems to have been the dubious projection of a later and more puritanical view of sexuality rather than Dante's vision because none of the people that Dante mentions were identifiable sodomites. [3]

My family built things. Like their father Raffaele, my father and uncle were agitated by a continuing urge to build. In 1955, they built a drive-in theater in the hollow below the old zinc plant in Slovan. It was called the Tri-State Drive-In Theater because it was only a few miles from the West Virginia panhandle which bordered both Pennsylvania and Ohio. But while my grandmother had been ahead of the curve when it came to business, her sons were slightly behind it. My grandparents moved to Slovan in 1915 when it was a boomtown, and the economy there peaked in the 1920s. Although World War II helped to end the Depression, the zinc plant was labor intensive and could only survive with cheap labor. However, the plant was unionized in the 1930s, and after the war ended, workers' demands for increased wages and benefits—along with the inefficiency of outdated technology—caused the plant to close in 1947. [4] Moreover, coal was losing its competitive advantage to other fuels and the last coal mines in the area were shut down by 1951. [5] The area's population went into a continual decline from its peak in the 1940s. The new drive-in theater caught the tail end of the enthusiasm for drive-in theaters.

My mother hated the Mungello family business partnership because of its irregular fluctuations of income and lack of certainty. She criticized it until eventually my father and Uncle Tony divided the property, with my uncle taking the Mary Ann Theater and the adjoining office building in Burgettstown and my father taking the drive-in theater and adjacent rental properties in Slovan. My father always felt a bond to Slovan and to the people of his boyhood home. For him Slovan was a humble sanctuary from a bigger world that he lacked the audacity to challenge. This was something my mother never could understand or accept.

The Mary Ann Theater operated for thirty-nine years until it was closed and was demolished in 1975 in order to construct a highway bypass through Burgettstown. My Uncle Tony received a financial settlement from the state. The drive-in had a much shorter existence. When business began to fall off in the early 1960s and my father had my college expenses to cover, he supplemented his income working as the chief juvenile probation officer of the Washington County court. My father sold the drive-in when he and my mother moved to Florida in 1966, but it was no longer a viable business and its closing was inevitable.

My Uncle Tony believed that my father had agreed to sell the drive-in to him. This was probably true, but my father changed his mind. The rest of the family felt that he had "double-crossed his brother."[6] However, the need for money and my mother's opposition to any more family business arrangements was what caused my father to sell the property to someone else. Once again, the explosive trait in my family surfaced. My uncle felt betrayed and never forgave my father. My father made excuses. At one point he said his children had opposed the sale, and at another point he said he did not want my Aunt Jessie to have it. Jeanette knew this was not the truth and said, "My brothers always lied to us."[7] When Jeanette asked on another occasion why he double-crossed Tony, my father said he was acting on behalf of my mother and said "she is the mother of my children."[8]

Flawed as my father was, he honored his marriage and betrayed his brother. In return, my mother drove him out of their home and remarried. My father never remarried. Flawed loyalties are nevertheless loyalties of a sort and they would make a fitting epitaph on my father's gravestone. The break in the long and close relationship between my father and his brother was never healed. When Jeanette asked Tony if he was going to Dom's funeral, he said, "I already did my crying."[9] My father was dead to his brother Tony.

Today the drive-in site sits empty and abandoned. My Uncle Tony died in 1994 and my Aunt Jessie died in 1996. Although my cousin Anthony Junior can be abrasive and still refuses to have any contact with my father's children, he showed great loyalty to his mother and took care of her during her last days. He told my Aunt Jeanette that he held her hand when she died.[10] He is married but is childless and the last of the Mungellos to have left the Slovan-Burgettstown area. My family's presence there, once so vibrant, is fading.

I spent many hours working at my father's drive-in theater, and I was introduced to mutual masturbation there by a slightly older boy named Jimmy who was one of my father's cronies. I was twelve and he was fifteen when we met, and we almost immediately became jack-off buddies. Jimmy chewed tobacco and his habit of spitting fascinated me. He was very thin and he was so embarrassed by his skinny legs that I never, ever saw him take off his jeans (the only kind of pants he owned). He was a poor boy. He eventually married and had children. To this day I remember him fondly as the boy who introduced me to sex play.

But boys' sex play was one thing and local class barriers were another. There were fairly clear small-town class divisions based on race, speech, personal cleanliness, education, and wealth. Jimmy always refused to come into my home, although I kept inviting him. He said that he just didn't feel comfortable there. He was acceptable to my mother because he was clean, unlike many of my father's cronies who my mother would feed separately at a table in the garage. One of these cronies was Frankie. Frankie was a hard-working, illiterate Italian-American who worked for my father. He lived with Gracie, the Mary Ann Theater cleaning woman, in a tiny house built for her in back of the theater. I doubt that they were married; marriage can be a luxury for the very poor. I never knew either of their last names. Frankie did not speak much, and when he did I could never understand him. Gracie talked more, and I could understand her even less. Both of them had speech impediments and also were missing a lot of teeth. I doubt that they could afford dentures. They were among the poorest of the poor in Burgettstown.

Attitudes toward race were complicated in my family. There were well-known cases of miscegenation in town. I knew a boy whose sister was half-black, which scandalized some people. Pennsylvania's public schools were not segregated, as they were in nearby West Virginia where they were integrated by the Supreme Court ruling of 1954. However, there definitely were informal but accepted racial barriers, such as the separate seating section in the rear right side of the Mary Ann Theater for "colored people." By contrast, our black cleaning woman ate lunch with us. My mother was unusual in that regard and she would eventually have a local light-skinned black woman, Mrs. Edna Webster, as her practitioner (spiritual counselor) in Christian Science. As a boy, I played with Edna's son Charlie, who had skin as white as mine and bright red hair. One of his attractive "colored" sisters became a high school cheerleader, a prominent position in this sports-loving small town. Mrs. Webster was a thin, attractive, intelligent, and ambitious woman. Life in those years must have been difficult for her.

In his youth my father had dark good looks and a strong body. He was five-foot-eight, an average male height for that time, and as he grew older, he became barrel-chested. Although his hair receded early, he maintained a touch of vanity into his old age. He was always going on diets and announcing his initial weight loss with great fanfare. I don't remember seeing him sick in bed for a single day of his life, although as he grew older, his naps on the living room recliner grew longer and his snoring grew louder. He rarely swore and he had a phobia of rats; he became upset by even the mention of them. Rats had been a problem during his boyhood in Slovan, and he apparently had a bad experience with them.

My father liked attractive women and some of them liked him. There seem to have been instances of his unfaithfulness to my mother. My Aunt Jeanette said to me that "many women went for your father."[11] She wrote: "Your father never drank or smoked, he may have enjoyed other women, but your Mom was at fault. She would go to [her parents' home in] Washington and stay for weeks. . . . She loved your father but one doesn't *change a man*."[12] After moving to Florida, my father suffered from an attack of Bell's Palsy that disfigured his face and from which he never fully recovered.

After he and my mother divorced, my father had girlfriends. I met one of them, an attractive woman younger than my father. This woman later claimed that he maintained his sexual vigor into the last years of his life even though he was becoming diabetic. In 1978 he tried to revive a postwar romance with a woman in Germany. The woman, Mrs. Florentine M. Calabrese of Andernach, was widowed and owned a small factory that she had apparently inherited from her husband. My father invited her to come live with him in New Orleans. In her letter of March 20, 1978, she declined his invitation with great gentleness. They had apparently been lovers. In 1979 when my father visited my family in Germany, he made a trip to visit her. Germany in 1979 must have seemed very strange to him after being there in 1946 as part of a victorious occupation army, and I imagine that his stature had diminished in the intervening years.

My father prided himself on being an inventive businessman. He was way ahead of his time in trying to secure potty parity for women. One of his proudest purchases was a woman's urinal for the drive-in theater ladies' room. I know about this because one of my jobs as a teenager was to clean the drive-in restrooms. Even from the perspective of a fifteen-year-old boy, it was clear to me that the fixture was to be straddled rather than sat upon, but that wasn't always clear to the women who used it. Nor was it clear which direction the woman should face in straddling it. Judging from the comparative cleanliness of the stall, it received much less use than the other two regular toilets whose floors were littered with the usual ladies' room detritus, including used Kotex pads carefully wrapped in wads of toilet paper. Most women either didn't know how to use this device or else choose not to. Some women who did use it took the time and effort to carefully fold toilet paper and spread it all around the porcelain edge of the fixture to sit on it when actually there was no seat because it wasn't for sitting at all.

The only other machine in the restrooms that fascinated me (I used to invent elaborate daydreams to entertain myself while doing the boring cleaning job) was the condom machine in the men's room, which appeared suddenly one day. I wouldn't dare ask my father what it was, but the other cronies who worked at the drive-in knew. The condoms cost a quarter each and some of them ended up being used and discarded on the drive-in's ground by cars parked in the back ramps. The guy who picked up the trash always made a point of telling me when he found one. We were obsessed by the topic, and Jimmy told stories about one woman in Slovan who would wash out and then reuse her boyfriends' condoms. One thing that I could never figure out was why a notice on the side of the condom machine stated "for the prevention of disease only." Even I knew that condoms were used to keep a girl from getting pregnant.

When my grandfather had taught my Uncle Tony to run the movie projectors at the old Penn Theater at the age of twelve, he was so small that he had to use a stool to reach high enough to thread the film into the machine. At the age of fourteen I was taught to run the drive-in projectors. I was substituting for my German cousin Paul, the regular projectionist, who was away one night in the summer of 1958. The film was a monumental one that matched my level of high anxiety—Cecil B. DeMille's *The Ten Commandments*. Only once during the film did a projector break down. I locked the doors and concentrated. Luckily, I was able to get it running again before the protesting car horns got too noisy.

NOTES

1. See Robert Hofler, *The Man Who Invented Rock Hudson: The Pretty Boys and Dirty Deals of Henry Willson* (New York: Carroll & Graf, 2005); Tab Hunter with Eddie Muller, *Tab Hunter Confidential: The Making of a Movie Star* (Chapel Hill, NC: Algonquin Books, 2005).

2. Dante's *Divine Comedy* mitigated the punishment of carnal sinners whose lust overcame their reason by placing them in the less horrific second circle of hell, below Limbo. Their punishment consisted of being eternally buffeted in darkness by fierce winds –unpleasant, but one of the mildest penalties suffered in hell. Dante's sympathy for these afflicted lovers was revealed in the famous people he placed in this circle of hell. See *The Comedy of Dante Alighieri the Florentine. Cantica I: Hell (L'Inferno),* trans. Dorothy L. Sayers. (Hammondsworth, England: Penguin, 1949), 97–103. Those in the second circle of Dante's hell being punished for lust include Dido, queen of the Carthaginians, whose infatuation with Aeneas caused her to commit suicide when Aeneas rejected her. The circle also includes Cleopatra (who loved both Caesar and Anthony), Helen of Troy, Achilles, Paris, and the tragic lovers Francesca de Rimini and Paolo.

3. Dante's third ring in the seventh circle of hell contains people who are condemned to eternal running as punishment for being slaves to their desires, but their desires were for fame and recognition rather than sex. The circle strangely omits the famous sodomites from history, such as the Athenian Alcibiades, Julius Caesar, and Alexander the Great. Richard Kay argues that those in the third ring of Dante's seventh circle of hell were guilty of unnatural vice in a political rather than sexual sense. They challenged the natural hierarchy of political authority. See Richard Kay, "The Sin of Brunetto Latini," *Medieval Studies* 31 (1969): 262–286. See also *The Comedy of Dante Alighieri,* 165.

4. David Demarest and Eugene Levy, "Remnants of an Industrial Landscape," *Pittsburgh History* 72, no. 3 (Fall 1989): 137.

5. John Michael Gabrielli, "The Economic and Social Development of an American Small Town: Burgettstown, Pennsylvania: 1773–1991," Bachelor of Arts thesis in history, Princeton University, Princeton, New Jersey, 1991, 81.

6. Jeanette Boake to the author, July 24, 2002.

7. Jeanette Boake to the author, July 2, 2004.

8. Jeanette Boake to the author, August 2, 2004.

9. Jeanette Boake to the author, August 2, 2004.

10. Jeanette Boake to the author, February 22, 2006.

11. Jeanette Boake to the author, May 1, 2006.

12. Jeanette Boake to the author, March 18, 2006.

Chapter Six

My Parents, 1937–1961

I remember the March cold in western Pennsylvania. My father was always eager to open the drive-in in the spring, although the nighttime temperatures in March were so cold that customers had to run their car motors to keep warm. But for those who used the drive-in as the local passion pit, that was only a minor problem. We were always waiting for the warm weather that would bring all the cars to the drive-in to fill my father's dreams. But I only remember the cold because the warm days with many cars of which my father dreamed never seemed to happen. I remember him pacing around the drive-in, waiting for the cars that never came.

My father was an impulsive dreamer. He would spend a year building a structure and then have his cronies tear it down in a few days. He was not a failure, but his life fell short of his dreams. In his youth he lacked the courage and daring to leave the area of his birth and upbringing. When he finally did leave it in 1966, it was because of my mother's nagging rather than his internal drive. After leaving, he always struck me as diminished in stature. This was apparent in his willingness in Florida to become a high school teacher, work that thirty years before he had spurned as worse than suicide. But in 1937 his youth and his dreams had been at their peak. By 1967 life's realities and my mother's complaints had worn him down.

My father also had a theatrical flair. I think some of the happiest moments of his life were during the early 1950s when he would get on the stage of the Mary Ann Theater on Wednesday "bingo night" and preside over the event to a packed theater. Typical of males in Italy even today, he was a careful dresser. But after leaving the Slovan-Burgettstown area, he lacked a stage. He had stage presence, but he lacked audacity. Audacity is something I inherited from my grandparents, not from my father.

My mother was five feet five inches tall, thin, shy, and pretty. She had been a sickly younger child who was spoiled by her parents. As a result, she remained immature and prone throughout her life to nervousness and hysteria, a trait that ran in her family. Her emotions did not flow from her in the spontaneous manner of Italians but were repressed in a more Germanic fashion until they rushed out in a neurotic fit. I saw the same high-strung pattern manifest itself in several of my German relatives (my grandfather and several aunts). My mother believed that Christian Science helped her control her emotions and perhaps it did; but she also used the religion to avoid being candid about her true feelings on the grounds that talking about a problem enhanced its power. I could never discuss what I really felt with her because she would never listen. Her emotional rigidity built a wall between us that never came down.

My mother's family came from east-central Germany in the Harz Mountain region, the setting of the famous Walpurgis Nacht. The family had one notable ancestor—a Lutheran pastor named Emil Schwarze (1750–1806). He and his wife Ida met a tragic fate when Napoleon's troops attacked their parsonage in Harzgerode in 1806. A maid hid under a bed and lived to tell the tale of how the French troops murdered my great-great-great grandmother and then carried off her pastor-husband as a hostage. He was never heard from again. I like to think that I inherited a spiritual and intellectual strain from him in addition to my middle name.

The Dittmars were more middle class than the Mungiellos, although America, "the land of opportunity," would soon remove the inequality between them. Among my grandparents' generation, all of the Dittmars were literate whereas none of the Mungiellos were. The Dittmars craved respectability and tended to be craftsmen, church cantors, organists, along with an occasional pastor. My great-grandfather August Dittmar (1839–1893) was a saddlemaker, a master craftsman who ran his own shop in Bernburg in which he sold his handmade leather goods. But when he died in 1893 followed by his wife Ida one year later, the family was thrown into a crisis. The leather shop was forced into a bankruptcy sale, and the youngest children needed care.

Shortly before these unexpected, traumatic events of 1893, the family posed for a formal portrait, all dressed up in respectable middle-class clothing. The parents are seated in front while two eldest sons flank the standing row of six children behind them. The debonair eldest son Fritz stands on the left side holding a top hat. Less dashing than his older brother, Otto stands on the right holding a more conservative Homburg. Otto would be the only one of the children not to immigrate to America. He stayed behind and fostered a family of six children who endured the twentieth-century chaos of World War I, hyperinflation, Hitler's Third Reich, and isolation in the Russian occupation zone, later communist East Germany. Beside Otto stands Emilie

(Millie), the eldest daughter who would be the first of the siblings to go to America. Beside Fritz stands poor Minna who brought the two youngest children to the US in 1895 only to fall ill and die within months of their arrival. Toward the middle stands the youngest daughter, Louisa, who would outlive two husbands and all of her siblings, dying in 1958. The youngest sibling of all is my grandfather, Gustav Emil, standing beside Louisa near the middle of the row.

Emilie (Millie) married Emil Leuschner in Radeburg in 1891 and returned with him to America. Leuschner had first emigrated in 1886 and became well known in Homestead, Pennsylvania, for his shop that painted carriages, rigs, and other horse-drawn wagons. He later switched to painting automobiles. The success of his Homestead shop generated the prosperity that allowed him and his wife to pay for the transatlantic transportation (in second class, not steerage like the Mungiellos) of his wife's three youngest siblings. Presumably these costs were paid for in the form of a loan that would be repaid, at least in part, when their parents' estate was settled.

Consequently, in 1895 Minna (then twenty-three years old) emigrated with Louisa (eighteen) and Gustav (fourteen) to join Emilie and her husband in Homestead. They left Bernburg on April 4, 1895, and traveled by train to Bremerhaven where they boarded the steamship *Oldenburg* for the crossing. Leuschner met them at the train station in Pittsburgh. The bankruptcy sale of August Dittmar's shop was not finalized until July 8, 1902. The sale price of 27,030 marks was reduced by outstanding debts to 3,846 marks, which, divided among the five remaining heirs, amounted to only 767.30 marks each.

Some of the members of my German family possessed an intellectual strain that produced technicians and mathematicians while others were artistic and spiritual. Prior to emigrating, they commonly wrote poetry and exhibited musical talent. This artistic strain found its fullest manifestation in my grandfather's eldest brother, Friedrich Dittmar (1864–1938). Fritz was a romantic dreamer whose dreams carried him to Chicago and New York where he Americanized his name from Friedrich to Fred. In Germany he had learned the trade of *Posamentier* from his saddle-master father. The term *Posamentier* is now archaic because it covered a range of skills (carriage builder, comb-maker, shoe maker, parchment maker, gold lace maker, etc.) that are little practiced today. In Chicago and New York Fritz pursued a career as an actor/opera singer with mixed success. Perpetually short of money, he often sent requests to his brother in Germany to check with the bank on the progress of the estate sale of their parents' shop in Bernburg. In the theatre off-season, each summer, Fritz supplemented his income by working as a *Posamentier*, using skills he had learned in his father's shop.

Fritz extolled life in America and encouraged his siblings to come, but when his sister Minna emigrated with their younger siblings Louisa and

Gustav, he was unable to make good on his offer to help them financially. Eventually his disappointments led him to complain about American materialism, saying "everything is about money—fame, honor, happiness, and love—everything is available for money. Even love depends on money." He grew nostalgic for the Germany where he claimed "ideal love still existed." After first encouraging his brother Otto to join him in America, he changed his mind and told Otto not to come, saying he wished that he had stayed in Germany. He claimed that he only felt joy in America when he had a large role in some theatrical production.

Fritz found solace for his unhappiness in Spiritism (also called Spiritualism), which was popular in late nineteenth-century America and Europe. Spiritists believed in reincarnation and in an active interaction between the living and the dead. They believed that the living could communicate with the spirits of the dead either through an instrument like a planchette or a medium. Fritz wrote enthusiastic letters to his family in 1898 and 1902 in which he described his communication with deceased relatives. In his letter of March 10, 1902, from New York City to his brother Otto in Germany, Fritz described how he and his wife Martha laid out the separate letters of the alphabet on the table and how Martha, grasping a piece of wood in her hand, would touch the various letters in a kind of trance until a message was communicated.

Nine months later he wrote of their use of a female medium to make contact with the deceased. The medium sat in a cabinet against the wall which was ringed with a heavy black curtain. The gas lights were dimmed and the medium went into a trance during which the participants sat in a circle singing religious songs. After twenty or thirty minutes a spirit would appear out of the cabinet. During these séances, the specter of his father, mother, brother, sister, and both of his own deceased small children appeared, and he was able to talk with each of them. The exchanges seem to have been comforting to Fritz. When he expressed his doubts about whether the spirit that claimed to be his mother was really her, he insisted that the spirit recite the poem she had written to him in her last letter. When she did, he was assured that it was her and he welcomed her with kisses and encouragement. He was comforted when the spirit of his recently deceased sister Minna appeared, crying and asking that they forgive one another for their last nasty letters, apparently over Fritz's failure to help his siblings with the money he had promised.

For a number of years Fritz fell completely out of touch with his sisters and brother in the Pittsburgh area, but then at the age of seventy, he appeared at an emotional family reunion at the large Leuschner family home in Homestead in 1934. In retrospect, he seemed to have been saying goodbye. After this, the family lost track of him and heard that he died four years later. Fritz had lived a secretive life, and one wonders if he was hiding something from the rest of the family. The artistic world he moved in was known to have been tolerant of homosexuality. One of the most prominent ways that men traditionally hid their same-sex attraction was to live in a remote city apart from the rest of their family where they could indulge this desire in secrecy. Certainly New York City in the late nineteenth century was reputed to provide more sexual opportunities for closeted bisexual men than any other city in the United States,

One venue where he could have made same-sex contacts was urban bathhouses (Turkish baths), then common in cities. These were sites that provided a convenient meeting place for married men who feared being seen in gay bars or other more public gay sites.[1] By 1902 the Ariston Baths, located in the basement of the Ariston apartment hotel at Broadway and West 54th Street, had begun to cultivate a homosexual clientele. The entry fee of one dollar eliminated the poorest clientele and prostitutes, creating a relatively safe middle-class environment. Upon entering, the visitor checked his valuables and was assigned a private changing room and a sheet to wear. Although the Ariston offered a swimming pool, steam room, sauna, messages, manicures, and a café, the main activity was sex in the dressing rooms, the dorm room, and the cooling rooms.[2]

As an actor working in the Broadway theater district, Fritz would have been aware of a Turkish bath like the Ariston, which was located between his workplaces and his home in 1902 at 218 E. 87th Street. I can't help but wonder if my birth in 1943, seven years after Fritz's death, might have served to provide a medium for a reincarnation of this same-sex desire since it frequently recurs in the same family. But this is just speculation. Less speculative is the outright claim by my Aunt Jeanette that one of my male cousins on the Mungello side of my family was gay.[3] I remember him as a shy boy and sweet. He is now very closeted and it would be cruel of me to out him. I suspect that there were other relatives as well who felt same-sex attraction but kept it hidden.

The other Dittmars in America lived less romantic lives than Fritz and occupied themselves with the hard work of making a living and raising a family. Indeed, their lives were far more stable and mundane than those of the Mungellos. The difference was that, unlike the Mungiellos in Roccarainola, there had been no volcano in Harzgerode to ignite their personalities.

My mother Lois was a good wife and mother in terms of doing practical things. Jeanette said she was a good cook and ahead of her time in cooking healthy vegetables.[4] However she was rigid and I felt that she loved me only to the extent that I did what she wanted. She lived by the values of her parents or her church, values that she had rigidly internalized. However, she was very generous. In 1979 she gave me $20,000 from her divorce settlement so that I could afford a down payment on a house for my family, even though she was living on a very limited income. (Long after both of my parents had died, I realized that the $20,000 was probably part of my father's contribution to their divorce settlement.) She and my older sister Marianne (named after our grandmother Marianna) had a stormy relationship from the time my sister was twelve until the day my mother died. I was less inclined to fight openly with my mother, but I did what I wanted.

I had some huge arguments about almost everything with my father during my adolescence. He was very Latin and tended to become angry easily and then just as easily forgive. One argument became so intense that at the age of sixteen, I decided to leave home. My father had once shown me a farm in West Virginia where he had gone when running away as a youth, and I guess running away from home was accepted as a male rite of passage in my family. It was the summer of 1960 between my junior and senior years in high school. My sister and her friend Donna Rozzo made me a bag lunch and drove me to an entrance of the Pennsylvania Turnpike where I hitched rides west, mostly from trailer truck drivers, across Ohio and Indiana to Chicago.

In Chicago I remember walking along a street numbered in the hundreds and yet being surprised that there were nothing but empty fields around. It was midnight and summer and exciting, as only life can be when you are sixteen and on your own for the first time. I decided to go to California and I hitched rides further west on the famous Route 66 to St. Louis. Prior to the building of the interstate highway system, Route 66 was the main highway linking the 2,000 miles between Chicago and Los Angeles. In the Great Depression, it became famous for poverty-stricken rural families trying to escape the Dust Bowl who loaded all of their belongings into their car and headed west on it.

Eventually I ended up in central Missouri near Fort Leonard Wood. I went into a bar, sat at the counter, and ordered a beer. A kindly barmaid served me, although I certainly did not look older than sixteen. Drinking it went to my head because I hadn't eaten much in the last two days. (I had nothing but a few carrot sticks left in my bag lunch.) The trip had been financed by a roll of quarters, funds that had been entrusted to me as treasurer of the high school Latin Club. The quarters were supposed to be used for a party that summer. As I sat there, I began to feel deflated and decided that the time was not yet right for me to leave home. So I turned around and hitchhiked back to Pennsylvania. Although I had gone over 700 miles from home, the whole trip took only a few days. I never told my parents where I had been and no one ever asked about what happened to the party for the Latin Club.

I always felt that my father loved me more than my mother did. I felt that while my mother would cut off her love if I did something she didn't like, I believed that my father would love me regardless of what I did. My father could be exasperating to deal with and he was not always honest in his business dealings. His sisters felt that he had cheated them out of their fair share of the Mungello family property, and they were probably right. It was his dishonesty that caused my grandfather to warn my Uncle Tony that my father took after their murdered uncle Filippo. Nevertheless my father's sisters continued to have regular contact with him and they traveled long distances to come to his funeral. As dysfunctional as they had been as a family without a mother, they still had strong family loyalty. My Uncle Tony was the only sibling who refused to attend my father's funeral because of his bitterness over the sale of the drive-in. My mother, by contrast, was impeccably honest but deficient in love. Loyalty to my wife, children, grandchildren, my brother, and my dogs is something I learned from my father. But I also absorbed some of his dishonesty.

Although my parents argued a great deal, their fights rarely became physical. Only once did I ever see my father strike my mother, and even then he was reacting almost instinctually. I remember it well although I was only six years old. They were arguing about money (a frequent point of contention) and as he was leaving, she threw a roll of quarters down the stairway at him, hitting him. He rushed back up the stairs and slapped her. But it only happened once. My family was verbally argumentative but not violent. The only gun I ever saw in my parents' house was a German Luger that my father had picked up while stationed in Germany. He had no bullets for it and I suspect he thought he would sell it. For us, violence was entertainment to be found in the movies. However, in their arguments, my mother would sometimes use us children as pawns. Once after an argument, she took us and left my father to live with my grandparents in Washington, Pennsylvania. That was very upsetting to me. My father eventually came to make up and brought us all home.

My father was equally to blame for their arguments, but my mother acted as though my father's family was the only ones that fought. However, I once saw my maternal grandparents have a bitter argument in which my grandfather ripped apart my grandmother's corsage out of anger. Rather than violence, both of my parents tended to deal with arguments by running away. Although my parents divorced in 1979, long after their children were adults, it was not my father's idea to do so. My mother admitted to me that she drove him out of the house. She betrayed a loyalty.

The only way my upbringing was different from most other small-town American boys of the time was that my father owned the local movie theater, the roller-skating rink, and the dance hall on Main Street, only a few blocks from our first house at 108 Archer Lane. Hollywood was making many family-oriented movies in the 1940s and 1950s, and my sister and I saw every film that played at the Mary Ann Theater in those years. The first seat in the first row of the theater was hers and the second seat was mine. We could also get unlimited amounts of free popcorn.

My parents built a new house on the other side of town and we moved there around 1950 when I was six. The house at the corner of Hindman and

Lincoln Avenues was built in a very modern, one-story ranch style. My father, who was always striving for originality, had the bricklayers turn the long red bricks inside out so that the exterior had a rough appearance. The house was in the nicest neighborhood in Burgettstown, and the move was a social step up for my family. The town's most prominent citizen, Dr. Audley Oliver Hindman, lived across the street. Years before during the Depression, he repossessed the building in Burgettstown where my grandparents operated one of their silent movie theatres. My sister and I got to know the Hindman family very well, which I suspect pleased my father. Since Burgettstown had only one grade school, I did not have to change schools when we moved. After spending seven years in the grade school, I moved to the high school for grades 8–12 and both schools were only a few blocks from my new home.

Since my father was a lapsed Catholic, my religious upbringing was left to my mother. In the same way that I was compelled to take piano lessons for seven years (and never touched the piano thereafter), I was compelled to attend Christian Science Sunday School for many years. My mother meant well, but I never did take to dance lessons, piano playing, or Christian Science. Christian Science is a demanding religion and I found the cold, New England mentality of its founder, Mary Baker Eddy (1821–1910), alien to my more Latin soul. Illness was viewed as being caused by a mental failure called "Error," which was something that could supposedly be controlled through prayer. To me, the burden of feeling guilty of false thinking on top of feeling sick seemed as unfair as was it was ridiculous. It was especially unsettling when my younger brother Mark almost died after his appendix burst and surgery was delayed because of my mother's religion. But one thing my mother did teach me was to take religion seriously. I have never lost my belief in God, although I stopped being a Christian Scientist soon after leaving for college.

NOTES

1. George Chauncey, *Gay New York: Gender Urban Culture and the Making of the Gay Male World 1890–1940* (New York: Basic Books, 1994), 204–225.

2. Daniel Hurewitz, *Stepping Out: Nine Walks through New York City's Gay and Lesbian Past* (New York: Holt, 1997), 177–178.

3. Jeanette Boake to the author, December 22, 2003.

4. Jeanette Boake to the author, January 19, 2005.

Chapter Seven

Leaving Home, 1955–1966

My high school years were the most difficult of my life. Football was a very important activity in Burgettstown. Because my father had been a high school super-jock who also played football in college, everyone assumed that I would be a good football player. But I was too small and had poor eye–body coordination. The coach kept sending me out to get passes that I couldn't catch. I was a terrible player and felt humiliated. This was not one of my dreams. Many years later, my younger brother told me that when he was out for football in high school, our father told him, "David never missed a practice." That's me. The same trait that is euphemistically called "disciplined" is pejoratively called "compulsive." After two years of trying, I gave up on football.

By contrast, I was a decent wrestler—not great but decent. Once in my freshman year on the junior varsity team, we had a meet in which my opponent was much stronger than I was. At fourteen years of age and 122 pounds, I was skinny and underdeveloped. It was all I could do to keep from getting pinned. But the worst part of it was knowing that I had to wrestle this same boy again at another meet later in the season, and when I did he pinned me. If you have never wrestled, it is hard to conceive the terror of having your shoulders being forced to the mat, while the naked gymnasium ceiling bulbs are glaring in your eyes. Meanwhile you try desperately to keep your shoulder blades off the mat while the spectators scream for a pin. In my sophomore year I wrestled at the 132-pound weight level and pinned someone else and won more matches than I lost, but after that I quit. Being part of a team has never mattered much to me.

I liked most of my academic subjects in school and made good grades, but it was clear that I was not going to excel in athletics. And yet I refused to be second-rate. After withdrawing from athletics at school, I fitted out a weight

room in a little cottage my father and I had built about 200 feet behind our
house. I became an utterly serious weight lifter; actually, bodybuilder would
be a more accurate term. I bought abominable-tasting food supplements
through a weight-lifting magazine run by Joe Wieder. Although the cottage
was unheated, I worked out after school during the cold winter months and
throughout the year.

I have a well-proportioned body. Although on the slight side, my muscles
responded well to the weights and I developed good definition. I realize now
that my bodybuilding was driven by my sexuality, but then, what isn't when
you're a horny teenager? Male pornography was almost unheard of in the
fifties, at least if you were a teenager in a small town in southwestern Pennsylvania. However, a new category of magazine was emerging that featured
lightly clad and even nude males: the male fitness magazine . Only frontal
nudity was excluded; usually a thin posing strap covered the genitals. One of
these magazines was called *Young Physique*. I remember my excitement
when I first saw a copy in Peachy Petrucci's Newstand in Burgettstown. My
obsession became to have my photos appear in *Young Physique*.

I found a photographer in Arlington, Virginia, who must have taken these
photos as a sideline, since like many people in Arlington, he worked for the
federal government. In the spring of 1961, when I was a senior in high
school, I visited my sister who was working as a secretary at the State
Department in Washington, D.C. I flew—it was my first plane ride and I
remember throwing up in the barf bag just before landing at Washington
National Airport. The next day the photographer picked me up outside my
sister's apartment and took me to his house where he had a studio in the
basement. I stripped and applied the body oil (I had already shaved my
body). Actually, he helped me apply some of it, but otherwise made no
sexual moves. I was seventeen.

There was nothing explicitly sexual, much less pornographic, in the
photos he had me pose for. (I would have been shocked if he had asked me to
take sexually explicit photos, and I am sure I would have refused.) In my
mind, the pictures simply emphasized the results of my bodybuilding program. I was aware of the sexual connotations of such pictures, but American
culture in the fifties was far more innocent than today and sex was conveyed
in implicit rather than explicit form. At most, the male physique pictures
were male versions of the sexually suggestive calendar pin-ups of females in
the forties and fifties. Both types of pictures were used by males in masturbation, as I knew from my own experience.

While I had a very strong sense that the photographer took photos of nude
young men because he was sexually attracted to them, I also sensed a very
strong undercurrent of fear of exposure on his part. I merely thought then that
he was just a timid and repressed government-worker type of personality.
Only later did I learn that between 1947 and the early 1960s the federal

government had been aggressively searching for and terminating the employment of anyone suspected of being homosexual. I had no idea then that the McCarthy Cold War search for security risks in government had been extended from communists to include homosexuals and that both had been hunted down by official agencies with a vengeance.[1] So this photographer had good reason to be afraid of being discovered taking bodybuilding pictures of a nude seventeen-year-old male in his basement studio.

I was surprised at how well the photos came out and amazed when *Young Physique* published three of them in its December 1961 issue, giving the shot of my naked backside a double-page spread. Their emphasis on that particular shot puzzled me. I don't think the idea of anal intercourse had yet entered my mind. I had failed as a football player but succeeded as a bodybuilder. I accepted the trade-off.

Just a few months before my sixteenth birthday, my father found a black 1941 Ford coupe in pristine condition. He helped me buy it and two days later when my buddies and I took it out, he had me promise that my older friend Butch Noah, who had a driver's license (I didn't), would do the driving. Shortly after we took off, I took over the wheel and promptly drove the car off the side of the road and flipped it into a deep ditch. All four of us (Butch, his brother Sambo, John Cunningham, and myself) were suddenly upside down on the inside roof, but luckily no one was hurt. My father didn't exactly think it was funny, but I think he got a charge out of me being so audacious. There is a certain tolerance—even expectation—of the misbehavior of a *ragazzo* (boy) in Italian families. My father also made me put the car back together over the next year, and he helped by locating still-new and unwrapped auto body parts in the dusty recesses of warehouses. When it was finished, I had it painted metallic bronze.

Unlike my father, who returned home, my dreams at seventeen began to carry me far beyond my hometown. In the summer of 1961 between the end of high school and the beginning of college, I decided to go to Atlantic City, New Jersey, to get a summer job. Those were the days before gambling casinos were allowed in Atlantic City and the place had a slower, more relaxed summertime atmosphere, although its glory days as a beach resort were long over. I remember packing some of my weights in the suitcase. I arrived in Atlantic City, carrying the heavy suitcase in my arms because the handle had been broken by the heavy weights. I soon found two young Iranians as roommates, nice guys whom I later lost touch with. We slept on mattresses without sheets.

It took a while, but I finally found a job at the Senator Hotel dining room. Old ladies thought I was cute and would slip me quarter tips behind their husbands' backs. I ended up as a barboy at the Ritz-Carlton Hotel, although I was legally underage at seventeen. It was a fun job and I learned a lot about liquor and bars. One thing I remember is how the bartender would make up the mixed drinks in advance in large bottles. One night I noticed a cockroach floating around in the bottle of whiskey sour mix. That did not stop him from using it.

One of the things I remember most from Atlantic City was seeing July Garland perform in the cavernous Convention Hall located on the Board-walk. She was someone I had seen in numerous musicals at my father's theater, including, of course, *The Wizard of Oz*. She was famous, and her Atlantic City concert was given a lot of advance publicity on the radio. I was intrigued enough to buy a ticket. At the time, Garland was in the midst of one of her many comebacks and in April she had given her famous concert at New York's Carnegie Hall. That concert was called "the greatest night in show business" and even allowing for show biz hyperbole, most critics be-lieve that the Carnegie Hall concert was the peak moment of her career.[2] The Atlantic City performance was part of a sixteen-city tour of this concert.

At the time, I had little knowledge of Garland's tragic, alcoholic, drug-filled life in which she was in a constant pendulum swing between obesity and drug-induced anorexia. Her unsuccessful search for love was symbolized in her theme song, "Over the Rainbow." Nor did I know at the time that her mixture of tragedy and talent had made her an icon for people with same-sex attraction as well as others who could empathize with her suffering. And yet our hearts often have a way of seeing things that our minds miss. Judy Garland's death at the end of the sixties would be one of the sparks for an iconic event in gay history. When she died in London of an accidental over-dose of barbiturates, her body was flown back to New York for the funeral which took place on June 27, 1969. That night, in the early hours of June 28, a riot occurred when police raided and harassed patrons at a gay bar called the Stonewall Inn. Such harassment had long been typical of police tactics, but when gays fought back, the riot marked a turning point in gay and lesbian history. Today it is celebrated with gay pride parades.

When I went to Garland's Atlantic City concert in August 1961, I remem-ber still being in my work clothes of black pants, white shirt, and black bowtie.[3] I stood, way in the back. She was an hour late in appearing, a typical event at her concerts. (She tended to suffer from intense pre-concert anxiety attacks and sometimes went on stage drunk and gave disastrous perfor-mances.) Suddenly she appeared—a pixie-like figure on an enormous stage—and she began to sing the words "When you're smiling, when you're smiling, the whole world smiles with you." An immediate and powerful bond formed between her and this vast audience as she sang these songs, most of which were about failed love. She ended up, of course, sitting on the edge of the stage, singing "Over the Rainbow."

At the end of the concert, I was caught up in the mass adulation of all these very well-dressed people who rushed down the aisles to the stage and reached out to touch her. I remember how soft and fragile her hand seemed when it touched mine. It would take me many years before I understood why I did that. When tragedy entered my life thirty-seven years later it was not just a case of bad luck. There was something in me compelling me to take the path that I took. I loved my wife Christine and my friend Carl most in life because of who I was. And because of who I was, it brought tragedy. When my hand touched Judy Garland's hand that day, it was like all the other hands reaching out to her there at the edge of the stage. It was a gesture of longing. Love and tragedy are never something we feel alone. In a sense, we are all looking over the rainbow.

At the end of that summer, I returned home before leaving for college. As a teenage romantic, I had refused to accept the well-intended advice of the school superintendent who told me Southern colleges tended to be "tainted" and I would do better to go to a Northern school. But I had my own ideas and went over a thousand miles to attend SMU (Southern Methodist University) in Dallas, Texas. I loved the big blue Texas sky and it was a good experience, although I had no idea that I would return thirty-two years later. However, at one point I was arrested. In the competition to have the most striking dorm room decorations, I took an eight-foot potted rubber plant from a nearby apartment lobby and was walking across campus with it when the Highland Park police stopped me. They arrested me and put me in a cell but didn't even lock the door. For "misdemeanor theft under $5.00" I was placed on disciplinary probation by the university. My mother was so appalled that she refused to speak to me; my father thought it was pretty funny, although he didn't tell me so at the time.

At SMU I was sexually attracted to males but was completely closeted. I lived in a corner second-floor room in Letterman's Hall and had a crush on my roommate, who was very blond. It was one of those hopeless situations because he was completely straight and made nasty remarks about some queer trying to reach under the restroom stall divider and feel his leg in the student union. He told the guy he would kill him if he didn't get his hand off his leg. He had no idea I was attracted to him. He used to get out of bed to answer late-night calls from his girlfriend and stand at the head of my bed with a raging erection showing through his briefs. I always had an urge to reach over and pull his briefs down. I'm sure he would have treated it as a joke. After we roomed together, he visited me in Washington, D.C., and we had a falling out. He couldn't understand why I had changed my mind about going to Europe with him. He was oblivious to the fact that I wasn't masochistic enough to watch him strip down to his briefs every night for two months in youth hostels across Europe.

In 1961–1962 at SMU, men who had sex with men were considered mentally ill. I remember all the hush-hush talk about one withdrawn guy in my dorm. In the same tone of voice used to describe a pathetic mental case, I was told that he had asked to blow some guy and was reported to the college administration. They let him stay on campus, but he was on some sort of probation and was clearly being watched.

After one year I transferred to George Washington University (commonly known as GW) in Washington, D.C., because I had become interested in politics. My sister and I shared an apartment in the Arlington Towers complex, just across the Potomac River from the Foggy Bottom area where GW was located. I found a part-time job on Capitol Hill in the office of Senator Joseph S. Clark Jr. (1901–1990), a Democratic senator from Pennsylvania. I would continue working there for the next three years.

I loved working on the Hill and walking through the halls of the Capitol filled with statues and history. I was, however, not very interested in becoming part of the networks of political power that usually attract people to work on the Hill. Most of the time, I was just a gofer, going to the attic to retrieve boxes, delivering envelopes, or updating the addressograph plates for the mailing lists. (I remember not including the new zip codes on the plates because I thought they were dehumanizing; I have always had certain Luddite tendencies.[4]) My part-time job wasn't even important enough to have my name listed in the published staff list.[5] Senator Clark was a wealthy liberal from an old blue blood family in Philadelphia who liked the masses much more in the abstract than in person. The only contact he had with the gofers in the office was when he needed some guy to carry his suitcase from the Old (now called Russell) Senate Office Building to the nearby Union Train Station.

Also, Senator Clark was always more of a senatorial critic than an insider. While I worked there he coauthored two books attacking the US Congress: *The Senate Establishment* (1963) and *Congress: The Sapless Branch* (1964). In 1965, when the payroll lists of the senator's office were published in several Pennsylvania newspapers, I was listed near the bottom with having received $268 in October–December 1964.[6] Nevertheless, someone from my home area of Pennsylvania complained about me getting a Democratic job when my father was a Republican. (My family had switched from Democratic to Republican as they moved into the business world.) However, in 1964 a prominent Italian-American judge named Michael A. Musmanno was running in the Democratic senatorial primary against Senator Clark's favored candidate, Genevieve Blatt. Clark had been a reform mayor of Philadelphia and he opposed Musmanno as a product of the corrupt Democratic city machines. But Clark's inherited wealth and privileged upbringing had made him insensitive to the realities of ethnic politics in America in the 1960s and failed to teach him the political danger of calling Musmanno "the biggest liar and egomaniac in the world." By his own admission, he "foolishly" gave a speech in Musmanno's home base of Pittsburgh to that effect, earning "the lasting enmity of the Italian community."[7] Blatt won the primary by only a few hundred votes, but Clark had alienated a number of Italian-American voters in Pennsylvania. With the name of Mungello, I was a token Italian-American on the staff, and it was probably judged unwise to fan the flames and fire me.

The senator's office staff was always very good to me. I think I originally got the job because the office manager thought I was cute (I was only eighteen when she hired me). She called me "Davy," had me bring her lunch from the cafeteria, and sometimes asked me to drive her home in my metallic bronze 1941 Ford coupe.

On August 28, 1963, the civil rights movement culminated in the March on Washington. Some 250,000 citizens, mostly African Americans, converged on the Mall in Washington in the largest demonstration the capital had ever seen. There was a lot of anxiety over the possibility of violence and President Kennedy initially opposed the march. Activity on Capitol Hill was brought to a standstill, and I remember wandering from the senator's office down to the Washington Monument with another office worker. The atmosphere was wonderfully peaceful, and whites numbered about one-fourth of the participants. I was interested in hearing entertainers like Peter, Paul and Mary, Bob Dylan, and Joan Baez perform. It was a long program and I couldn't get near to the Lincoln Memorial where Martin Luther King gave his famous "I Have a Dream" speech later that day.

While I was at GW, I participated in Students for a Democratic Society (SDS), largely because of a friend in Chinese class named Ed Bowers. At that time, the SDS chapter at GW was mainly a cultural and political discussion group, reading books like Paul Goodman's *Growing Up Absurd* and Herman Hesse's *Steppenwolf*. But it did organize the first political protest I ever participated in. In October 1963 during my junior year, Madame Ngo-dinh-Nhu, the sister-in-law of South Vietnam's President Ngo Dinh Diem, made a three-week visit to the United States in an attempt to raise support for her brother-in-law's government. Unfortunately, she was terribly miscast for the role and quickly became known as the "Dragon Lady." Students staged protests at her appearances at Harvard and Princeton and elsewhere.

The national office of SDS tried to use Madame Nhu's visit to organize a series of demonstrations against American policies in Vietnam.[8] However, most members of SDS were far more interested in domestic issues like civil rights and poverty. Paul Booth was unable even to rally his fellow SDS Swarthmoreans to participate. Had he done so, I might have met Carl Wittman six years earlier. But if I had, I doubt that much would have come of the meeting. It was as if the coordinates of our fate knew that the time was not yet ripe for our meeting.

As part of the protest against US policies, I formed part of a picket line on October 18 in front of the National Press Club in downtown Washington, D.C., which was not far from the GW campus. A group of us marched with signs, protesting the policies of the South Vietnam government. It was pretty tame stuff, except that at one point the organizers asked for volunteers who were willing to be arrested for sitting down and blocking the entrance. The sit-in would follow the method of passive resistance used in the antisegregation demonstrations in the South. I had sat in a jail cell over the theft of a rubber plant in Dallas, but I was not willing to do the same over Madame Nhu and so I was not among the seven demonstrators who were arrested.

In the summer of 1964, between my junior and senior years at GW, I worked as a camp counselor, where I met a remarkable woman named Lois Goodrich (1908–1984) who had journeyed in a covered wagon with her parents from central to west Texas in the early twentieth century.[9] She later moved to New York City and developed an innovative approach to children's summer camps described in her book *Decentralized Camping* (1959). Instead of coming together in large central units (a dining hall, crafts center, or archery range), campers spent most of their time in small units of eight or nine with two counselors and they did most of their activities at a separate and remote camp site. Goodrich and her fiercely devoted female staff ran Trail Blazer Camps like a matriarchy.[10] Located in the Kittatinny Mountains of northwestern New Jersey, the girls camp was on one side of the lake and a smaller boys camp was on the other side. In retrospect, it strikes me that the girls camp was a precursor of the lesbian separatism that later emerged in gay politics in the seventies.

Trail Blazer Camps served poor children from New York City, most of whom had never had any exposure to nature. As counselors we studied the campers' social work files before they arrived. We kept a goat at the remote campsite as part of the plan of decentralized camping to expose the campers to animal life. I had milked cows before, but goats were different in that they are milked from the rear and their milk does not have to be pasteurized. I also remember taking the boys on a long hike into the Kittatinny Mountains and getting lost.[11] I eventually found the way, but it was upsetting to find that I could not orient myself among all the hills and trees. In a letter Goodrich wrote to me in early 1965 inviting me back as a counselor, she described me as creative and impatient.[12] I think she understood me pretty well.

During my senior year at GW I had my first sexual experience with a woman. The young woman was pretty and blond and a year older than me. We had not spent much time together and she invited me to her apartment, which was near Washington Circle. We had sex on her living room floor and although I enjoyed it, I remember it simply because it was my first experience. I don't even recall her name. However, I do remember being concerned because I hadn't used a condom. A few weeks later, I saw her on campus and asked her if she was pregnant. She said no, but thanked me for asking. (Abortions were much harder to get in 1965.) She was nice. I hope she found happiness with someone.

While I enjoyed working on the Hill, I learned I wasn't really interested in politics. At GW I had found a major I loved—philosophy. At that age I was absolutely serious about following an idealized image of the ancient Greeks in pursuit of the True, the Good, and the Beautiful. I was an undergraduate aesthete who (like Oscar Wilde) was infatuated with the idea of life imitating art rather than art imitating life. I also wrote a lot of poetry that (like my wrestling ability) was only decent, not great. I became interested in the "inscrutable" Orient and took a Chinese language course because the aesthetics of the characters fascinated me.

After graduating in June of 1965, I decided not to go on in philosophy because I considered myself a poet who was not interested in a field dominated by the dry Anglo-American analytical tradition. I wanted to study Chinese philosophy, but there were few graduate programs at the time that offered it. Although I had not majored in English, I entered a graduate program in English literature at the University of Connecticut at Storrs. I found the countryside around Storrs beautiful but isolated, and I missed the girl I had been dating, Christine. Once she visited me in my rented room and I remember being on the floor, pulling her merino wool skirt up her thighs while we tried to keep the noise down so my landlady would not hear. I also remember the November day when a lecture in literary criticism seemed so tedious and irrelevant that I decided to drop out of graduate school and go to Europe.

Because of my strong family ties, Europe had an almost magical appeal to me as the home of my ancestors. Although Christine and I were becoming serious as a couple, she had almost two years to finish at GW, and I was drawn to Europe by this romantic feeling of blood. So right after Thanksgiving, I climbed aboard an Icelandic Air plane (then the cheapest way of getting to Europe) and flew from New York to Copenhagen. A former college roommate of my sister's named Bette Gahres was renting a room from a Danish family near the central train station, and I rented a room from the same family. For the next two months, I walked endlessly all over Copenhagen and wrote poetry in a freezing-cold room. I read J. D. Salinger's *Catcher in the Rye* and instantly related to Holden Caulfield and his dislike of phonies. I was fascinated by the prostitutes who walked the streets around the train station.

In January of 1966, my friend Bette and I hitchhiked across the snow-covered countryside to Paris. The German autobahns were fine for rides, but when we got onto a side road in France, none of the French drivers would pick us up. We ended up splurging for train tickets and arrived in Paris with minor cases of frostbite on our feet. It was freezing cold in Paris and we were constantly seeking out heated cafes to stay warm. I remember the homeless people sleeping on the streets wrapped in layers of newspapers. I had to decide what I was going to do about the military draft and the Vietnam War, about which I had mixed feelings. I remember sitting on a bench near the

Louvre reading about the growing Vietnam conflict in the *International Herald Tribune*. In part because of Christine, I decided to go back to the US.

After I returned to the United States, I took a language exam with the army in order to see if I might qualify for Chinese study at the Foreign Language Institute in Monterey. I did well on the test but remained undecided. My local draft board called me to take the physical, which I did in Pittsburgh. However, during the process, the form asked whether I felt sexual desire toward men and there it was, staring me in the face, the big question.

My first experience in restroom sex had occurred several years before in the basement of the old GW library on G Street in the fall of 1962. Because of the oppressive homophobic attitudes of the 1950s and 1960s, sex between men was driven underground into places like public restrooms, commonly known among gays as "tearooms." The anonymity of the contact as well as the risk involved added to the element of excitement for more adventuresome males. I have always been a risk taker and risk taking combined with sex produced a double-whammy kind of high. I think this is what some people seek in drugs or from parachuting out of airplanes, but I get it from sex. Society tried to discourage this activity, and vice squads spied on suspected sexual activity by using peepholes in public restroom walls or by having young, good-looking police officers make suggestive sexual motions in order to entrap unsuspecting men. Those who took the bait and responded were arrested and charged with public indecency or lewd behavior.

These arrests would be bundled together under the category of a "morals charge." Such arrests were commonly reported in local newspapers, and the human damage they inflicted on those charged far outweighed the statutory punishment for the misdemeanor charge. The arrested men were often married or prominent citizens and the public scandal destroyed reputations, broke up marriages, ruined careers, and sometimes ended in suicide. Nevertheless, such sexual activity continued and certain restrooms were said to be safe from vice squad surveillance.

In the fall of 1962 I was not yet nineteen and extremely naive, but I did notice that whenever I used a stall in the basement men's room of the GW library, someone else would occupy the next stall and begin tapping his foot and then gradually move it closer until his foot was touching mine. Then a hand would slide under the partition. I was both shocked and fascinated. Although I initially repulsed such approaches, I continued going back to this restroom. Over time, my youthful modesty was overcome and I began to respond to these overtures by moving my foot toward the other guy or reaching under the stall. I found this sort of sex a convenient way to release the powerful drive that was attracting me to males, but I was also disturbed by it because I thought I wanted to marry and have children. In fact, I became so disturbed about this conflict in my sexual feelings that I turned to psychotherapy for help.

My first effort to get rid of these same-sex feelings through psychotherapy was when I was a freshman at SMU. I discreetly asked my psychology instructor if he knew of a therapist who could help me. (What is today discredited as "conversion therapy" was then widely accepted.) He referred me to the University of Texas Southwestern Medical School in Dallas and I had several sessions with a psychiatrist there. Later, when I was at GW, I spent 200 hours at the Georgetown University outpatient clinic in an effort to rid myself of same-sex attractions. When I was called up by my draft board in 1966, I telephoned my former Georgetown psychiatrist who said that my diagnosed "anxiety reaction" would not prevent me from serving in the military.

Even having confronted my feelings for so long, I felt uneasy about how to answer the question on the military induction form. Should I answer that question on the form with a lie, as most other men in my situation at that time probably did, or should I tell the truth? If I told the truth, would word get back to my parents and others in the small town where I lived? Finally, I decided to check yes. Later on, during the exam, I was called in to speak with a psychiatrist who asked me some questions. A few weeks later, I received a notice from Local Board 164 in Washington, Pennsylvania, dated February 14, 1966. The second of the two blocks on the form was checked. It said: "found not acceptable for induction under current standards." I have preserved that envelope and 4-F notice for fifty years and have kept secret what happened. Today men with same-sex attraction can serve in the military, and that truly makes this notice a haunting ghost of the past.

NOTES

1. David K. Johnson, *The Lavender Scare: The Cold War Persecution of Gays and Lesbians in the Federal Government* (Chicago: University of Chicago Press, 2004), 1–14.

2. Gerald Clarke, *Get Happy: The Life of Judy Garland* (New York: Delta, 2000), 354–355. The original concert recording by Capitol Records won five Grammy Awards and was reissued in 2001 as a fortieth anniversary edition.

3. David Shipman, *Judy Garland: The Secret Life of an American Legend* (New York: Hyperion, 1993), 414–415.

4. A Luddite is someone who opposes the introduction of new technology. It is derived from a supposed Ned Ludd and English workmen who in 1811–1816 tried to prevent the introduction of labor-saving machinery by destroying machines and burning factories.

5. *Congressional Staff Directory 1963*, comp. and ed. Charles B. Brownson (Washington, DC: Government Printing Office, 1963), 73.

6. "State's 2 Senators Have 75 Employees," *Standard-Speaker* (Hazleton, Pennsylvania), May 17, 1965, 3.

7. Steven G. Neal, "Reflections of a Crusty Reformer," *Today* (*Philadelphia Inquirer* Sunday magazine) January 7, 1973, 27.

8. Kirkpatrick Sale, *SDS* (New York: Random House, 1973), 119–120.

9. William G. Vinal, "Still More Outdoor Leaders I Have Known," *Journal of Outdoor Education* 4, no. 1 (1969): 8.

10. From 1931 to 1952 Trail Blazer Camps had been called Life Camps because their owners during that time were the publishers of *Life*, *Time*, and *Fortune* magazines.

11. In 1943, Henry Luce, the publisher of Time-Life magazines, visited the Life Camps and got lost in the same area as I did twenty-one years later.

12. Letter from Lois Goodrich, February 10, 1965.

Chapter Eight

Christine, 1946–1968

I have gone through stages in my life in which my objects of sexual attraction have changed. When I was younger, I liked blondes. The two great loves of my early life were natural blondes who were flaxen-haired in their youth. Later in life I liked dark Latinos. For many of us, opposites attract and the American melting pot was forged in beds spread from sea to shining sea.

Christine's family was different from mine. They were more affluent than my family, but they had less passion. Christine's father, Robert Henry McKegg, who called himself "modestly successful," retired early at fifty-seven years of age so that he and his wife could move to Florida where they built a new house that backed onto the sixth green of their golf club. Golf was their passion and their lives revolved around it.

Both of Christine's parents were born in England. Her mother, born Clarice Morris (1911–1992), was the youngest child in a close, working-class English family. In 1913 when Clarice was two years old, the family emigrated from Wolverhampton, an industrial city near Birmingham, to Bethlehem, Pennsylvania, where her father, Benjamin Morris, worked as a tool-and-die man at Bethlehem Steel. Later the family moved to Brooklyn. The Morrises tended to die early, usually in their sixties, because (Christine claimed) of clogged arteries from eating too many overcooked meat roasts whose fat drippings were later fried with bread.

Clarice had a quiet manner, auburn hair, freckles, a trim athletic figure, and a natural grace. Although she smoked cigarettes and the skin on her face became wrinkled, she remained a very attractive woman into her old age. There was something concentrated about both her body and her personality. But she was intimidated by her husband and his family who looked down on the working-class background of her family. Instead of openly fighting back, Christine's mother steamed inwardly. Over the years, her resentment over this and other things grew into a bitterness that, in the typical English style, she kept just below the surface. But occasionally she would voice her resentment with an intensity so shocking that I could only laugh to deflect the embarrassment I felt. I liked Clarice very much. Although she was not physically demonstrative, she conveyed a warmth toward those she liked, and I always felt that she liked me. She was intensely loyal to her children, a trait that she passed to Christine, who, in turn, passed it to our own daughter Lisa Elise.

Christine's paternal side of the family consisted of very proper middle-class Britons who had emigrated from a suburb of Liverpool. They cultivated and proudly retained their plummy British accents long after living for many years in the United States; the right British accent in America had—and still has—a cachet in the US. The McKeggs were Scotch-Irish by descent and there was a tradition of going to sea in the family. Christine's great-grandfather, William Henry McKegg, worked for the Irish coastguard, then under English control. He met his future wife, Mary Campbell, in the Irish seaport town of Carrickfergus, near Belfast. She claimed descent from the Campbells, the most powerful of the Scottish clans and notorious for their treacherous slaughter of the MacDonalds of Glencoe in 1692.[1] The McKegg family was remarkable in producing three sons (Henry, Alfred, and Alexander) in a single generation who all became ship captains.

One of these sons was Christine's grandfather, Alfred Hugh McKegg (1875–1946), who was born in the coastal town of Howth, near Dublin. He went to sea at fourteen years of age as an apprentice on sailing ships. In time he obtained his Master Mariner's license and eventually became a ship captain for Furness, Withey & Co., Ltd. Among the McKegg family pictures is one of Captain McKegg as a young man in his twenties, taken in the seaport of Bristol. On the back of the picture, he recorded his progress in advancing rank in his distinctively elegant handwriting, crossing out the previous rank as he advanced: 3rd mate *Syrian Prince*, 1st mate *Trojan Prince*, 3rd officer *s/s Swedish Prince*, 2nd officer *Russian Prince*. In 1900 he married Minnie Evangeline McKay in the Anglican parish church of St. Margaret of Foxteth Park, Liverpool. The young couple lived in Wallasey, a western suburb of Liverpool on the River Mersey.

Captain McKegg commanded cargo ships, except for a single shipload of Italian emigrants that he carried from Genoa to Ellis Island; while Christine's grandfather was a captain, my grandfather was a lowly steerage passenger on ships like this. During World War I in the Mediterranean Sea, a German submarine shot away the radio of Captain McKegg's vessel and forced the crew to abandon their ship. The Germans proceeded to board his vessel and sink it with two charges of dynamite. The German submarine captain radioed for assistance for Captain McKegg's crew, afloat in life boats, who were rescued after forty-eight hours and taken to Gibraltar. Family lore has it that a second ship commanded by Captain McKegg's older brother Henry (called Harry) was torpedoed on the very same day in the Mediterranean.

Because Captain McKegg's work kept him away from his family for three to six months at a time, the family welcomed his transfer to a land-based position in the United States. Late in 1918 he began his work as a marine supervisor for the Bay Ridge Operating Company, a subsidiary of Furness, Withey in Brooklyn. His expertise in handling cargo was applied to loading and unloading cargo there, and he was also involved in computing the weight of heavy cargo, such as Baldwin locomotives. Captain McKegg preceded his family to the United States where he bought a completely furnished house—including even the silverware—at 960 79th Street, Brooklyn, a semi-detached house with a driveway on their family's side. His diminutive wife Minnie (only five feet and one-half inch tall) and four children (including eleven-year-old Robert Henry) travelled first class on the S.S. *Royal George* from Liverpool to New York. They arrived in March 1919 and, unlike my relatives, they disembarked in the Lower Bay of New York Harbor, going through customs there and avoiding Ellis Island.

Christine's father, Robert Henry McKegg (1908–2004), was a physically unimposing man. He was only medium in height, on the thin side, and he went bald in his thirties. His one distinguishing feature, aside from his large hooked nose, was his striking blue eyes. He had met Christine's mother when he was seventeen or eighteen and she was only fourteen or fifteen. He went to work for Sacony Vacuum Oil Company (later Mobil Oil Company) in 1927. In 1935, in the middle of the Great Depression, he and Clarice were married. Prudently, they waited to have children: they were British. Their first child, Alfred Hugh, was born in 1942, and Christine followed in 1946.

Sacony Vacuum-Mobil Oil Company transferred Mr. McKegg (which is what I always called him) to London for two years. He went to England in April or May of 1950, and Christine, her mother, and brother followed in June aboard the *Queen Elizabeth*. Christine's mother felt distinctly uncomfortable among the first-class passengers. She was young and insecure; she lacked a college education and had little travel experience. In addition, she had to restrain the childhood exuberance of her two small children, including trying to prevent little Hugh from sticking his head out the porthole. When she and the children returned on the liner *United States* two years later, she insisted on booking second-class cabins.

England in 1950 was still recovering from World War II, and ration books limited access to childhood favorites made from eggs, sugar, and butter; as a substitute for candy, Christine ate meringues. The family lived in an unattached house at 29 Holland Avenue in Cheam, near Sutton, in the southern suburbs of London. Because the McKeggs belonged to the aspiring British middle class, Mr. McKegg and his family felt it was imperative that both children attend boarding schools where they could acquire the proper pronunciation of the King's English, along with other distinguishing marks of class. Her brother was sent off to Homefield School, a boarding school in Sutton. Little Christine, who had just turned four in March, was boarded at Glenrothy Nursery and Kindergarten School, only a hundred-and-fifty yards down the street from where her parents lived. Elocution, drama, dancing, and pianoforte were key parts of this juvenile curriculum.

This was an excruciating experience for Christine's mother, who spent a lifetime being intimidated by the McKeggs' higher class values. She was so distraught about parting with her small daughter that she spent hours walking down Holland Avenue and looking through the fence, trying to catch a glimpse of her flaxen-haired little girl in the school yard. Christine's later memories of the school were limited, though mainly positive. She spoke fondly of Miss Lillian Thomas, who ran the school, and she remembered sharing the tub with other children during baths. She also remembered eating interminable servings of cooked cabbage which she foreswore for the rest of her life. But the aim of the boarding school had been achieved: she acquired a beautiful King's English accent. Like many musically talented people, she had an excellent ear for mimicking sounds. This worked well in cultivating a proper British accent—and also helped to undo it. After returning to their home in America in the summer of 1952, she completely lost her accent and—much to the McKeggs' horror—mimicked a Long Island accent. Later, like a chameleon, her ear would adapt to local accents wherever we lived.

Her musical ear enabled her to hear sounds that I could not hear. She had perfect pitch. This was a key to her singing ability. She loved singing in groups and preferred to sing harmony rather than melody. When she came to Washington, D.C., in 1965 to attend GW, she joined a folk trio consisting of her brother Al, who played a guitar, and Dinah Gray (now Dinah Wiley). They called themselves the Al McKegg Trio, and they sang at various long-gone clubs in the D.C. area, including the Brickskeller, Lute and Lyre, and Potter's House. 1965 was close to the end of the wave of popular folksingers: groups like Peter, Paul and Mary and The Kingston Trio became international stars. Folk music's lapse in popularity came with the increasing use of electric guitars and with the emergence of wildly popular rock groups like the Beatles. The peak of the Al McKegg Trio's success came when they won a weekly competition at the Cellar Door in Georgetown. The trio split up in 1966 when Dinah married Patrick Prentice and Christine married me.

Later Christine would love singing as an alto in church choirs, though she sometimes despaired at the poor musical quality of popular church music. She especially enjoyed singing in church choirs in Germany where the musical tradition remains rich. When we made our last move to Waco, Texas, she joined the traditional choir of Saint Paul's Episcopal Church, which she liked very much. When she was dying, she asked to be buried in her church choir robes.

I first met Christine on a steamy humid summer day in 1965 in Washington, D.C. I was sitting in Brownlee's bar in the 2100 block of Pennsylvania Avenue, a favorite GW student hangout, with my good friend Patrick Prentice. Patrick had all the style that I admired but could never duplicate. His whole life centered around his poetry. He was very Irish in a dark sort of way with a dimpled smile, sexy in the eyes of many women and also me. Besides his poetry, he thought, slept, and ate women. He had a steady girlfriend in Dinah who he would eventually marry (and divorce). Dinah was about as level-headed as Patrick was soaring. There was a story that Dinah would go around trying to sniff up Patrick's inopportune farts at social events. She was always trying to put his life in order. After their divorce, she went to law school and became a government attorney, while Patrick stayed in the GW area, seducing women with his smile and charm and poetry. A few years ago a friend told me that Patrick was still there, now writing television documentaries. She saw him dancing with an attractive woman many years younger than him. He'd gone completely bald, but he had enough energy to dance the night away.

I was attracted to Patrick, although I never enjoyed beer or cigarettes or marijuana or women as much as he did. But Patrick played an essential role in my life because on that hot, steamy day in July of 1965, he introduced me to Christine. We were sitting in a booth and I was facing the door, so I saw her come in first. She walked into the bar with her sister-in-law Barbie, looking for some relief from apartment hunting. Christine was transferring from Lasell Junior College, then a women's college in Massachusetts, to GW to finish her junior and senior years. She saw Patrick and came over to our table. I can't say that at first I was all that struck by her, although she was a natural blonde and I liked blondes. She was wearing an ugly dress and sandals. And she was interrupting a conversation that Patrick and I were having about our poetry (at that time there was nothing more important than our poetry). But Patrick knew her and invited her to sit down. He didn't know her well and his view of her then was pretty well summed up in the remark that her hips were so wide that babies would just drop out of her. That was vintage Patrick. But he meant well and, anyway, he was always friendly to attractive women.

I don't remember much more about that first meeting. We were all drinking schooners of beer, which in 1965 sold at Brownlee's for 25 cents. To many people, the place would seem like a dump, but in the warm, fuzzy way that makes places like Brownlee's standard establishments around most college campuses. Brownlee's doesn't exist anymore and I haven't seen Patrick for years, but together they gave me that meeting with Christine that grew into the most important relationship of my life.

Why did I marry? I can tell you exactly why: to have a family. My family is the most important thing in my life. I mean my ancestors, grandparents,

mother and father, sister and brother, aunts, uncles, cousins, nieces and neph-
ews, wife, son and daughter, grandsons and granddaughter. When I married,
I chose someone who was attractive and who would make a good partner. I
had been blessed/cursed with a raging libido that enabled me to be bisexual,
even though my sexual orientation inclined toward males. But sexual passion
was not the most important thing for Christine. I always felt a little uncomfortable when she referred to our sex as "making love" because most of my
sexual feelings were more tied to passion than to love.

I thought I loved my wife when I married her, but it was not a very deep
sort of love. In fact, I believe I loved her most intensely thirty-one years later
when she died. We had built a life together, and when she died it was
shattered into small pieces that could never be put together again. Some of
the most beautiful, incredibly idealistic words in the English language are
from the marriage ceremony, namely, the promise (or is it a goal?) "to love
and to cherish, until death do us part." Maybe purists will say that I fell short
of that promise. But I still loved my wife.

Christine had beautiful facial bone structure. She had a nervous habit of
moving the left side of her lips over her teeth with her hand and chewing on
the inside of her mouth. She was fun to be with and I remember one night
going swimming with our clothes on in the Reflecting Pool near the Lincoln
Memorial. I loved to watch her smoke a cigarette. She made me feel calmer
when I was with her. I loved to feel the smooth skin with the light dusting of
blond hair on the inside of her thighs. Although we were together for over
thirty-two years, it always felt, in one sense, as if I were making love to her
for the first time because that first image of her young body never left me.

In March 1966, after my military status had been resolved and I was no
longer draftable, I moved into a third floor room at 1817 F Street NW. This
was on the edge of the Foggy Bottom area of Washington, then filled with
tree-lined streets and picturesque but deteriorating brick row houses, many of
which have since been gentrified. I found a job teaching English in a prep
school called the Woodward School for Boys in the nearby Central YMCA
on G Street. This was the famous YMCA where poor Walter Jenkins, the
longest-serving aide to President Lyndon Johnson, became the main character in a national scandal after being arrested for indecent exposure in the
basement men's room during the 1964 presidential election. Actually, Jenkins had been fellating another man, but newspapers then would never have
included such a detail because it was deemed too shocking to American
sensibilities. That does not mean that oral sex was not widely practiced in
America; it simply wasn't talked about. Most people in America would have
been amazed to know that D.C. was filled with many such tearooms in the
1960s. The aggressive political climate of the capital generated (and still
does) a lot of furtive male sex. [2]

Christine and I were married on June 12, 1966, in the chapel of the First Congregational Church in downtown Washington, D.C. (Carl Wittman, in counterpoint, was married four months later in New Jersey.) On that day Christine looked the most beautiful I'd ever seen her. These indelible images seem to be part of the mystique of marriage and I had the same impression of my daughter on her wedding day almost thirty years later. Christine's parents would have preferred a large wedding on Long Island, but she decided (in the style of the time) on a small affair. Our reception was at the Mayflower Hotel and Patrick Prentice was my best man. I felt strong and filled with hope. I expected sexual obstacles in the marriage but felt confident that I could overcome them.

Our first apartment at 603 18th Street NW was one of those fascinating places that my old college roommate, Lon Hanke, had a knack for finding and he passed it on to us. It was part of the former servants' quarters for a large house that fronted on F Street, incredibly just one block west of the Old Executive Office Building, which is next to the White House. Our apartment entrance was on the first floor, the living room and kitchen were on the second floor, and the bedroom and bathroom were on the third floor. We liked that apartment very much. It had a white metal picnic table on an ivy-covered brick patio just outside the front door. It was within easy walking distance of GW where Christine was finishing her senior year, and it was next door to the YMCA prep school where I continued to teach English.

The only unsavory features of the apartment were the garbage smells and other offensive odors from the kitchen of a Korean restaurant that poured into the side living room window facing the back alley. The view from that window also featured the second-floor YMCA weight room (in those days not yet air-conditioned) with audible grunts and the crashing of weights on the floor. I enrolled in a third-year evening class in Chinese at GW and began applying to graduate programs in Chinese studies. I was accepted at the University of California at Berkeley.

I had hoped (without much basis) that after marrying, I would be able to control my same-sex desires. But, of course, shortly after my marriage, those feelings resurfaced. At the time I viewed them as pathological and was very upset by them, and so I contacted my former Georgetown University psychiatrist. The only thing I remember about his response was that since he was now in private practice, he was concerned about collecting a fee for any consultation. Wisely, I chose not to see him. It most certainly would have been worthless to have been treated again for an "anxiety reaction" when my same-sex desires were originating from my very nature. Some problems cannot be solved and simply must be lived with. Once again, I found release in the basement tearooms on the nearby GW campus.

During the year that Christine and I began our married life together in the apartment at the corner of F and 18th Street, I was unaware that we were living two blocks away from what had once been the center of Washington's homosexual world.[3] Lafayette Park, on Pennsylvania Avenue directly across from the White House, had been a focal point for same-sex cruising and socializing since the late nineteenth century until 1950. In the 1930s, the New Deal expansion of government made the capital a magnet for young, single job seekers from all over the Depression-era United States. Many of them were queer, and this created a flourishing homosexual and lesbian subculture in Washington. Rooming houses and restaurants in the area around Lafayette Park became meeting places for queers. One of the most popular places was the YMCA on G Street, next door to the apartment in which Christine and I lived and where I taught.

The free wartime atmosphere that fostered this same-sex subculture began to change after World War II ended. A crackdown on sex crimes began in 1946 followed by the U.S. Park Police launching a "Pervert Elimination Campaign" in Lafayette Park in 1947.[4] Following media headlines and congressional hearings, the Miller Sexual Psychopath Law ("sexual psychopath" being synonymous with homosexual) was signed into law by President Truman in 1948. The driving force in this persecution was the Cold War. Unlike the highly publicized exposure of former communists in the 1950s, few people today realize that the search for homosexuals did not end when the communist witch hunt did; it was even more vehement and longer-lasting.

Shortly after Senator Joseph McCarthy made his famous speech in Wheeling, West Virginia, in February 1950 saying that the State Department employed 205 communists, the senator presented to the Senate chamber a list of eighty-one "loyalty risks."[5] Two of the cases on that list involved homosexuals whom he linked with communists. Public suspicion was aroused when the State Department announced that during the preceding three years (1947–1949), ninety-one homosexuals had been terminated at the State Department as security risks. The State Department created an aggressive program to uncover homosexuals, eventually dividing loyalty-security risks into separate categories of political and sexual deviants.[6] By the 1960s the State Department had dismissed approximately 1,000 employees accused of homosexuality. Extrapolating from statistics, it is estimated that as many as 5,000 suspected queers or lesbians may have been terminated from federal employment in the early years of the Cold War.[7]

The Washington, D.C., morals squad was notorious in its pursuit of homosexuals in Lafayette Square and other cruising areas. Enticement and entrapment techniques were commonly used and merely making eye contact with another man in such areas frequently led to arrest. Physical brutality by the police was common. The threshold of guilt was lowered from sexual behavior to sexual identity. The mere admission of homosexual tendencies was sufficient to be convicted of disorderly conduct, solicitation, or assault.[8] Police interrogators insisted that an accused man reveal the names of other homosexuals as proof that he had broken with his past. Government agencies were informed of any employee who was arrested or merely named in an interrogation, and the result frequently was suspension. Once dismissed on grounds of homosexuality, it was difficult for the victims to find another job in the federal government. Chronic unemployment and despair in the aftermath of their arrests led to numerous suicides.[9]

The government's success in suspending employees on homosexual grounds was based upon the paralyzing shame and fear of those arrested and their hesitancy to contest the suspensions. Gradually, those terminated employees began to hire attorneys to fight these cases and that led to several court victories. Another milestone occurred on April 17, 1965, when seven male and three female members of the Mattachine Society of Washington picketed the White House for homosexual rights.[10] Although I was finishing my course work at GW only a few blocks away, I was unaware of this picketing. If I had known, I would have been curious but certainly would not have joined the picket line. Finally, in 1973 a ruling by the Washington US Court of Appeals forced the Civil Service Commission to end its exclusion of homosexuals from government. The victory of Washington homosexuals was typical of the capital's mentality and how it focused on job security rather than any change in queer identity.

I think I wanted to get out of Washington because I sensed that the atmosphere there was intellectually confining. People in Washington were too driven by power to foster the kind of creative thinking that leads to a cultural and spiritual movement. Had I stayed, I would never have met Carl and witnessed the founding of the gay liberation movement. Washington was not a place that freed men's souls.

Christine graduated from GW and we left Washington, D.C., in our new red Camaro convertible in June of 1967. Like millions before us (and, unknown to me, like Carl that very same summer), we became participants in the great American dream of seeking our fortune by going West. My dream was fulfilled: The San Francisco Bay area was where I launched my career, where my children were born, and where I met Carl. It was an exciting new beginning, but we almost didn't make it. The U-Haul people had rigged up a makeshift hitch for a trailer that was too large for the Camaro. While descending a mountain on Interstate 80 between Cheyenne and Laramie, Wyoming, the trailer started to fishtail wildly. As we careened down the mountain, the car began to go out of control, and I was forced onto the shoulder of the median strip. Luckily, the car slowed and I was able to regain control. We felt fortunate. The only other thing that I remember about that trip is that as soon as we came to the Nevada border, Christine started playing the nickel slot machines at every stop. She was like that. She always got a bang out of life.

We arrived in San Francisco in June 1967 along with thousands of Flower Children who were migrating there from all over the country, leaving behind their middle-class homes, parents, and personal cleanliness and seeking love instead of war. Bathing was replaced by patchouli oil. It was the scent of the sixties. Drinking alcohol was replaced by smoking marijuana and downing tablets of LSD. Hare Krishnas (more middle-class kids, but dressed in saffron-colored robes with shaved heads instead of long hair) were dancing in the streets, pounding bongo drums, singing the mantra "Hare Krishna, Hare Krishna, Krishna, Krishna, Hare Hare, Hare Rama, Hare Hare, Rama Rama." It was almost impossible to walk down certain streets without being panhandled several times. Regular employment and marriage and savings accounts were all rejected in favor of living in the streets or in the parks or crashing in some stranger's apartment and eating handouts.

What the hippies did most of all was love freely, though it was almost entirely of the boy-girl variety. In some ways, they didn't realize just how vanilla their tastes really were. Later, the lightness and fun would wear off and, along with the shift to more serious drugs like heroin, many hippies would begin to self-destruct. But that ugliness came later. In June of 1967 when Christine and I arrived in the Haight-Ashbury district to stay with our good friends, Patrick and Dinah Prentice, the Flower Children were still light and happy, and so were we.

Our first apartment in Berkeley was on Oxford Street, on the north side of Cal campus. Christine found a secretarial job in the Berkeley office of the Educational Testing Service (ETS) of Princeton, New Jersey. After one year, in June of 1968, we were able to find a student apartment to manage on the south side of campus at 2534 Benvenue Avenue. This was the far more active side of campus, near to most of the shops—and the hippie scene—on Telegraph Avenue. Students lived cheaply then and Christine was able to quit her boring job at ETS and work part-time at an antiques shop owned by Bob Dobbins on nearby College Avenue. We discovered the federal food stamp program and after qualifying as residents of California, my tuition fees were reduced to the in-state level, which were low at the time.

Although I was not particularly political, it was hard not to get involved in political demonstrations at Berkeley during the late sixties. Things like the noontime rallies on the Sproul Hall steps became as much part of the daily routine as the morning fog and the afternoon sun. Many of the rallies were marked by someone burning his draft card in protest against the Vietnam War. The most memorable of the antiwar rallies I took part in was the attempt to shut down the draft induction center in neighboring Oakland. This occurred as part of Stop the Draft Week (October 16–21, 1967), organized in part by Students for a Democratic Society. The pacifist slogan "Hell no we won't go" had been modified to the more aggressive "Hell no nobody goes!" and the violence escalated accordingly. Students joined nonstudent protestors to create a protest group of 10,000 that was met outside the induction center by helmeted police wielding batons. Although we were political demonstrators, there was also an element of blood sport present. One sensed that some of the demonstrators were trying to provoke the police, and at times they succeeded. One also sensed that some of the police enjoyed bloodying the protestors.

The following year, 1968, was politically turbulent in America, and this turmoil was accentuated in Berkeley. The Vietnam Tet Offensive of January was followed on March 31 by President Lyndon Johnson's unexpected announcement that he would not run for reelection and, four days later, April 4, the assassination of Martin Luther King.

A massive student strike at Columbia University in New York City began on April 23. Robert F. Kennedy was assassinated at the Ambassador Hotel in Los Angeles on June 5 after winning the California Democratic primary to run for president. Later that summer, the Democratic Convention took place in August in Chicago amid wildly publicized protests and internationally televised police repression. That year in Berkeley was punctuated by street demonstrations and violence. On July 4, 15,000 people flooded the streets for a "victory rally" in the form of the "First Annual Telegraph Avenue Independence Day Street Dance and Rally."[11]

There is something in the landscape of the San Francisco Bay area that is strikingly similar to the Bay of Naples. Both bays are among the most sensually beautiful in the world. Both face west surrounded by an enormous blue sky and arid hills lit by a brilliant sun that each evening sinks into the sea. Except for the times I have been in Naples, I have never felt so alive as I did in Berkeley. My ancestors had lived so many centuries near the Bay of Naples that its solar rhythms had been absorbed into my genes. I don't know if these rhythms had been suppressed for a time by the colder, inland terrain of southwestern Pennsylvania, but once I was in Berkeley, it was as if the elemental forces of love and passion in my blood were reawakened. And so I came to California twenty-five years after my grandfather Raffaele Mungiello. In the spring of 1969 my passion was awakened and, for the second time, I fell in love.

NOTES

1. Micheil MacDonald, *The Clans of Scotland: The History and Landscape of the Scottish Clans* (London: Grange Books, 1991), 85.

2. Another famous tearoom incident involved Congressman Jon Hinson, a Republican of the Fourth District of Mississippi. He was arrested on February 4, 1981, in a men's restroom well known for sexual activity in the Longworth Office Building for fellating a black employee of the Library of Congress. He consequently resigned. See John Howard, *Men Like That: A Southern Queer History* (Chicago: University of Chicago Press, 1999), 272–277.

3. David K. Johnson, *The Lavender Scare: The Cold War Persecution of Gays and Lesbians in the Federal Government* (Chicago: University of Chicago Press, 2004), 41–51.

4. Johnson, *The Lavender Scare,* 55–64.

5. Johnson, *The Lavender Scare,* 15–16.

6. Johnson, *The Lavender Scare,* 75.

7. Johnson, *The Lavender Scare,* 166.

8. Johnson, *The Lavender Scare,* 174–177.

9. Johnson, *The Lavender Scare,* 156–160.

10. Johnson, *The Lavender Scare,* 199–200.

11. Steve Chain, "Telegraph Avenue in Berkeley: After the Barricades, Let the People Decide," *Ramparts,* August 24, 1968, 22–27.

Chapter Nine

Carl, 1943–1963

Carl Wittman and I lived lives in counterpoint, like two different melodies that converged for a short time in the most intense way. We were related not by blood but by the elemental force of our sexuality. And yet our lives soon diverged because our backgrounds and personalities and imaginations were too different to be reconciled.

Carl and I both came into the world in 1943. It was a good year to be born American because Americans were filled with confidence and conquering everything in sight. American soldiers were liberating Europe from the Germans and pushing Japanese forces back across the Pacific. The upbeat American musical *Oklahoma* opened on Broadway while Bing Crosby's recording of "I'll Be Home for Christmas" was heard by millions of separated soldiers, lovers, and mothers. The first antibiotic, penicillin, began its work as a wonder drug that healed previously incurable bacterial infections like syphilis. The Yankee baseball player Joe DiMaggio became a hero by volunteering for the Air Corps.[1] *Casablanca* won the Oscar for best picture, and its theme song "As Time Goes By" became a standard in American music. A sentimental movie about a boy and a dog, *Lassie Come Home*, was enormously popular.

Carl was born at the beginning of 1943 in northern New Jersey. I was born in southwestern Pennsylvania at the end of 1943. He was born into a politically leftist family whose father was an attorney. I was born into a family struggling to realize the American dream of moving from illiteracy to a doctorate in three generations. His family gave him a positive self-image but failed to teach him how to love. My family gave me a mixed self-image but a passion for family. Carl was gregarious and political while I was introspective and creative. He became a leader in a major New Left organization of the 1960s and of the gay liberation movement of the 1970s. I became an academic who wrote books about Chinese history.

So what was it that, twenty-five years after our births, brought us together in a place 2,500 miles away from our homes with an intensity that could not last? Was it our physical awkwardness as boys and the consequent humiliation that we shared? Was it the force of our minds and personalities? Was it the attraction in our genes, or was it fixed in the stars? Did someone high in the sky design the coordinates of our lives such that twenty-five years after our birth we would meet? Of course, I don't know the answers to these questions. But I do know that when we did meet, I was compelled by a powerful force to love him and, though I left him, to never forget him. It is a force that stays with me to this day, shaping my life, even though the Carl that I know has existed entirely as a memory for forty-seven years while the real Carl is dead.

Carl Peter Wittman was born on February 24, 1943, in Hackensack, New Jersey. His grandfather, an Austrian German, had immigrated to the United States in the later part of the nineteenth century. This grandfather had an adventuresome spirit; there is a family photograph of him panning for gold in Alaska. Some of the gold nuggets he found were passed down through the family. Eventually, he settled in the small town of Paramus, in Bergen County, New Jersey, now a suburb of New York City. There he built a stone house with his own hands and drove to Hackensack with a horse and buggy. His son, Walter Thurston Wittman (1914–1994), became a respected local attorney, a civic leader in Paramus and a member of the Chamber of Commerce, even though he was a committed communist. This son married Jeannette (known as Nettie) Freeman (1910–1994) from upstate New York, a woman four years older than him, who shared his leftist sympathies and was active in the community.[2] It is because of his mother that Wittman could trace his ancestors in the British Isles.[3]

Carl had an older sister, Jane, born seventeen months before him in August 1941. They had a contentious relationship as childhood siblings. They were raised in Paramus, a town that grew from a population of less than 4,000 in 1940 to over 23,000 in 1960, unlike my hometown of Burgettstown, which during these same years had a stagnant population. They lived at E-42 Century Road. A cousin remembers the Wittmans as a fascinating family who were very good to her and her family.

The Wittmans were part of a close-knit group of five or six families in Paramus who were political leftists; however, they never tried to implement their political beliefs. Once Carl as an idealistic college student confronted them about their armchair leftist politics. Why had they never done anything political? Their answer was that they were afraid because of what had happened to the Rosenberg family. Julius and Ethel Rosenberg were communists who had been executed in 1953 in one of the most famous and controversial espionage cases of the Cold War. The Wittmans feared that what had happened to the Rosenbergs' two sons could happen to Carl and his sister. Ironically, Carl became friends with the eldest Rosenberg son, Michael Meeropol, at Swarthmore College.

Carl began an active sex life with men at fourteen. He was closeted but not passive—he once told me about an older man he took back to his parents' home for sex. He felt that kids could take care of themselves and that they became "sexual beings way earlier than we'd like to admit. Those of us who began cruising in early adolescence know this, and we were doing the cruising, not being debauched by dirty old men."[4] Carl's view, as in so much of his life, was a radical outlook completely at odds with today's sometimes hysterical view of abused minors as vulnerable victims.

An adoring younger cousin remembers Carl as having a blond crewcut, a big smile, and wide eyes. She remembers him being popular and playing sports, but on this last point her hero worship deceives her. In the last thirteen years of his life, Wittman took up folk dancing and, as with so much else that he did, he became a leader—a teacher of English and Scottish dance. Just before his death, he wrote an essay entitled "Loving Dance" in which he recalled his humiliating awkwardness during high school days in athletics and school dances. Because he carried these searing memories with him as he grew older, when he taught dance, he felt called to reach out to the clumsiest dancers. Each of his dance classes would contain some physically awkward people. Sometimes these were male athletes who were otherwise graceful on the basketball court and sometimes these were people who were simply physically awkward in everything that they did. He believed that they sensed his sympathy for them and wrote:

> And they are right. For I am among them. I got chosen last (or, thank God, next to last, leaving the final indignity to someone I despised even more) when teams "chose up" at high school gym class. I slouched and leaned, trying to make this big awkward body as small as possible, so my classmates wouldn't be reminded how useless it was in the things which counted: athletics and school dances. When I kept being asked why I held myself as if I had a stomach ache, I might have said; obviously, to cover my shamelessly queer genitals.[5]

Carl was proud of his family, though it is not certain that he loved them. They fostered in him a strong self-image that would later make him a leader in leftist organizations like the Students for a Democratic Society (SDS), the draft resistance, the gay liberation movement, folk dancing, and ecological activism. His aunt Betty (later Elizabeth) Freeman (1919–2006) was one of his mother's younger sisters and worked as a guidance counselor at Paramus High School. There was a special bond between this professional, unmarried woman and her nephew, and he was closer to her than to anyone else in his family.[6] In 1969, when his marriage was ending, she was the first member of his family to whom he came out as a gay man. She would later reciprocate by coming out as a lesbian and moving to Oregon to be with him; later still she would follow him to North Carolina where she witnessed his death.

Carl graduated from Paramus High School in June of 1960, ranking sixth in a class of 193. In September he entered Swarthmore College in southeastern Pennsylvania, a prestigious liberal arts college of Quaker origins with a reputation for leftist politics. During his freshman year, he became friends with a group of likeminded leftists, including Miriam (Mimi) Feingold (currently Miriam Real), and Michael Meeropol. Only a small group of friends knew that Meeropol was the Rosenbergs' son. Carl had expressed a fleeting sympathy for his situation, but he was contemptuous of Meeropol's fear of getting arrested in a political demonstration and having his identity revealed.

In the spring semester of their freshman year, Wittman began to reject Meeropol when he realized he could not dominate him. At 5 feet 9 inches in height with brown hair, Meeropol fit the pattern of a smaller, dark-haired male to which Carl was attracted throughout his life. However, Meeropol was obliviously heterosexual and Carl may have sensed this.

Wittman is remembered from his college days as a leftist with a Marxist bent who searched for an economic interpretation of historical and political events in history classes. There were faculty complaints about the "communism" of some freshmen. Carl majored in history and took several economics courses but withdrew from the honors program because of his increasing involvement in political activities.[7] He was heavily involved in the student newspaper *The Phoenix* and later served as editor-in-chief; even later he would write a column with a leftist perspective for the paper.

In the early sixties the Swarthmore Political Action Club (SPAC), a group of thirty to fifty undergraduates, had been involved with peace and disarmament issues. In 1962 when Paul Booth tried to convince SPAC to become an SDS chapter, the idea was rejected. However, in the fall of 1963 Carl returned from the SDS summer convention and played a crucial role in reorienting SPAC into a more activist direction as one of the most active SDS chapters in the country.

SDS was one of the main vehicles for the radical idealism that emerged among American youth in the second half of the twentieth century. It was based on a politics of values that initially involved pacifism and disarmament (during the Cold War), racial equality, the redistribution of wealth, and above all the decentralization of authority. At first, SDS fought against the injustice of poverty and racial segregation and later against the injustice of the war in Vietnam. Finally, it fought against the injustice that suppressed women. However, when SDS faltered in fighting the injustice that suppressed homosexuals, Wittman withdrew from his former comrades and helped to forge the new gay liberation movement.

NOTES

1. Betsy Dexter, *You Must Remember This 1943* (New York: Warner Books, 1995), 26.

2. Jeannette Wittman was on the steering committee of the College Needs Council of Bergen County. John W. Slocum, "Bergen Is Urged to Add College," *New York Times*, October 5, 1958, 82.

3. Carl Wittman, "Loving Dance," in *New Men, New Minds: Breaking Male Tradition, How Today's Men Are Changing the Traditional Roles of Masculinity*, ed. Franklin Abbott (Freedom, CA: Crossing Press, 1987), 82. Wittman's essay "Loving Dance" originally appeared in *RFD* 4 (summer solstice 1975): 31–34.

4. Wittman quoted in Charles Shively, "Wittman, Carl (1943–1986)," in *Encyclopedia of Homosexuality*, vol. 2, ed. Wayne Dynar (New York: Garland, 1990), 1400.

5. Wittman, "Loving Dance," 81–82.

6. Carl Wittman, taped by Marsha Emerman, Ashland, Oregon, 1980.

7. College transcript of Carl Peter Wittman, Office of the Registrar, Swarthmore College, issued October 12, 2001; private letter of Carl Wittman to Miriam Feingold, dated January 30, 1964, from Ann Arbor, in Miriam Feingold Papers, 1960–1967, State Historical Society of Wisconsin, Archives Division, Social Action Collection, sheet 391.

Chapter Ten

The Movement, 1963–1967

In the 1960s, it was common to hear young people talk about "the movement." When they said "the movement," they were referring to all of the different struggles they were engaged in to change the world as they knew it. For some, it meant a political struggle against American racism, poverty, and militarism. For others it involved a counterculture of recreational drugs, unrestrained sex, and rock music. Above all, the movement meant freedom to do things that had been forbidden. It meant attacking parents, customs, attitudes, institutions, government, organizations, and churches that had restricted freedom.

The movement attacked attitudes that segregated people by skin color as well as attitudes that frowned on males with long hair. Reactions to both of these attacks were strong and at times violent. Images of guard dogs attacking civil rights protestors in Alabama as well as images of flag-waving, short-haired, hard-hat construction laborers fighting long-haired war protesters were etched on the youthful consciousness of my generation. There were also movement images of public nudity and the lyrics of the Broadway musical *Hair*. The movement attacked American patriotism and the military while peaceniks (both hippies and Vietnam War protestors) advocated peace and disarmament. Bypassing the Judeo-Christian teachings in which they had been raised, adherents of the movement saw the 1960s as the beginning of the astrological Age of Aquarius in which world freedom and brotherhood would abound. People in the movement attacked political liberals who believed in gradual reform because they believed that radical politics, not reform, was needed.

The movement attacked the very American idea that linked wealth with happiness and instead cultivated a simple, anticommercial lifestyle. The movement attacked taboos toward premarital sex and cultivated free love. A "love-in" referred to people gathering to express indiscriminate affection and oftentimes sex. The movement attacked the nuclear family as oppressive, and it cultivated new liberating communal arrangements for family and child-rearing. I remember feeling that I should live in some sort of commune. It was a social pressure to conform but all in the name of nonconformity. It was like the pressure I felt a few years later from fellow Christian Charismatics to speak in tongues: spiritual liberation was offered through group conformity. I resisted both living in a commune and speaking in tongues.

The movement was intentionally abrasive and used shocking language as a weapon. A word like "fuck" was cultivated by people who had to struggle to overcome a carefully instilled, polite aversion to the use of foul language. When most movement people said "fuck," there was something forced about it, as if they were making a statement rather than expressing a feeling. The movement attacked suburbia, careers, discipline, and even cleanliness. All these were despised as middle class, even though (or perhaps because) most of the adherents of the movement had emerged out of homes that had en-shrined those very values. Some of the people involved in the political move-ment opposed the use of drugs and saw them as a distraction from the need to concentrate on fighting racism and the war in Vietnam.

Of course, not all the values of the movement fit together in harmony, and some were contradictory. People were selective about which values they chose, and that is why the movement meant different things to different people. Nevertheless, people like Carl, Christine, and me were all shaped by the movement, and we all participated in it to varying degrees. Carl advocat-ed its politics, Christine sang its songs, and I freed my soul.

Most historians trace the beginnings of the movement to the fight against racial segregation in the South. The civil rights movement for African Americans began in 1956 when Martin Luther King Jr. led a boycott of segregated buses in Montgomery, Alabama. In 1960 King's method of non-violent civil disobedience was first used when four black students sat down with a Bible in a whites-only section of a department store cafeteria in Greensboro, North Carolina. Carl became involved in the civil rights move-ment in the summer of 1962 when he traveled with a group of students to Jackson, Tennessee, where he participated in an American Friends Service Committee (AFSC) project involving black voter registration. [1]

In the spring of 1963 Carl and other SPAC members became involved in the Cambridge movement to protest segregation and unequal employment and housing in Maryland's Eastern Shore. Working together with blacks in SNCC (pronounced "snick" and standing for Student Nonviolent Coordinat-ing Committee), they participated in marches that led to mass arrests and violence between the demonstrators and police and eventually tear-gassing by the National Guard. Attorney General Robert Kennedy negotiated a com-promise settlement. Carl and his close associate Vernon Grizzard felt this settlement confirmed that the civil rights movement was incapable of dealing with the problems of blacks. They believed (and here we see the Marxist influence of Carl's background) that black oppression was rooted in economic, not political, inequalities. [2]

Carl's move into national politics came at the end of September 1963 when he participated in the quarterly SDS National Council meeting in Bloomington, Indiana. His presence is recorded in the earliest known SDS group portrait, which twenty-four years later appeared on the front page of the *New York Times Book Review*. [3] This group photograph, taken by C. Clark Kissinger, shows Carl standing far in the back, behind everyone else. Only part of his face and blond hair are visible, reflecting not only his height but also a self-effacing quality. In striking contrast, Tom Hayden is fully visible, slightly apart from the rest of the group on the left side, striking a dramatic pose. Vernon Grizzard, whom Carl had a crush on, is standing beside him. Todd Gitlin, who later became a prominent sociologist, is standing in the row in front of Carl. Following this meeting, Carl made a six-week road trip, visiting Cambridge (Massachusetts), Washington, D.C., the historically black West Virginia State College, and Chicago. [4] As he went from place to place, he observed local organizations and tried to energize people.

Carl's leadership was more personal than public in the sense that he excelled in individual and small group discussions. By these means he recruited people who would have a deep commitment to the movement. Whereas some SDS leaders, like Tom Hayden, were very forceful with charismatic personas, Carl belonged to a group of SDS leaders who were less outspoken and worked behind the scenes.

Compelling testimony of Carl's influence as a recruiter and organizer comes from Cathy Wilkerson. Her name became famous in March of 1970 when three SDS faction Weathermen accidentally exploded the bombs they were making in the basement of her father's Greenwich Village townhouse at 18 West Eleventh Street. [5] The explosion killed the three bomb makers and effectively ended what remained of the more radical arm of SDS. Wilkerson was in the townhouse at the time, but she and Kathy Boudin escaped injury and both went underground for a while. [6] Later she resurfaced, served less than one year of a three-year sentence, and eventually became an inner city math instructor. When she had first arrived as a freshman at Swarthmore in the fall of 1962, she was interested in becoming involved in a political movement but was naive and insecure. [7] She attended a few SPAC meetings but stopped because she was intimidated by the "articulate, intellectual males" who spoke with such passion and she had trouble understanding what they were saying.

Wilkerson had a difficult relationship with most of the men in SDS. She felt they were contemptuous of her because of her outside status and limited knowledge. Wittman was the only one who treated her differently and spoke to her about politics in a way she could understand. Later that winter he approached her about going with him and some other students to Cambridge, Maryland, to support the civil rights struggle there.[8] She went and the trip transformed her political life.

In the fall of his senior year (1963) Carl decided to try and develop a broader approach that combined civil rights and an antipoverty campaign in industrially depressed Chester, Pennsylvania, only two miles from the Swarthmore campus. Others became involved, and in November SPAC joined with blacks in Chester to support a broad range of demands. Their picketing, sit-ins, and arrests produced the first major violent action by a white college group in the North.[9] By January political organizing was taking Carl on long organizing trips away from campus. In Ann Arbor, Michigan, home of the largest SDS chapter, he spoke with "Hayden and Co." about activities for the year after graduation. At this point he had a positive impression of Tom Hayden. He was "enthusiastic about working with him the following year, maybe in Chicago or Detroit, Baltimore or Newark."[10]

Meanwhile, demonstrations continued in Chester. On March 31, 1964, 107 people, including Carl and a number of Swarthmore students, were arrested on charges of "affray, illegal assembly, and refusing to move on orders of an officer."[11] Since the total for bail was over $125,000, they had difficulty raising it. Carl's letter from jail dated April 2, 1964, revealed how energized he was by the experience. He was filled with plans for the future and stated that by June he would probably be working for SDS, either in campus organizing, at the national office, or in the field, possibly in Cleveland, Chicago, or Newark. However, after spending a week in jail, he came out depressed and even cried briefly over the fact that the jailed students had not used their time in jail productively but had just amused themselves.

Carl's early letters and essays fail to reflect the warmth of his personality. His essays tend to be polemical in tone. His three letters to Mimi Feingold preserved in the Feingold Papers at the Wisconsin Historical Society are surprisingly devoid of warmth, even though he addresses them to "Mims," signs them "love," and is writing them to the woman he will marry in less than three years. His letters reveal lots of enthusiasm for political projects, praise for some people, and criticism of others.

Do we ever get over our undergraduate crushes? I had an undergraduate crush on my freshman roommate Ronny Hames. And as typically happened in the bad old days when we all hid our same-sex attraction, the object of my crush and the object of Carl's crush were both obliviously straight. When I first met Carl in 1969, he told me about his unrequited undergraduate love. When I later asked various people from his Swarthmore days who that might be, the near-unanimous response was Vernon Grizzard. During their junior or senior years they became quite close and Carl sometimes referred to Grizzard as "my shadow." But Grizzard was oblivious to Carl's same-sex feelings, and when he eventually learned about them he withdrew from Carl. Grizzard later returned to Florida where he attended law school, married, had a child, and lived in Tallahassee for thirty-four years until suffering an early death in 2011.[12]

Throughout his life, Carl had crushes on a number of men. But his feelings for Grizzard developed before he came out. In fact, while he was at Swarthmore, he remained in the closet, though he was sexually active off-campus. It was easy to find partners for casual sex in nearby cruising spots, but it was something that he felt compelled to hide from his classmates. In the early sixties, even on a liberal campus like Swarthmore, same-sex feelings were still "the love that dare not speak its name."[13] Revealing them would have destroyed Carl's ability to recruit for political causes.

At the National Council meeting in New York City in December 1963, SDS decided to shift its organizing emphasis from college campuses to poor communities and, according to Tom Hayden, "leave all that academic crap behind it."[14] Carl drafted a position paper for this shift entitled "An Interracial Movement of the Poor?" and passed it on to Hayden for editing and some additions.[15] "An Interracial Movement of the Poor?" is a synthesis of ideas from the Old Left and the civil rights and the labor movements.[16] It presented a strategy for blacks and whites working together to deal with poverty and racism.[17] This strategy was implemented through Economic Research and Action Projects, commonly known by their acronym ERAP (pronounced "ee-rap"). ERAP projects began in the summer of 1964 in ten (eventually thirteen) cities: Baltimore, Boston, Chester, Chicago, Cleveland, Hazard (Kentucky), Louisville, Newark, Philadelphia, and Trenton.[18]

Anti-intellectualism was a prominent part of the New Left. Some SDS members dispute that characterization and believe it is based on a misunderstanding. One SDS defender admitted that their thinking was based on their own experiences rather than other people's theoretical writings but claimed that they analyzed things before they sought to change them. Anti-intellectualism was expressed by Carl in the ERAP proposal as an extension of *The Port Huron Statement* (1962), one of the most important guiding documents for SDS and the New Left as a whole. SDS attacked American universities for reinforcing the status quo rather than serving as a source for social criticism and change.[19] Wittman expressed this type of anti-intellectualism in his paraphrase of Karl Marx: "our major problem is not to analyze the situation, but to change it."[20]

The Clinton Hill neighborhood of Newark had undergone dramatic demographic change from 1950 to 1960.[21] The ERAP project concentrated on the "lower hill" area of the neighborhood that was populated almost entirely by blacks with the lowest family incomes and highest unemployment. Newark's urban renewal policies included demolishing low-cost housing, forcing many blacks to relocate to Clinton Hill. However, because much of Clinton Hill

was also scheduled for demolition, landlords neglected to make needed re-
pairs and garbage service deteriorated. The plumbing and heating systems
also deteriorated while rats and roaches proliferated. Into this area came the
youthful and somewhat naive SDS organizers seeking to foster an interracial
movement of the poor.

The Newark Community Union Project (NCUP) in the Clinton Hill
neighborhood was one of the largest ERAP projects and was loosely directed
by Wittman and Hayden.[22] However, there was a lot of tension between
Hayden, Wittman, and Barry Kalish, who were all competing for leadership
of the group.[23] SDS was filled with alpha males who competed with one
another. Hayden and Wittman were both forceful personalities, though they
came from very different backgrounds. Hayden came from an Irish Catholic
working-class family and attended a large public university while Carl came
from a politically sophisticated, atheistic, Marxist family and attended an
elite private liberal arts college.

Hayden found it easier to relate to women than to men and complained
about difficulties interacting with other men. Disagreements were so intense
that sometimes, in situations involving Carl, Hayden could not even communicate when they reached an impasse.[24] While Carl had a sunny disposition
and sweet smiles, he also seemed to have a secret.

The secret was Carl's sexuality. The radicalism of SDS members in the
early and mid-sixties was limited to political, social, and economic concerns
rather than personal issues and relationships. Only later would gender equality and sexual orientation become important issues, and even to this day there
is a reluctance among former SDS members to discuss anyone's sexual orientation. But for Carl the personal was political.

One Newark project participant, Corinna Fales, remembers Carl's sunny
disposition and sweet smiles but recalls that part of him seemed to be kept
intentionally private or hidden.[25] Carl and I shared a powerful sex drive that
was impossible to suppress. It was an inseparable part of who we were and a
key to explaining our lives. Given the strength of this drive, all we could do
was to express these feelings in secret and hidden ways. Consequently, each
of us would periodically disappear in search of men for sex. Hitchhiking was
one way of doing this. Carl met men through hitchhiking on the New Jersey
Turnpike. At the age of sixteen, I ran away from home and hitched rides from
Pennsylvania to Missouri. I was too closeted to have sex with anyone, but the
desire was a driving force.

Hayden was unaware of Carl's same-sex orientation, partly because Carl
was hiding it and partly because Hayden was not sensitive enough to pick up
on the signs that gays tend to give off. In the mid-1960s, American society
associated homosexuality almost exclusively with effeminacy, but Carl was
not effeminate.[26] Carl remembered that soon after the Newark project began
in 1964, Hayden "announced that there was to be no homosexuality or mari-

juana on our community organizing project, and then proceeded to borrow my room to bed down with his latest woman."[27] Hayden does not remember making that announcement, but he was worried about what the community would think of the SDS organizers.[28]

Hayden later admitted that he was ignorant about homosexuality at the time. Possibly some insensitive comments on his part conveyed a certain homophobia to Carl. Eventually, Hayden realized that Carl was gay, and this realization caused him to withdraw from his former collaborator. In his memoirs and informal comments, Hayden later expressed regret over how he reacted to Carl's sexuality.[29]

In the summer of 1965, one year after establishing the Newark project, Carl and a few others left Newark to establish a new project in nearby Jersey City and Hoboken. Carl favored a looser form of organization than Hayden and more contact with area residents. Maybe he also wanted to get away from Hayden's homophobia and feel freer to cruise for sex. In Hoboken, organizers found jobs in an attempt to get to know residents in their local workplaces and to support themselves. Carl worked first as an orderly in a local hospital, then in a print shop, and finally as a welfare worker. A second reason for the break-off involved an attempt to more fully implement the biracial aims of "An Interracial Movement for the Poor?" While Newark turned out to be mainly black, Hoboken was mostly white. A new project was established there in June 1965. (The many Italian-Americans in Hoboken included the branch of my Mungiello family that retained the name's original spelling.) The Hoboken project initially consisted of only four regular organizers: Helen Garvy, Vernon Grizzard, Jill Hamberg, and Carl.[30]

SDS members were very idealistic. Carl's cousin Marya Warshaw recalls visiting the Hoboken project on several occasions, until an argument over Bob Dylan switching to an electric guitar made her feel unwelcome.[31] She thought Dylan going electric was a great idea, but the SDS people were purists and regarded the switch as a sell-out to the materialism of a consumer society. When Grizzard left to go back to school in 1966, Mimi Feingold moved in with Carl.[32]

When Carl first revealed his same-sex attraction to ERAP coworkers, it came almost in the form of a denial. (How different from the unapologetic tone he would use in writing "A Gay Manifesto" three years later!) The first person he appears to have told was one of his female coworkers in Hoboken. In the fall of 1965 he gave this coworker a copy of James Baldwin's novel *Giovanni's Room* to read. Afterward he asked what she thought about the character being gay. After seeing that the reaction was fairly neutral, he revealed his gay feelings.

Anyone who wants to learn about the oppressive feelings of queer men in the fifties and early sixties can read about them in *Giovanni's Room*. It is one of the great classics in gay literature because the author, James Baldwin, understood oppression on two counts: he was both black and gay. To escape American racial prejudice, he fled to Paris in 1948 where he lived for six years. He fell in love with a Swiss man named Lucien Happersberger and continued the love affair even after Happersberger married.[33] Baldwin transformed his experience into *Giovanni's Room* (1956), except that the American David was white instead of black and his male lover Giovanni was Italian instead of Swiss.

In the book, when David was unable to accept his same-sex feelings for Giovanni and tried to break away to marry a woman, Giovanni falls apart, commits murder, and is sentenced to death. At the end of the book, David's same-sex feelings for men are finally revealed to his fiancée in a tawdry bar scene and soon afterward she leaves him as he faces his responsibility for Giovanni's execution. Such was the oppression and tragedy associated with homosexuality in the fifties. For Carl this book had great meaning in confirming his own feelings of homosexual isolation and in serving as a future political platform for the gay liberation movement.

The person to whom Carl showed *Giovanni's Room* felt that she was a trial balloon for Carl's plan to reveal his gay feelings to Mimi Feingold. He was going to a demonstration in Washington, D.C., where he would see Feingold. They had been a couple at Swarthmore and Carl wanted to revive the relationship, with marriage in mind. He had apparently convinced himself that he was bisexual rather than exclusively gay and that his sexuality was fluid enough to manage a marriage. And he wanted to have children.

This story has special meaning to me because I had strikingly identical feelings and desires. But while I succeeded, Carl did not. He failed because, as he later admitted, his desires were largely the wishes and expectations of others that he had internalized. My desires to marry and have children were more my own. The particular way the male body is constructed makes it hard to fake sexual passion. The legendary Victorian advice to "lie back and think of England" might help a woman who undergoes sex as a conjugal duty to fake passion, but it is less helpful to a man with erectile problems. Some men try to deal with the problem by fantasizing that their sexual partner is a man rather than a woman. Carl wanted so much to be a bisexual that he convinced himself he could function sexually with a woman, at least in the context of a marital relationship. One wonders when that awful moment of realization came when he saw that he could not manage it?

Carl wanted to get away from the homophobia of his fellow radicals, but he had also absorbed some of their homophobia. He was filled with all these contradictory feelings, including self-loathing. He once wore a woman's dress to an SDS meeting. These contradictory feelings led him to make a self-destructive announcement to his fellow SDS members. Early in 1966, Carl surprised the Newark and Hoboken project people by announcing not only that he was gay but that he loved Mimi Feingold and they were going to be married. One witness described Carl as saying that he was marrying because his homosexuality was like a broken record and he wanted to create a symphony. The clear intention was to have children. Three years later after the marriage had disintegrated, he tried to explain in a letter to his Aunt Elizabeth why the marriage had failed:

> In the last year or so, I've realized more and more that some of my desire to get married was a way of telling the world that I wasn't homosexual—I had rationalized by saying that homosexuality could be a sick thing—but at least at this point I have to find out what was really my motive in getting married vis-a-vis this, and get straight in my head how much I've been inhibited and intimidated by what everyone has always been telling me—that I have to be married to a girl in order to be happy and normal. [34]

Ironically, I was with Carl when he wrote this letter. It was the week in March 1969 when we had driven from the San Francisco area to Wolf Creek, Oregon. I remember him staying up late one night to write a letter to his aunt and being upset about it when he finally came to bed.

Mimi Feingold is described by those who knew her at the time as being small with short, dark hair, a bundle of energy. She seems to have been a female version of the smaller, dark-haired males who attracted Carl. At Swarthmore, she had been part of "the four," a group of recognized leftists on campus that included her roommate, Charlotte Philipps. She and Carl became close during his freshman year.

Feingold graduated from Swarthmore in June of 1963, a year before Carl. In 1963–1964 she was active in CORE (Congress of Racial Equality) promoting voter registration and community organizing projects in Louisiana, and she completed her MA in history at the University of Wisconsin at Madison in 1966. [35] The wedding of Feingold and Carl took place on October 1, 1966, in a sheep pasture at the farm of the prominent leftist and pacifist Dave Dellinger (1915–2004) in Clinton, New Jersey. (At Swarthmore, Carl had been friends with Dellinger's son, Patch Dellinger.) It was a very sixties-style alternative wedding, with its outdoor country setting, informal dress ("in the interests of comfort"), and potluck food ("in the interests of participatory democracy"). [36] The intentionally medieval theme of the wedding reflected the idealistic desire of the SDS movement to return to the more humanistic fundamentals of an earlier and simpler age.

For Carl, for whom the personal was political, his marriage was a political event. It involved the union of a power couple and the wedding celebrated the movement as much as it did the couple's marriage. But just as personal politics was the driving force that brought the couple together, so would personal politics cause their marriage to unravel.

By the summer of 1967 the ERAP projects were disintegrating under both internal and external pressures. Overworked, underfed, and increasingly in conflict, SDS organizers began to crave more sleep and amenities, simple things like orange juice for breakfast and an end to tuna casseroles.[37] After 1965 the growing Black Power movement and their vocally militant separatism made it increasingly difficult for white ERAP organizers to work with community blacks. The riots in Newark in 1967 marked the end of ERAP's efforts in black communities.[38] As the community organizing in slums fell apart, SDS shifted its emphasis back to college students and college-educated professionals. However, the major efforts of SDS from 1965 on were concentrated on opposing the war in Vietnam and militarism in American society.

The collapse of ERAP projects in the summer of 1967 marked a shift in the leadership of SDS. The old guard had tended to originate out of northeastern families of Jewish intellectuals and Old Left parents who had gone to prestigious colleges. The new leaders attended public universities and emerged from working-class families in the American heartland where leftist ideas had a much more practical orientation.[39] The emergence of this "prairie power" in the Midwest and South was led by the SDS chapter at Austin, Texas, home of the University of Texas.[40] There was considerable tension between the two groups. Unlike the old guard, this younger group was more identified with the counterculture and with the use of psychedelic drugs.[41] The fact that the new guard was more anti-establishment and anarchistic may help explain the more radical shift in direction that SDS took in 1967.

To this day, friendships among many former SDS members remain strong; they continue to have contact with one another, and there is a general reluctance to publicly criticize other former SDS members. Most are now professionals or recently retired and located in the coastal urban areas of the Northeast United States or California. The old enemies of the sixties (centralized authoritarianism, militarism, racism, sexism, and ecological abuse) continue to unite them in an informal way. However, they are not a monolithic group, and some former SDS members are harsh in their criticism of the group. Bill Hartzog is one such critic. He was born in Ohio and was, according to Kirkpatrick Sale, "the pure personification of prairie power."[42] After an unsuccessful run for the SDS presidency in 1966, Hartzog refused military induction and went underground, migrating to Canada where he has remained. He was eventually pardoned by the Carter administration in 1978 and now works as an attorney in Montreal.

Some former SDS members have voiced criticism of Wittman. Part of the criticism was aimed at Wittman's personality and style and his treatment of Mimi Feingold, which some regarded as cruel. Another part of his criticism was aimed at a misreading of history by Carl and several SDS members who believed that a national revolution was imminent. They refused to accept that the United States was not ripe for revolution. In fact, most of American society did not care about revolution.

According to his critics, Carl substituted his remarkable self-confidence for his lack of political and historical understanding. He was intellectually coercive and forced his ideas on people. (Several former SDS members expressed the view that Carl was manipulative, but this view was by no means unanimous.) Carl was said to be intolerant and his personal style was to make people feel bad if they disagreed with him. I saw an example of this when I was with him in 1969. He practiced a sort of soft bullying based on moralizing. He made someone feel bad if they didn't share his morality, which he presented as the only true morality. But SDS was filled with moralists who condemned others for their immorality. By 1980, Carl came to recognize the flaws of this uncompromising morality. However, in the 1960s his sense of will was so powerful that he believed he could *will* change, *will* revolution, even *will* a change in his sexual orientation (from gay to bisexual when he married), and *will* his own death (which he later did through suicide).

Carl has his defenders. One of them remembered Carl as a very charismatic organizer who was politically astute, exuberant, outgoing, and friendly with a good sense of humor.[43] However, even this defender admitted that Carl could be intimidating.

Carl's contribution to SDS was as a leader of one of the strongest campus chapters and one of the most important of the student civil rights campaigns. His involvement in the civil rights struggle at Cambridge and Chester gave him the experience and authority to draft a plan for urban organizing in the north (ERAP).[44] But since SDS was essentially a student organization, Carl and others who were no longer students became unsure in how they should relate to it. From this perspective, Carl's withdrawal from SDS made sense, although it was also done for the simple reason that he was getting older and moving on, like other members of the SDS old guard.[45] But there was another reason for Carl's withdrawal and that was his dawning realization that SDS was hostile to him at his most fundamental level—his sexuality.

NOTES

1. Mab Segrest, *Memoir of a Race Traitor* (Boston: South End Press, 1994), 54.

2. Wesley Hogan, "How Democracy Travels: SNCC, Swarthmore Students, and the Growth of the Student Movement in the North, 1961–1964," *The Pennsylvania Magazine of History and Biography* 126, no. 3 (July 2002): 450–451.

3. *The New York Times Book Review*, June 21, 1987, 1. The portrait appeared as part of a review by Hendrik Hertzberg of James Miller's *Democracy Is in the Streets: From Port Huron to the Siege of Chicago* (New York: Simon & Shuster, 1987). The nineteen members in the portrait, including Wittman, are identified on page 33 of the review.

4. Hogan, "How Democracy Travels," 462.

5. Cathy Wilkerson, *Flying Close to the Sun: My Life and Times as a Weatherman* (New York: Seven Stories Press, 2007), 265–348.

6. Wilkerson, *Flying Close to the Sun*, 349–377. See also Susan Brady, *Family Circle: The Boudins and the Aristocracy of the Left* (New York: Knopf, 2003), 203–207, 255, 279, 290.

7. Cathy Wilkerson to the author, December 19, 2001.

8. Wilkerson, *Flying Close to the Sun*, 46–47.

9. Kirkpatrick Sale, *SDS* (New York: Random House, 1973), 104.

10. Private letter from Carl Wittman to Miriam Feingold, Miriam Feingold Papers, January 30, 1964, Wisconsin Historical Society, sheet 392.

11. Private letter of Carl Wittman to Miriam Feingold, dated April 2, 1964, from Broadmeadows Prison in Pennsylvania, Miriam Feingold Papers, sheet 418.

12. Obituary of Vernon Townes Grizzard III (1944–2011), *Tallahassee Democrat*, October 14, 2011.

13. This famous allusion ("the love that dare not speak its name") to same-sex feeling is from the last line of the poem "Two Loves" (1892) by Lord Alfred Douglas. Douglas was probably making an allusion to the medieval Latin name for sodomy as "*piccatum illud horrible inter Christianos non nominandum*" (that horrible sin unmentionable among Christians). Douglas and Oscar Wilde were famous lovers who became entangled in a notorious London trial in 1895 that sent Oscar Wilde to jail for homosexual offenses. See Neil McKenna, *The Secret Life of Oscar Wilde* (New York: Basic Books, 2005), 88, 173, 238; Douglas Murray, *Bosie: A Biography of Lord Alfred Douglas* (New York: Hyperion, 2000), 35–36.

14. Jennifer Frost, *An Interracial Movement of the Poor: Community Organizing and the New Left in the 1960s* (New York: New York University Press, 2001), 18.

15. Email from Tom Hayden, November 19, 2001. Frost, 27, refers to Wittman as the author and Hayden as the editor. In his letter to Mimi Feingold of April 2, 1964, Wittman referred to this paper: "Hayden and I are writing a major paper on the subject of biracial alliance on economic issues . . . I'll enclose a copy as soon as Hayden gets it completely drawn up." Wittman to Feingold, Miriam Feingold Papers, April 2, 1964, sheet 419.

16. A historian of this movement, Jennifer Frost, states that the "Interracial Movement of the Poor?" "owed much to Carl Wittman, the son of Communist parents and an avid student of history." Frost, *An Interracial Movement of the Poor*, 27.

17. Sale, *SDS*, 105, notes that although the paper is "long, discursive, and well-nigh unreadable, it nonetheless had an impact on many in SDS circles."

18. Frost, *An Interracial Movement of the Poor*, 47, 50; Sale, *SDS*, 113–114.

19. SDS said that universities "must make debate and controversy, not dull pedantic cant, the common style for educational life." Students for a Democratic Society (SDS), *The Port Huron Statement* (1962) (Chicago: Kerr, 1990), 10, 15–16, 75, 77.

20. Letter from Carl Wittman to Paul Booth, February 18, 1964, Tamiment Institute Library, New York University, New York, Students for a Democratic Society Records, 1934–36; 1946–1966, series 2B, box 19, folder 1, quoted in Frost, *An Interracial Movement of the Poor*, 47. Karl Marx's original statement was "The philosophers have only *interpreted* the world, in various ways; the point, however, is to *change* it." It is found in Marx's "Thesis on Feuerbach," written in 1845 and published in Friedrich Engels' essay *Ludwig Feuerbach and the End of Classical German Philosophy* (1888). See Robert C. Tucker, ed., *The Marx-Engels Reader*, 2nd ed. (New York: Norton, 1978), 145. I thank my colleague Dr. David Hendon for helping me to identify the source of this quotation.

21. In part, because of massive migration of blacks from the South to the North, the Clinton Hill neighborhood of Newark went from being predominantly white to 56 percent black in 1950–1960 while the population increased from 33,400 to 41,289. Frost, *An Interracial Movement of the Poor*, 59–60.

22. The Newark ERAP project included, in addition to Hayden and Wittman, Connie Brown, Steve Bloch, Corinna Fales, David Gelber, Carol Glassman, Larry Gordon, Jill Hamberg, Barry Kalish, and Michael Zweig. Frost, *An Interracial Movement of the Poor*, 58.

23. See the project report "Newark" by Carl Wittman and Carl Hayden, in *Students for a Democratic Society Bulletin* 3, no. 2 (October 1964): 15–17.

24. Tom Hayden, *Reunion: A Memoir* (New York: Random House, 1988), 421.

25. Telephone and e-mail interview with Corinna Fales, September 30, 2001.

26. Later, one of Carl's strongest concerns would be with helping young gay men who were coming out to find more authentic and natural models because many of them came from remote areas where the only available gay model was a drag queen. Telephone interview of Frank Nelson, September 9, 2001.

27. Carl Wittman, "Us and the New Left," *Fag Rag* (Boston), Fall 1978, 22. Also see Frost, *An Interracial Movement of the Poor*, 155.

28. Email message from Tom Hayden, November 19, 2001.

29. Hayden, *Reunion*, 130; email from Hayden, November 19, 2001.

30. Garvy had been working as the assistant national secretary at the SDS national office in New York City and had visited the Newark project. Other participants such as Nick Egleson, Ingrid Kraus, and Mike Zweig joined the Hoboken project only for the summer.

31. Telephone interview of Marya Warshaw, October 5, 2001.

32. In 1966 Michael Lesser, who was working full time in organizing district number 1199 Hospital Workers Union, joined the Hoboken project on an informal basis. Telephone interview of Michael Lesser, September 28, 2001.

33. James Baldwin, *Giovanni's Room* (New York: Random House, 1956); Colm Tóibín, *Love in a Dark Time and Other Explorations of Gay Lives and Literature* (New York: Scribner, 2001), 195–198.

34. Letter of Carl Wittman to Elizabeth Freeman, Wolf Creek, Oregon, March 25, 1969, cited in Segrest, *Memoir of a Race Traitor*, 56.

35. Feingold Papers, biography.

36. Wedding announcement, Miriam Feingold Papers, State Historical Society of Wisconsin, Archives Division, Social Action Collection, sheets 539–540.

37. Frost, *An Interracial Movement of the Poor*, 154–155.

38. Frost, *An Interracial Movement of the Poor*, 152. One of the last fruits of the Hoboken ERAP project was the 97-page pamphlet by Jill Hamberg, Paul Booth, Mimi Feingold, and Carl Wittman entitled *Where It's At: A Research Guide for Community Organizing* (Boston: New England Free Press, 1967).

39. Robert Pardun, *Prairie Radical: A Journey through the Sixties* (Los Gatos, CA: Shire, 2001), 2, 114–115, 166–67.

40. Doug Rossinow, "The New Left in the Counterculture: Hypotheses and Evidence," *Radical History Review* 67 (1997): 86–87.

41. Todd Gitlin, *The Sixties: Years of Hope, Days of Rage*, rev. ed. (New York: Bantam, 1993), 212–214, 225.

42. Sale, *SDS*, 282.

43. One former SDS participant concedes that the notion of doing community organizing among the poor was naive, and the unemployment levels of the poor in 1964 were already receding. However, ERAP had other aims as well; for example, the Cleveland ERAP project had four aims: welfare rights, a housing project, a garbage-removal strategy called GROIN, and an emphasis on playground creation. Social organizers have a passion for acronyms. ERAP organizers at Newark and elsewhere used the acronyms JOIN (Jobs or Income Now) versus— somewhat humorously—GROIN (Garbage Removal or Income Now) to express the debate between organizers who wanted to emphasize employment and wage issues versus those who wanted to emphasize community issues such as refuse removal, traffic lights, and playgrounds.

44. Hogan, "How Democracy Travels," 470.

45. Some members of SDS who were no longer students formed a new organization in 1968 called Movement for a Democratic Society. MDS attempted to appeal to middle-aged professionals who wanted to maintain a relationship to the movement. Massimo Teodori, ed., *The New Left: A Documentary History* (Indianapolis: Bobbs-Merrill, 1969), 483.

Chapter Eleven

Liberation, 1967–1969

In the summer of 1967 Carl and I both moved from the East Coast to the San Francisco Bay area. We were young and the sky wasn't big enough to measure our dreams. Some people of our generation went to California because they were disillusioned, and others were just searching. My grandfather had gone there, my aunts had gone there, and now I went there.

After the Hoboken project fell apart in the summer of 1967, a number of SDS members moved to California to make a fresh start. Helen Garvy moved first, and she encouraged Wittman and Feingold to come visit. They did and stayed. Carl drove out to the West Coast with Jill Hamberg while Feingold came later. The newly married couple lived in an apartment on Albion Street in the Mission district of San Francisco. While there, they assembled a harpsichord from a kit together.

Carl, like all healthy men of our generation, faced the prospect of being drafted into the military. He had a long struggle with Local Draft Board #4 in Hackensack (one of 4,000 local draft boards in the United States) that began in 1965, soon after his graduation from Swarthmore. I can't think of anyone less temperamentally suited to the military's regimented activities and hierarchical command structure than Carl. He also opposed being drafted on moral grounds because of his opposition to the Vietnam War. After withdrawing from SDS and going to San Francisco in mid-1967, he became deeply involved with the resistance movement . He spent a lot of time with resistance group in San Francisco, worked at Draft Help, and was active in organizing a resistance conference in Oregon and another in Washington.[1]

In 1968 Carl and sixteen other men refused induction at the Oakland induction center. Although it was typical for antiwar activists to publicize such refusals in order to stoke opposition to the war, Carl chose not to share his intentions with the resistance group in order to avoid that sort of attention.

When I met him in 1969, he was facing the prospect of going to jail for his resistance. In this, as in so many decisions in his life, he took control of his own fate and had indicated his determination by writing to his draft board on April 29, 1968: "Now there is no fear, no doubt, I am calling the shots."[2]

In an article published in *Liberation* magazine in 1968, Carl described how the resistance movement meant much more to him than merely opposition to the Vietnam War. For him, the draft was merely one of many forms of oppression in American society that affected male-female relations, child-raising, homosexuality, and aggression.[3] Most of his attack was aimed at the nuclear family. He attacked the roles of mother and father, of parent and child, and asked, "Is a heterosexual couple the only correct agency for raising children?" Part of his attack stemmed from negative feelings about his own family, and part of it came from his feelings of being excluded from family life because of his same-sex attraction.

Carl and I were attracted to one another by a strong sexual force, but we were very different. He attacked the family, I revered it. He rejected his marriage, I found meaning in mine. He believed that "social institutions, not evil or weakness, are the sources of our fears and limitations." I believe that love is more important than any social institution and that evil is a powerful force. Carl and I each made our choices and, for each of us, they were right.

The move to the West Coast was a watershed in Carl's life. Although he had come out and revealed his same-sex attraction to fellow SDS members, there were many people, including his own family, who did not know. They still thought he had conventional sexual feelings, and from the outside his marriage seemed to confirm this impression. The San Francisco Bay area in the late sixties was a place where Carl began to live out his sexual dreams in a way that even today, almost fifty years later, strikes many, including his former SDS comrades, as shocking.[4]

I met Carl in a men's restroom in the Harmon Gymnasium on the University of California Berkeley campus. It was at the very end of February in 1969 and the weather in Berkeley was spring-like. This restroom was a well-known hookup site for gay men. The need to use a public toilet as a meeting place was typical of the oppressive state to which same-sex desire had been driven in the sixties. Carl and I were in adjoining stalls, and we made contact by looking through a small hole in the metal partition. I scribbled a note on a piece of toilet paper and handed it under the partition. He scribbled back, asking if I had a place to go. I said yes, but not without some hesitation. Christine and I had an apartment only a few blocks off campus on Benvenue Avenue. But soon after getting married in 1966, I'd brought some guy home to our apartment in Washington, D.C., and Christine returned unexpectedly. I vowed never to do it again and I had never done it again, until Carl asked me if I had a place to go.

Unlike my first meeting with Christine, I was immediately smitten when I first saw Carl that day. What I remember most about him were three things: his blond hair, his smile, and his constant blinking from wearing ill-fitting contacts. Why was I so overwhelmed by him? I think I was looking for someone like him. Christine and I had decided to have children and I was happy about that, but I was also afraid. Getting married is one thing, but having a child really is the beginning of a path with no turning back. I wasn't sure I was ready to go down that path. (Men in my family did not abandon their wives and children, and I had absorbed that value absolutely.) Carl would turn out to be a last fling, my last moment of hesitation, before going down that path.

We walked to my second-floor apartment and there is that moment I remember, of me standing in the living room while he sat on the couch and unzipped me. If moments could be collected in life like pressed flowers, that moment would be in a special collection. It was the beginning of a brief but (at least for me) intense affair. Carl felt awkward in his large body and was attracted to my smaller size. I was dark and attracted to his blond hair. Our attraction to one another reminded me of Aristophanes' light-hearted theory of love in Plato's *Symposium*.[5] We were like two males seeking our missing halves in the other.

Afterward Carl and I walked along a footpath on the Berkeley campus near Strawberry Creek and the Eucalyptus Grove. I can still smell the Eucalyptus trees. He had to go back to San Francisco and I had to go to class. When we said goodbye, close to Fulton Street, we kissed. Oddly, I do not remember the first time I kissed Christine, but I do remember the last kiss in 1997. It was 10:00 in the morning and the sky was overcast. But I only remember the last kiss that I gave her. How odd then that I remember so well the first kiss I gave to Carl.

In 1969 (even in Berkeley), two males standing on the path of a busy campus kissing in the middle of the day was a shocking sight. I had long gotten over my adolescent exhibitionism and so this was a daring thing for me to do. Even with Carl's involvement in the gay liberation movement, it was probably also a daring a thing for him to do. A few years later he mentioned to a friend how hard it was not to be able to walk down a street in San Francisco holding hands with the person he loved. Not that he wouldn't kiss another man on the street, but he resented the stares it attracted. When I kissed Carl on that path on the Berkeley campus I felt the door was opening into a very new and exciting way of life. But at the same time, I knew that entering that door would hurt someone. This betrayal of my wife is my first great regret.

The most hurtful thing I ever did to Christine was to leave her for a one-week trip to Oregon with Carl. The reason for the timing was logical, if selfish. It was the break between the winter and spring academic quarters at Berkeley. But the trip also fell on her birthday, March 24. In 1969 she turned twenty-three. So I went on the trip with all the appropriate apologies and she said it was all right, but it wasn't. Twenty-three is young, especially when you are carrying your first child and wondering if the father of that child still loves you. Later I would come to feel that this was the cruelest thing I ever did in my life. I couldn't bring that trip to mind without thinking of Christine, pregnant and abandoned on her birthday in that apartment, and I would cringe with shame and guilt.

The only other time I remember kissing Carl was in Oregon. We had taken my car, the sporty, red 1967 Chevy Camaro convertible. We were driving with the top down and we kissed in the front seat. It was a very public kiss and also a kiss of defiance, thrown at the world for all to see. It was exciting, but it was not sweet.

There was a mystique about Carl that fascinated me. His life and personality were almost the exact opposite of mine. He was very sociable and friendly while I was intense and liked solitude. He came from a family of dedicated leftists and had been very involved in radical politics while my family had been absorbed with the practical business of running theaters. I was creative and spiritual in a way that (at this point in his life) he was not. He opened up a whole new world to me, a world whose participants I had only seen from afar. When we drove to Oregon in March 1969, we stopped at Eugene and slept on John Froines' living room couch. Froines, then employed as an assistant professor of chemistry at the University of Oregon, had just been indicted as one of the Chicago Eight. This was a colorful group of personalities that included Jerry Rubin and Abbie Hoffman of the Yuppies and Bobby Seal of the Black Panther Party. They became famous defendants in a trial that grew out of violent demonstrations at the 1968 Democratic Convention.[6] Carl knew several of the Chicago Eight personally, including Rennie Davis and Tom Hayden from SDS and David Dellinger, the senior radical in the group.

Carl came from a very political family at odds with the anticommunist trends of the fifties while I was politically naive. I came from a family that was only mildly political and still very much in touch with its roots in Europe. I had never experienced anti-Italian prejudice. I didn't know that innocent Italian immigrants had been attacked by the Ku Klux Klan in western Pennsylvania in the 1920s, much less lynched throughout the South during the years 1891–1910.[7] Although my father had been called "hunky," the derogatory term for immigrants who lived in Slovan in the 1920s and 1930s, I had never heard the term. I knew nothing about 1,500 Italian resident aliens in New York, California, and Louisiana being arrested in 1942 and 10,000 Italians on the West Coast being forced to relocate.[8]

Carl came from a prospering urban area in northern New Jersey while I came from a small, stagnant town in the southwestern Pennsylvania countryside that was being bypassed by the American dream. His parents lived in close proximity to New York City and were more sophisticated than mine. My father's college degree and family property made him one of the more prominent citizens in the small town where I was raised, but he was really only a big fish in a very little pond. Although our family's living standard was modest in comparison with the outside world, in our small world it was relatively affluent and I rarely felt deprived of anything.

Carl was a political activist while I loved ideas and books and studying. He didn't particularly like graduate students, but he liked me. At the time, he was living a life that struck me as incredibly free. Whereas I was in the middle of a long graduate program at Berkeley, he was breaking up with his wife, actively involved in the gay liberation movement in San Francisco, and living cheaply off his earnings as a male "model" from an ad in the *Berkeley Barb*. His life held a compelling attraction for me.

Prostitution is an alien, distasteful, and immoral practice to many people, and these attitudes are not limited to conservative Christians. Some liberals and feminists view prostitution as abusive (with poor women mainly in mind). Many gays are hostile to male prostitution because it changes an affectional relationship into an exploitive one. For many people, love and money—like oil and water—do not mix. Both leftist revolutionaries and conservative rightists have attempted to suppress prostitution along with homosexuality. Carl was a free spirit who refused to be bound by these negative attitudes.

The liberal atmosphere of the San Francisco Bay area had long made it a mecca for people with same-sex desire. In the late sixties, the cultural climate there was radicalized by the movement, epitomized in the development of the underground press, beginning with the *Village Voice* of New York in 1957. In the sixties, the number of underground newspapers expanded to over a hundred and included the *Berkeley Barb* with its weekly circulation of 60,000.[9] The reporters and writers on such newspapers were willing to live on subsistence wages in order to further their goals of creating a better world. However, like many highly political alternative newspapers, including the *East Village Other* and the *Los Angeles Free Press*, the *Berkeley Barb* depended on graphic sex ads to finance its publication.[10] The *Berkeley Barb* was full of pictures of naked people, news articles on sexual liberation, feature articles on sex, and sex ads. The latter included classified ads under "models," which were transparent ads for mostly male prostitutes.

Male prostitution in the United States has remained one of the activities most resistant to commercial consolidation. The *Berkeley Barb* no longer exists, but male prostitutes remain, largely in the form of individual entrepreneurs feeding on the new Internet technology. Most, but not all, male prostitutes come from working-class and poor families. Many were abused as children and have low self-esteem. Most male prostitutes are motivated primarily by money. Some are lazy and many are pathological liars. However, a few sell their bodies for the experience and some (like Carl and me) for the adventure. Maybe it was due to the Berkeley atmosphere in the sixties, but the "models" who advertised in the *Berkeley Barb* tended to be highly individualistic. Their earnings were fairly limited, even adjusting for the fact that in 1969 the federal minimal wage was $1.60 per hour (versus $7.25 per hour in 2015) and the average per capita income was only $5,032 per year (as opposed to $54,629 per year in 2014).[11] "Models" who advertised in the *Berkeley Barb* in 1969 typically charged $15–$20 (roughly equivalent to $100–$150 in 2015 dollars) per hour.

The *Berkeley Barb* first began grouping ads under the category of "model" in the issue of February 16–22, 1968. Carl's first ad appeared in the issue of January 24–30, 1969, just a month before I met him. It was a typical ad but also individualistic: "BLOND 6 ft well built, hung; odd hours ok 826-7891."[12] The reference to "odd hours" reflected his unusual lifestyle; he lived by his own clock. After we met, I was so influenced by Carl that I decided to follow his example and placed my own ad in the *Berkeley Barb*: "PAUL with dk eyes 5'8", 137, young, slim, muscular, lithe 841-7303."[13] The poet in me couldn't resist inserting a word like "lithe," although most prospective clients who read it could barely pronounce the word, much less know what it meant. When I ran the ad the second time, I took out "lithe" and replaced it with "body."[14] I guess my idealism was slipping.

You need a strong libido to be a male prostitute and mine was strong enough except on a few occasions. One still sticks in my mind. I hitched a ride across the Oakland Bay Bridge to San Francisco and knocked on the door. The thirtyish man who answered was friendly and nice, but he was obese and physically repulsive. When I could not get an erection, I felt I had failed him. He was very nice about it and paid me anyway, but that failure bothered me.

Carl and I enjoyed each other's company, but it was a sex-driven relationship. Once we were buying groceries at the Safeway on Telegraph Avenue in Berkeley and we met a black man who offered to pay us both for sex. We took him back to my apartment (by that point Christine had taken the car and left California), but I did not enjoy having sex that way. It's different when you're with someone you love. In Plato's *Symposium*, Socrates said that sexual attraction between two people is the first step on a ladder that leads upward. As we advance up the ladder, our love becomes less and less a feeling and more and more an idea. Eventually we reach the top of the ladder where we have a final revelation of love in its most absolute and immortal form, the idea of absolute Goodness. It is "an everlasting loveliness which neither comes nor goes, which neither flowers nor fades . . . the same then as now, here as then."[15] But absolute love cannot be reached unless we take that first step, which is purely sensual. In my entire life, I have never found a better explanation of what happened between Christine, Carl, and me.

The third time I ran the ad in the *Barb*, it was filled with symbolism.[16] My relationship with Carl was coming to a climax and our ads symbolized this by appearing together near the end of the list of about eighty modeling ads. The *Barb* usually ran the ads in the order in which they were received and I vaguely recall Carl and I going to the *Barb* office on University Avenue in Berkeley and placing them together (models worked on a cash basis). In some ways, the symbolism was as sentimental as two names linked together inside a heart and carved into a tree or school desk. It was the last modeling ad I placed in the *Barb*. Soon afterward, I decided to end my relationship with Carl and asked my wife to return from the East Coast where she had fled to family and friends when our marriage seemed to be disintegrating.

Carl's ads continued to appear on an almost weekly basis for the rest of 1969. He altered the ad in slight ways. The phone number was changed from 826-7891 to 826-7314 in the April 25–May 1, 1969, issue, probably indicating the move that he made on Liberty Street from the house at number 121 to the apartment at number 171 when he and his wife broke up. In late June the ad was changed to "MODEL blond 6 ft. 165 lb odd hours ok. Friendly, hip 826-7314."[17] In August it became: "MALE MODEL—Blond 6'-165–23 Tanned, nice body. Friendly. Hip. ODD HOURS OK. 826-7314.[18] His tan probably came from working outside at the Wolf Creek commune in Oregon. Except for deleting the word "tanned," the ad stayed the same for the rest of the year. His age was twenty-six, not twenty-three, but sex ads are typically filled with minor mendacities.

Several people who knew Carl fairly well remained unaware of his work as a prostitute, but he told me about it the first day we met. He knew that some of his friends would be scandalized by the fact—and some who later learned of his activity *were* scandalized. Recent treatments of him as a founder of gay liberation attempt to sanitize his image by omitting his work as a male prostitute, even though they are aware of my published description of this activity.[19] But prostitution was a natural part of Carl's conscious attempt to free his sexuality, a variation on the sixties' leftist theme of the personal being political.

For younger men with same-sex feeling and for those who are attracted only to the opposite sex, it is difficult today to conceive of the emotional repression that those of us with same-sex erotic feelings felt in the fifties and sixties. It was like having hazel eyes in a country where hazel eyes had been condemned. It was possible to hide our hazel eyes with colored contact lenses, but we always knew the real color. There is also a dangerous tendency among people with same-sex feeling today to assume that the bad old days of homophobia are behind us forever. And yet the record of history indicates that tolerance of same-sex activity has ebbed and flowed in the past. If history is a reliable guide, a repressive homophobia is likely to return at some point in the future.

Carl had a very strong sense of his own worth. That had been, in part, a gift from his family. But it only went so far because his parents, like many Old Left people, were homophobic. For many years Carl tried to live in a straight world, suppressing crushes on school buddies and meeting males for sex anonymously. But gradually he came to realize that he had to reveal what he really felt inside. As he did so, the slouch of his earlier youth faded and he began to stand straighter, as if the burden of his repressed sexuality had been lifted.

Mimi Feingold was, like Carl, a red diaper baby who had been raised by communist parents. Less than two years after Mimi and Carl had been married, the marriage disintegrated and, according to numerous witnesses, Mimi was devastated by the breakup. Several years later she told a friend that she had been naive and had not understood what was happening in her marriage to Carl. Although I have never met her, I feel tremendous sympathy for what she must have been going through. She had believed that Carl could manage a marriage with a woman. But then, even Carl had believed it. The marriage failed. Soon after Carl and I met in Berkeley, I drove into San Francisco to see him. Later that night, I remember dropping him off outside his home in the Mission District when he and his wife were in the final stages of their separation. He seemed sad when he spoke of it.

Why did Carl in 1966 come out sexually and announce his marriage to Mimi at the same time? It seems bizarre, until one considers several factors. First, there was the pressure he felt from his family and from society to marry. On the other hand, he was a warm, caring man and he may really have wanted children. Then there was Carl's powerful will. In the same way that he applied the force of his will to political movements, so too did he attempt to apply the force of his will to his marriage.

Unlike today, there was no venereal disease in the sixties that could not be cured. The term "STD" (sexually transmitted disease) had not yet been invented to accommodate the range of sexually contracted illnesses that would surge with the proliferation of sexual activity in the 1970s. Chlamydia, genital herpes, genital warts, hepatitis B, trichomoniasis, and intestinal infections such as *shigella* and hepatitis A were problems yet to be. The first case of full-blown AIDS was still a decade away. For many of us with same-sex desires, sex was like a glass of water. Thirst was simple. You drank the water and then you forgot about it. It was rarely a memorable event.

On the Berkeley campus in the late sixties practically no one was out as a gay man, but there was a lot of furtive male sexual activity in certain restrooms. In 1965 seven men were arrested in the Bancroft Library basement restroom for homosexual activity and the door of every other stall was temporarily removed.[20] Most of the stall doors were restored by the time I arrived. The campus men's rooms with homosexual activity were in the basement of the Student Union, the basement of Wheeler Hall, and on the first floor of the Life Sciences building. Doe and Bancroft Libraries had three tearooms—in the basement, upstairs next to the History of Art Department, and on the third floor of the Annex. Harmon Gymnasium had four tearooms—two in the basement and two on the first floor.

Sexual activity in these restrooms peaked from noon to 4:00 pm. Not all of the participants were students. Some, like Carl, were visitors. Others were faculty. I encountered two of my professors there. One day I was sitting in a stall and glanced up to find an eminent historian of Russia peering at me through the crack in the stall door. I was shocked, as only someone young enough to be prudish could be. I thought this sort of activity was reserved for guys in their twenties.

In my youth I had sexual contact with hundreds of men, possibly even a thousand, and I suspect that Carl might have exceeded me. It sounds like a lot, but this number was by no means unusual and, given the era, I was neither a superman nor a superslut. The outlook prevalent in gay cultures in New York and San Francisco in the seventies was "so many men, so little time," so that 200 sexual contacts a year for a gay man in his twenties and thirties was common.[21] It was a form of sexual athletics.

Even greater numbers of sexual contacts have been recorded by numerous gay men, although some gay writers have a dubious record when it comes to documenting sexual encounters. In his book *And The Band Played On*, Randy Shilts (1951–1994) made famous the story about the spread of AIDS by the French-Canadian airline steward Gaetan Dugas (1953–1984), whom he dubbed "Patient Zero." Shilts claimed that Dugas' combination of striking good looks, voracious sexual appetite, and employment with Air Canada enabled him to spread AIDS across the United States through frequent sexual encounters. When Dugas was allegedly interviewed by a medical researcher in 1981, he claimed over 2,500 sexual partners at the rate of 250 per year for the last ten years—and he was only twenty-eight.[22] In fact, Shilts had invented Gaetan Dugas: he was a literary fabrication based on an epidemiological study and hypothesis of transmission by a "Patient Zero" compiled by Dr. William Darrow and colleagues at the Center for Disease Control in Atlanta.

Darrow later repudiated his study, but the myth of Dugas as Patient Zero lived on.

However even Dugas' numbers pale by comparison with the claims of the famous gay author Edmund White, who claimed that his usual pattern while living in New York in the sixties was to have sex with a different man every night and to contract gonorrhea once a month.[23] White's numbers have to be regarded as dubious because he had by then adopted a postmodern style of blurring fiction and nonfiction in his writing.

Perhaps the unreliability of these gay writers on the numbers of sexual contacts is linked with a certain fantasizing. But even if precise numbers are not known, it is clear that the general level of promiscuity among gay men from the late sixties to the early eighties was high while the danger from sexual diseases was thought to be low. (During my period of greatest promiscuity, I never caught anything worse than crabs.) Of course, not all gay men were or are promiscuous and some have a very limited number of sexual contacts.

Sometimes I wonder if Carl and I were part of an era of sexual freedom whose time has come and gone and that I'm one of the few left to tell the story. I may not have embraced the absolute freedom that Carl championed, but I never doubted that it was a valid choice. And yet thirty years after Carl's essay "The Gay Manifesto" appeared, one of the most controversial voices of gay life condemned the central values of the gay liberation movement. What Carl believed was absolute freedom, Andrew Sullivan has called promiscuity. For Sullivan, by promoting the "tragic lie" that all avenues of sexuality are equally good, "gay liberationists . . . constructed and defended and glorified the abattoirs of the [AIDS] epidemic."[24] He saw the AIDS epidemic as the inevitable result of gay liberation's "ideology that human beings are mere social constructs and that sex is beyond good and evil." Sullivan's criticism of gay liberation has been harshly criticized by many gays. And my instinctual defense of Carl is complicated by the fact that I share many of Sullivan's beliefs in the saving power of commitment and marriage and God. Both Carl and Sullivan are advocates; I am not. While my background and instincts led me toward commitment and marriage and God, another part of me was drawn toward freedom that seemed like a glorious pagan sun in the sky. I will always be grateful to Carl for showing me the intensity of that light.

Carl and I both grew up in an era when there were strong pressures to be attracted to women. The radical political movement of the sixties in which he participated was homophobic. Surprisingly, many hippies (and here I am speaking of the original late-sixties Haight-Ashbury variety) were homophobic. I once had a young hippie from Haight-Ashbury come to Berkeley in response to my ad and pay me for sex because in San Francisco he had to pretend to be hetero among his fellow hippies. The sixties slogan "make love, not war" applied mainly to heterosexual love. Carl and I both responded to these pressures by marrying, though his marriage was short-lived and there were no children. Mine lasted thirty-one years and produced children. Not that I felt perfectly at ease. I did have sex with guys outside of marriage, but except for that once in Washington, D.C., and a second time with Carl, I didn't bring them home and I never loved any of them, except Carl. And that is why Carl was the only one who ever threatened my marriage.

Carl and I were together for scarcely three months. With our wives living in our homes, we were reduced to spending a lot of time in my Camaro. Only on the one-week trip to Oregon in March of 1969 did we really spend entire days and nights together. We enjoyed one another's company. We laughed, we kissed, we slept in the same bed, we had sex, and we worked in the garden at Wolf Creek; I listened to the stories of his life, I comforted him when he cried, I loved him. Oftentimes the fantasy we project on a stranger evaporates when we get to know him. With Carl, it was just the opposite: the fantasy increased with contact. Like all fantasies, it was nourished more by the imagination than by the actuality. And yet a fantasy can be far more powerful in shaping our lives than an actual experience. A fantasy is not a fiction. A fiction is a falsehood that doesn't exist. A fantasy is an elaboration of the reality that exists in our imagination. For me, Carl was that kind of fantasy.

NOTES

1. Carl Wittman, "Waves of Resistance," *Liberation* (November 1968): 29. One of Wittman's coworkers at Draft Help in San Francisco was Arlene Goldbard. See http://arlenegoldbard.com/blog/archive-012005.shtml, p. 6.

2. Quoted in Mab Segrest, *Memoir of a Race Traitor* (Boston: South End Press, 1994), 59. Wittman's letter of April 29, 1968, to Local Draft Board #4, Hackensack, New Jersey, is preserved in the Swarthmore College Peace Collection, subject file #1, box 5.

3. The source of information and quotations in this and the next paragraph is Wittman's essay "Waves of Resistance," 29–33.

4. See Linda Hirschman, *Victory: The Triumphant Gay Revolution* (New York: HarperCollins, 2012), 87.

5. Plato, *Symposium,* trans. Michael Joyce, in *The Collected Dialogues of Plato,* ed. Edith Hamilton and Huntington Cairns (Princeton, NJ: Princeton University Press, 1961), 542–546.

6. The federal Department of Justice headed by Attorney General John Mitchell prosecuted these eight men on the grounds that they constituted a conspiracy to disrupt the Chicago Democratic Convention. They included Rennie Davis, David Dellinger, John Froines, Tom Hayden, and Lee Weiner of the Mobilization Committee; Jerry Rubin and Abbie Hoffman of the Yippies; and Bobby Seale of the Black Panther Party. Kirkpatrick Sale, *SDS* (New York: Random House, 1973), 541–542.

7. Stefano Luconi, *From Paesani to White Ethnics: The Italian Experience in Philadelphia* (Albany: State University of New York Press, 2001), 46; Jerre Mangione and Ben Morreale, *La Storia: Five Centuries of the Italian American Experience* (New York: HarperCollins, 1991), 200–213.

8. Rose D. Scherini, "When Italian Americans Were 'Enemy Aliens,'" in *Una Storia Segreta: The Secret History of Italian American Evacuation and Internment during World War II,* ed. Lawrence Di Stasi (Berkeley, CA: Heyday Books, 2001), 10–21.

9. Massimo Teodori, ed., *The New Left: A Documentary History* (Indianapolis: Bobbs-Merrill, 1969), 495–496.

10. Eric Bates, "Chaining the Alternatives: What Started as a Movement Has Become an Industry," *The Nation,* June 29, 1998, 12.

11. Data from World Development Indicators (WDI), October 2015, World Bank, http://knoema.com.

12. *Berkeley Barb,* January 24–30, 1969, 17.

13. *Berkeley Barb,* March 14–21, 1969, 21.

14. *Berkeley Barb,* April 18–24, 1969, 26.

15. Plato, *Symposium,* no. 211, page 562.

16. *Berkeley Barb,* April 25–May 1, 1969, 26.

17. *Berkeley Barb,* June 27–July 3, 1969, 16.

18. *Berkeley Barb,* August 1–7, 1969, 17.

19. See "Raised Voices among Pretty Manners: Profiles of Ten LGBT Activists for Social Justice," http://www.outhistory.org, August 25, 2014. My article describing Wittman's activity as a male prostitute is "A Spirit of the 60's," *The Gay & Lesbian Review Worldwide* 15, no. 3 (May-June 2008): 20–22.

20. Konstantin Berlandt, "Minorities—'2700 Homosexuals at Cal,'" *Daily Californian,* November 29, 1965.

21. Randy Shilts, *And the Band Played On* (New York: St. Martin's Press, 1987), 307.

22. Shilts, *And the Band Played On,* 83.

23. Edmund White, *The Farewell Symphony* (New York: Knopf, 1997), 63. The literary critic Reed Woodhouse accuses White of a subtle kind of lying in his fiction. See Woodhouse's *Unlimited Embrace: A Canon of Gay Fiction, 1945–1995* (Amherst: University of Massachusetts Press, 1998), 263–295.

24. Andrew Sullivan, *Love Undetectable: Notes on Friendship, Sex, and Survival* (New York: Knopf, 1999), 52–53.

Figure 1. The author's maternal grandparents and their six children on the occasion of their twenty-fifth wedding anniversary on Mary 29, 1889, in Bernburg, Germany. Seated: Ida Schwarze Dittmar (1842–1894) and August Dittmar (1839–1893). Standing left to right: Friedrich, Minna, Louisa, Gustav Emil (the author's grandfather, eight and a half years old), Emilie Anna, and Otto.

Figure 2. The tombstone photograph of the author's granduncle Filippo Russo (born 1889 in Roccarainola, Italy) who was murdered in East McKeesport, Pennsylvania, on December 5, 1919, by a Black Hand criminal organization. McKeesport Cemetery, 2002.

Figure 3. The Penn Theater (ca. 1950) in Slovan, Pennsylvania, built around 1920 by the author's grandparents, Raffaele and Marianna Mungello. The theater was closed in 1946 and demolished in the early 1950s. The attached building on the left side was built after Marianna's death in 1926 and contained a medical doctor's office on the first floor. The doorway between the theater and doctor's office led to apartments on the first and second floors. The Mungello family lived in one of the second-floor apartments while the author's parents, Dominic and Lois Mungello, established their first home in the adjoining apartment in 1939. One of the eight large smokestacks from the zinc plant is visible on the far right of the theater on a hillside overlooking Slovan.

Figure 4. Graveside photograph at the burial of the author's grandmother, Marianna (née Russo) Mungello, at the Fairview Cemetery between Slovan and Burgettstown, September 1926. The Mungello family stands behind the coffin, beginning at the head of their mother (from left to right with heads bowed): Evelyn, Jeanette, Helen, Dominic, Anthony, Mae, and Raffaele. The woman wearing the black hat and standing between Helen and Dominic is Maria Russo, the widow of Filippo Russo and sister-in-law of Marianna. The three flower bearers on the left (Catherine Capozzoli, Frances Tucci, and Anna Tucci) were ticket sellers at the theaters. The two men standing in the front row to the right of Raffaele Mungello (Eugene Livi and James Ross) were projectionists at the theaters. To the right of them and wearing a bow tie is Henry Gerrero, who played the piano during the silent films.

Figure 5. The author's father, Dominic Mungello, wearing his Union High School letterman's shirt, in Slovan, 1933.

Figure 6. The Mary Ann Theater façade in Burgettstown, Pennsylvania, at the time of its opening in 1937. Built by Raffaele Mungello and his son Anthony, the façade was done in a striking pale green Art Deco style that was very prominent in American architecture of the 1920s and 1930s. In 1949 an office building was added on the left side of the theater. In expanding this structure, the Mungello sons Anthony and Dominic duplicated their father's ground plan of the Penn Theater in Slovan. The structure was demolished in 1975.

Figure 7. The Mungello sisters (left to right): Evelyn, Helen, Jeanette, and Mae, in Slovan, Easter 1944.

Figure 8. The author's grandfather, Raffaele Mungello, after his move to southern California, Los Angeles, 1946.

Figure 9. Body-building photograph of David Mungello, seventeen years of age. Arlington, Virginia, April 1961.

Figure 10. The author's aunt Evelyn (née Mungello) Kelley, later Knowland, holding a medallion recognizing Mrs. Elizabeth Hensey Yorty, wife of the Los Angeles
mayor Sam Yorty, as the guest of honor at St. Casimer School Fashion Show
Luncheon in Burbank, California, August 1963. Evelyn chaired the event and sent
this picture to her family to mark her rising social status. The photograph was
taken one year before she met former senator William F. Knowland.

Figure 11. Carl Wittman's senior photograph from the 1964 Swarthmore College yearbook, The Halcyon. Courtesy of the Publications Department of Swarthmore College.

Figure 12. David Mungello, as a graduate student at the University of California, Berkeley, 1967.

Figure 13. David and Christine Mungello, in the mellow, yellow style of the 1960s, in Berkeley, California, 1968.

Figure 14. David Mungello, carrying the red banner of the Committee of Concerned Asian Scholars as part of a mass demonstration to protest police violence in the Peoples' Park incident, Berkeley, California, May 1969. The red banner, hung between two bamboo poles, was made in imitation of banners carried by Red Guards in the Chinese Cultural Revolution, a movement that was romanticized and misinterpreted by Western political leftists in the 1960s.

Figure 15. Christine Mungello, with our amah Lian Taitai in the background, Taipei, during the summer heat, Taiwan, 1971.

Figure 16. Christine Mungello, fellow Lingnan College teacher Paul Bailey, our children Michael and Lisa, and the author (kneeling) on Lantao Island, part of the British Crown Colony of Hong Kong, 1974. At that time, Lantao Island was a remote and undeveloped area, reachable only by ferry. A Trappist monastery and dairy farm are visible in the background. Since then a new Hong Kong Airport and Disneyland have been built on the island.

Figure 17. Carl Wittman in his Scottish kilt, at the Wolf Creek gay commune, Oregon, ca. 1975.

Figure 18. Billie Rohrer (Pepe, born Miguelito Alvarada), soon after his adoption from El Salvador by the author's sister, Marianne (Mimi) Rohrer and her husband William G. Rohrer II, Haddon Township, New Jersey, February 1975.

Figure 19. Christine and David Mungello, shortly after Christine's fatal diagnosis of metastatic breast cancer, 1996. SolasGallery.com.

Figure 20. David Mungello with his grandchildren: Madison Sue Pflum, Austin Pflum, Holden Howard, David Mungello, Dylan Pflum, and Jordan Pflum, Dallas, Texas, November 2015.

Chapter Twelve

Leaving Carl, 1969

Leaving someone you love is the hardest thing to do. I have done it twice in my life. The second time I did it, I had no choice: Christine was dying and she left me. But the first time I did have a choice. While Carl and I were like two different melodies that played together in counterpoint, Christine and I were like a single melody played with harmonic chords. In singing, Christine always preferred singing harmony over melody while in life I "sang" only melody because I refused to do back-up.

The most decisive moment in my life was a May night in 1969. That was the night I realized that, while Carl had a beautiful smile, his smile was aimed at many people, not just me. I was sitting in a circle of five guys in Carl's apartment on Liberty Street in San Francisco while a marijuana joint was being passed around. I was there because I was so infatuated with Carl that I had separated from my pregnant wife who had left me to travel 3,000 miles back East in search of refuge. But that night for the first time I saw that Carl was not focused on me as much as on having group sex.

A slightly older fellow I didn't know was sitting on my right, and a younger, dark-haired guy was sitting on my left. He was a new friend of Carl's and it may have been Stevens McClave, with whom Carl later had a relationship. Or maybe it was just another smaller dark-haired guy that Carl was attracted to. I never particularly liked smoking marijuana, but it was unsociable to pass. Maybe the drug depressed me, but I suddenly missed my wife.

Carl had been excited about what he called "an orgy," but I never enjoyed group sex that much. A sudden sadness overwhelmed me. I got up, went over to Carl, knelt down and quietly said that I missed my wife and had to leave. He was very nice about it. He was always very nice. In my youthful idealism, I believed that the most intense passions of sex were like the passions of the

119

soul. Sometimes they are, but on that spring evening in the Mission district of San Francisco, I realized that sometimes the passions of sex were just physical. Carl was much sweeter and kinder than I was, but he could not love. Perhaps later and with another man he was able to love, but not then and not with me.

I have never been a passive personality. When I left his apartment that night, I also left behind one way of life and chose another. It's not that I never looked back and I certainly had lapses, but I had made my choice and I pretty much stuck with it. After she returned, Christine and I never talked about Carl—ever. I once raised the subject, but she didn't want to discuss it and I had undergone enough psychotherapy to know that talking about something can sometimes not only be fruitless but can even feed the demon. As for love, my first loyalty was to her and my family. The fantasy of what life would have been like following Carl remained, but it was sealed off in a private part of my soul. It tugged at me for years. Sometimes it was an angel and sometimes it was a demon.

I went back to Berkeley but the next morning, I felt so bad about leaving Carl that I returned to the Liberty Street apartment to apologize for not participating in the orgy. Carl and the fellow who might have been McClave were the only ones still there. We had a nice chat, but something had changed in my mind and I had made my decision. I did not tell him, but since his feelings about our relationship were not as intense as mine, I don't think it mattered that he learned of it only gradually.

Like my father with his extramarital romances in post–World War II occupation Germany, my romance with Carl gave me a glimpse of a very different life that I might have had, living as a gay man. But like my father, I could not leave my family. This was partly cultural. Southern Italian respect for the institution of marriage was shared even by mafiosi who commonly keep mistresses but were still condemned for deserting or divorcing a wife.[1] Like my father, I too was not the divorcing kind, even if I was more adventuresome and tortured than my father. I heard the siren of freedom singing and I was drawn to it, but I got away.

I think I came far closer to leaving my family than my father did. If I'd come to believe that Carl loved me as much as I loved him, it would have made for an even more agonizing decision but, ultimately, I believe it would have been decided by the birth of my child eight months after I met Carl. I believe that once I held my little girl in my arms, I could never have abandoned her, never left my wife so that another man might raise my daughter. The decision I made in the spring of 1969 was probably the most momentous decision in my life. I do not regret it.

The spring of 1969 was a tumultuous time. In April Christine had left because I was choosing Carl and rejecting her. She drove back to the East Coast alone to visit her parents in Florida and then friends and relatives in the Washington, D.C., area. I am sure she did not tell her parents all the details of our separation. They were very reserved and British. That April was also a bad month for me because the China historian whom I was working most closely with at Berkeley, Joseph R. Levenson (1920–1969), drowned on April 6. He was canoeing with his three sons on the swollen Russian River when the canoe capsized in the rapids. His body was not found for weeks.

Professor Levenson was not only a brilliant and eminent scholar, but he was also very kind to me. Soon after arriving on campus in 1967, I knocked unannounced on his office door and asked him to supervise an individual readings course and he had agreed. I never found anyone else who could replace him as a mentor. Levenson had studied in the late forties and early fifties at Harvard under Professor John King Fairbank (1907–1991). Fairbank was a famous China scholar who had been accused of communist sympathies and interrogated by the Senate Judiciary (McCarren) Committee in 1952, but he emerged unscathed. He was part of the academic world that I was hoping to move into, but in the world I was leaving, memories of the swash-buckling movie actors Douglas Fairbanks (1883–1939) and his son Douglas Fairbanks Jr. (1909–2000) still lingered. I had seen many of their movies in my father's theaters. In Levenson's last seminar, I remember referring repeatedly to the Harvard China scholar as "Fairbanks." In a voice of some exasperation, Professor Levenson finally corrected me: "Mr. Mungello, the name is 'Fairbank,' not 'Fairbanks.'" Upward mobility is not without its stumbles. I was properly humbled. As I eagerly moved into this scholarly new world, I suppose that part of me never lost the imprint of all those movies that I saw in my family's theaters. . Ironically, many years later a friend told me that the family name of Prof. Fairbank had originally been Fairbanks with an *s*.

Community events were traumatic as well. That spring a mixed group of hippie and radical political types (both groups were as indigenous to Berkeley as students) decided to create a park out of an empty lot owned by the University of California. The lot was located in the South Campus area, just behind businesses on Telegraph Avenue and was bounded on three sides by Dwight, Bowditch and Haste Streets. It was only two blocks away from our apartment at 2534 Benvenue Avenue. The University had purchased the lot and had the quaint, brown-shingle houses torn down as part of an attempt to clean up the blight in the area through an urban renewal plan. The original intention had been to build dormitories on the lot, but funding and other obstacles had intervened, so that a new plan was created to make an intramural soccer field there.

From April 20 until May 15 people began to plant shrubs, trees, flowers and vegetables with joyful hippie abandon, and the area became known as People's Park. Given the politicized atmosphere of the late sixties in Berkeley, a confrontation was probably inevitable, and on May 15 the university brought in bulldozers and began to build a fence around the property. Violence ensued and the Alameda County Sheriff's Office bused in a number of deputies, known unaffectionately as "Blue Meanies" in reference to the blue overalls and helmets from the Beatles' movie and song "Yellow Submarine." At the end of the day, a hundred demonstrators had been injured, mainly by shotgun blasts: thirteen required hospitalization and one died.[2] The next day Governor Ronald Reagan ordered 2,000 National Guardsmen into the area. This action and the tear gas strike against demonstrators on campus by a National Guard helicopter brought national publicity to the event. In the following week, over a thousand people were arrested in Berkeley.

Although it was strange to see National Guardsmen lined up under Sather Gate, for those of us who lived and studied in Berkeley, the People's Park incident seemed merely one more event in an ongoing series of political demonstrations. In my own field of Chinese history, opposition to the Vietnam War had given rise to a generational conflict between students and professors that produced a new student-led study group dedicated to alternative academic approaches to Asian studies. Nearly fifty graduate students in this group forged a chapter of the Committee of Concerned Asian Scholars. In late May, we marched as a group along with a mass demonstration protesting the violence of the People's Park incident. I helped carry a large red banner (modeled after those used by Red Guards in the Chinese Cultural Revolution) emblazoned with the name "Committee of Concerned Asian Scholars" that hung between two long bamboo poles. My friend Jason Bishop took a picture of me carrying the banner. In the sun-worshipping Berkeley style of the time, I am shirtless and having fun.

Today it is widely accepted that there is a gay identity and that men with same-sex feelings share something that transcends sexual desire. However, in 1969 ideas about same-sex feelings were far more in flux. There was another reason why I left Carl beside the fact that he didn't love me as much as I loved him. There was something very uncompromising (and irrevocable) about Carl's gayness. I left him because being gay (at least in the way that Carl lived it) was so militant I believed it would have involved breaking with my family. I did not realize then that there are other ways of being gay that do not involve breaking with one's family. However, Carl's philosophy (which he was then formulating for his "Gay Manifesto") was very antimarriage and antifamily and the choice seemed very stark to me at the time. The campaign for gay marriage that developed many years later was in some ways a complete reversal of the attitudes of earlier gay liberationists. For me, the choice was either being gay or staying with my family. There is an old Neapolitan expression for referring to one's family as "blood of my blood" (*sange dò sange mio*).[3] I understand this completely. My family was too much part of who I was to ever leave it.

I had to convince Christine of my commitment to our marriage before she would return to California, which she did in June of 1969. After she returned, I could never bear to see Carl again. Our first child, Lisa (Elise), was a little girl with curly golden red hair to which the maternity ward nurses tied a yellow ribbon. She was born in November 1969. Early in 1970, Carl unexpectedly dropped by our apartment in Berkeley with a friend (possibly McClave), but I was not home. Christine did not know who he was, but she may have guessed. Our good friend Jason Bishop was there and told me about the visit. For my wife and myself, my affair with Carl was so tumultuous and painful that it was marked by silence. But for me, the memory of my relationship with Carl remained something very precious.

NOTES

1. In the late forties and early fifties, Mafia business associates pressured the singer Frank Sinatra to reconcile with his first wife, Nancy Sinatra. See Anthony Summers and Robbyn Swan, *Sinatra: The Life* (New York: Knopf, 2005), 178.

2. The left-wing magazine *Ramparts* devoted the cover and twenty-six pages to covering the People's Park Incident. See *Ramparts* (August 1969): 34–59.

3. Richard Gambino, *Blood of My Blood: The Dilemma of the Italian-Americans* (New York: Anchor Books, 1975), 4. In a variation on the Neapolitan dialect, the expression "blood of my blood" in standard Italian today is "*sangue dò sangue mio.*"

Chapter Thirteen

Moving On, 1970–1973

My life over the next ten years consisted of a series of travels and residences on three continents. When I tell people the places where we lived (Taipei, rural Maryland, Hong Kong, New York, Germany, and Iowa), they are impressed, but the reality was more mundane. We had very little money. My own values had been a fit for the sixties culture because I placed little value on wealth or acquiring possessions. My hair was a little long and I was perfectly content getting my clothes by rummaging through the boxes of trendy castoffs in the used clothing stores on Telegraph Avenue in Berkeley. I was interested in spending time in the bookstores and reading. I enjoyed being alone because my imagination has always been the most exciting place I know.

I was always concerned about damaging my mind with the recreational drugs that began to proliferate in the late sixties such as marijuana, hallucinogens (LSD, peyote, psychedelic mushrooms), amphetamines, Quaaludes, and heroin. Many of the hippies that we knew in Berkeley had exchanged study and bathing for drugs and patchouli oil. The term "fried mind" is not used much today, but it was quite common in the late sixties to describe the zombie-like behavior of people who had used too many drugs.

I have always felt different. Among heterosexuals, I felt gay. Among gays, I felt bisexual. Among my skeptical fellow academics, I felt different because I believed in God. Among Christians, I felt alienated by my fascination for Buddhism. Among gays who felt bitter toward their families, I was an outlier. My mind was creative and driven and it did not accommodate well to game plans devised by other people. I would soon pay a price for my intense individuality.

The academic world may be liberal in the political sense, but it is extremely conservative in terms of creativity. There is a common academic aphorism that not more than 15 percent of a scholarly book may be truly creative. Never having found anyone to replace Professor Levenson as a mentor, I pursued my own intellectual interests. I was also arrogant and too proud of having published an article in a respected academic journal as early as the fall of 1969, unusual for someone less than halfway through his graduate program.[1] There were still great gaps in my knowledge of Chinese history. Consequently, my oral comprehensive exams for the doctorate in history in the spring of 1971 were less than stellar, and I had to come back and repeat them a year later. The oral comprehensive exams were the next-to-last stage in progress toward a doctorate. After passing them, one moved on to writing the dissertation.

In the meanwhile, Christine and my daughter and I went to Taipei for language study as we'd planned, but I was extremely discouraged. It was a bad omen that the charter flight leaving from the north field of JFK Airport in New York was twelve hours late in departing. The most vivid memory I have of arriving in Taipei late at night in July 1971 is the foul stench that seemed to follow us everywhere. I was depressed and difficult to live with, and my usually optimistic wife at times lost patience with me. I remember how crowded the public buses were. People crushed up against you so tightly that you could breathe in what they had eaten for their last meal. Although our bodies were pressed against one another, it was totally unsexual. On the other hand, I remember how charming the guys were holding hands, something that even gay guys on the streets of San Francisco seldom did. It was an old world custom for male friends, not only in China but also in Italy.

We rented a house on a street with a very auspicious Chinese name—Wolongjie (Sleeping Dragon Street), Lane 17, No. 17. "Sleeping Dragon" was a Daoist nickname for Zhuge Liang (Kong Ming), the legendary military strategist in the most famous Chinese historical novel, *Romance of the Three Kingdoms (Sanguozhi yanyi)*.[2] Although I was an impoverished American graduate student, costs in Taipei were then low and the value of the American dollar was high. We were able to afford a three-bedroom Japanese-style house (since replaced by a high-rise apartment building) with a servant's room and live-in amah named Lian Taitai (Mrs. Lian) who cooked fantastic Chinese food. I think we paid her the equivalent of US$38.50 a month. The goldfish pond in the backyard was delightful, except that I had to fight the occasional snake or two that appeared in it. It was in Taipei that Christine found her first job teaching English as a Second Language (ESL) at Zhengzhi Daxue (College of Political Science). It was so like her to adapt to a situation and make the best of it. Thereafter, she taught ESL almost everyplace we lived.

I spent a lot of time exploring the streets of Taipei, looking for old books in used book stalls. I was also watching for signs of gay Chinese men, but the culture was so different and my language skills were so shaky that I walked right past them without noticing. Same-sex male love had a long history in China, but it had been suppressed as un-modern in the twentieth century by the "modernizing" influence of Western homophobia and communist revolutionary puritanism. At that time, it was viewed as a morals offense both by the Nationalists on Taiwan and the Communists on the mainland. On the mainland, sexual contact between males was brutally punished, sometimes with a bullet through the head.[3]

Although I did not find any gays in my wanderings throughout Taipei, I later heard about them from other Americans. In 1983 the novel *Niezi* (Whore's Son) by Bai Xianyong was published, giving a detailed picture of the gay life that existed in Taipei at the very time I lived there. In Taipei in 1971 gays were typically ostracized by their families and some of the outcasts clustered together to form a "glass [i.e., see-through] community," from which the book's English title *Crystal Boys* comes.[4]

The center of gay life in Taipei in 1971 was New Park (Xin Gongyuan), a downtown park less than three miles from my home. I passed it many times, oblivious to the gay life there. In the previous year the police had raided the park several times and arrested sixty men for violating "good mores."[5] Many of these Chinese gay men in New Park survived as male hustlers. Given my foreign status and the fact that Taiwan was under martial law until 1987, it's unlikely that I would have risked having much contact with them, even if I had known they were there. Fifteen years later when I was in Shanghai, things were changing. I made eye contact with several Chinese gays in a park, although it was impossible to do anything because other people were everywhere and we had no private place to go: lingering communist distrust of foreigners in 1986 made my hotel room off-limits. The legal ban on same-sex acts was not lifted on the Chinese mainland until 1992.[6]

In November 1971 we were back in Berkeley, this time at 2607 Ellsworth Street, just a short distance from our previous apartment at 2534 Benvenue. We came back early because I was in a rut academically and Christine didn't want to give birth to our second child in Taipei. She preferred to use the same facility where our daughter had been born, the University of California San Francisco Medical Center. They offered a complete maternity package, including prenatal exams, for $250, and that fee could be reduced by giving blood. We had no trouble finding friends to help us donate. Blood was one thing we all had plenty of. Our son, Michael Campbell, was born on February 11, 1972.

I passed my oral comprehensives in the spring and we wanted to get our children out of Berkeley. The drug scene was getting nastier. Father George

F. Tittman, who had baptized our daughter at St. Marks Episcopal Church, was soon to be murdered not far from where we lived.

One of the more remarkable aspects of radicals of the late 1960s and early 1970s was their back-to-the-land effort—a return to traditional values of nature, farming, and homespun arts all while cultivating innovative social and sexual lifestyles. These involved the liberation of both women and gays and also New Age spirituality. It included a strong interest in Asian religions like Buddhism and Daoism. While the liberation aspect began in urban areas like San Francisco and New York, the ideals of living off the land, protecting the natural environment, learning basic crafts, and cultivating spirituality caused many radicals to move into the countryside where communes and communal farms proliferated.

Christine and I also participated in this movement, first, by living in the Maryland countryside for a year (1972–1973) and later by living in a religious commune during the summer of 1975. The valley surrounding the village of Brownsville, Maryland (just a few miles northeast of Harpers Ferry, West Virginia) is one of the most beautiful valleys I have ever seen. It felt like a dream come true when we spent the year living there on the edge of the village while I wrote my dissertation—four adults, four children, and an assortment of dogs and cats, living in this plain country house, cultivating a large garden and surviving with federal food stamps. We became friends with our country neighbors and attended the local Church of the Brethren, a traditional and yet pacifist Christian church.

During the year we were there I did cross-legged Buddhist meditation on a daily basis. I completed my doctoral dissertation, "Leibniz and Confucianism," and finished the PhD in 1973. But all was not idyllic in Pleasant Valley (the actual name). During that year, the marriages of my brother-in-law and his wife and another couple who were good friends both disintegrated.

Whenever I'm stressed to the point that my right ear begins to throb and sudden deafness threatens to return (it did once already), I get in a cross-legged (half-lotus) position on the floor, close my eyes, and imagine that I am floating on a blue lake surrounded by trees on a perfectly still day. As I merge with the still surface of the water, my anxiety begins to melt away, at least for a while. I learned this technique practicing daily Buddhist meditation in the Maryland countryside during 1972. For me, God is in the country.

The back-to-the-land movement involved a rejection of materialistic values (wealth, possessions, and well-paid but boring jobs) and the cultivation of simplicity, interpersonal relationships, nature, art, and spirituality. We used only mild drugs like marijuana, which we grew and which I rarely smoked. In Maryland we were all related by blood or marriage, and so the arrangement for us was less radical than the gay communal experience Carl had in Oregon. But by moving to the country he and I were living parallel lives, even though we were not in contact with one another.

When we lived in Taipei in 1971 Christine and I had visited Hong Kong with my sister Marianne. We liked it so much that we wanted to return and live there some day. With my doctorate completed, we tried to find work in Hong Kong teaching in church-related institutions. Although I had spent six years in graduate training at one of the best universities in the world, I was naïve about practical things like job-hunting and this led to some laughable mismatches. The weirdest mismatch we had was driving to nearby Salunga, Pennsylvania, for an interview with the Board of Missions and Charities of the Eastern Mennonites, a fairly strict Christian group. The interview was going okay until they discovered that Christine smoked. In those days, smoking was far more widely practiced and accepted in American society than today, but not for the Mennonites. The absurdity of the situation suddenly struck us. There we were, Berkeley types, interviewing with the Mennonites! I remember saying something ridiculously stupid like "although my wife smokes, I still love her." The interview ended, we got in the car, and laughed all the way back to Pleasant Valley.

NOTES

1. David E. Mungello, "Neo-Confucianism and wen-jen Aesthetic Theory," *Philosophy East and West* 19, no. 4 (October 1969): 367–383.

2. See Luo Guanzhong, *Three Kingdoms: A Historical Novel,* abridged ed., trans. Moss Roberts, (Berkeley: University of California Press, 1999), 159.

3. Bao Ruowang (Jean Pasqualini) and Rudolph Chelminski, *Prisoner of Mao* (Harmondsworth, England: Penguin, 1973), 189–190. I later published a book on the topic of foreign homosexuals in China entitled *Western Queers in China: Flight to the Land of Oz* (Lanham, MD: Rowman & Littlefield, 2012).

4. Pai Hsien-yung , *Crystal Boys,* trans. Howard Goldblatt (San Francisco: Gay Sunshine Press, 1990), 7.

5. Jans Damm, "Same Sex Desire and Society in Taiwan, 1970–1987," *China Quarterly* 181 (2005): 75.

6. Mungello, *Western Queers in China*, 5.

Chapter Fourteen

Back to the Land, 1969–1977

In the 1970s my counterpoint in life, Carl, once again became part of the vanguard of a movement, one less political but more sexual, artistic, and spiritual than SDS had been. As he shifted his focus over the years 1971–1986 from San Francisco to a rural region in southwestern Oregon and later to Durham, North Carolina, earning an income was never a major concern for him. He preferred jobs that interested him, whether that meant working in a printing shop, cultivating vegetable and flower gardens, hustling as a male prostitute, teaching Native American history in a community college, or even leading a country dance group. His main concern was to develop a movement of gay people that would foster a healthy sense of gay identity and, at the same time, win acceptance in society at large.

The famous Stonewall Inn Riot of June 28, 1969, in New York is regarded by many as marking the beginning of the gay liberation movement, but Stonewall was merely a crystallizing event for forces of change that had been building for some time in American culture. Carl's greatest achievement was to express the aspirations of this movement in his article "A Gay Manifesto."[1] In 1968 he circulated a draft of this work among friends, although it did not take final form until May 1969, one month before Stonewall.[2]

For Wittman, the ultimate model for the "Gay Manifesto" was Karl Marx's *Communist Manifesto* (1848), which called on the workers of the world to unite in a revolution aimed at abolishing private property and creating a classless society. The style of writing of the "Gay Manifesto" is similar to the SDS's *Port Huron Statement* (1962), which Wittman also called a "manifesto."[3] *The Port Huron Statement* criticized American society for its racial bigotry, its Cold War attitudes, and the enslavement of the universities to serving the status quo, but it made no mention of sexuality.[4] "A Gay

Manifesto" (at 5,500 words) is much shorter than the *Port Huron Statement* (28,000 words), more colorful in tone, and more focused on a single issue—homosexuality. It was first published at the end of 1969 in *The San Francisco Free Press*, an underground newspaper filled with pictures of nude males and aimed at a gay readership.[5] Wittman's manifesto was widely reproduced and for many quickly became the "bible of Gay Liberation."[6]

"A Gay Manifesto" was reprinted in the February 1970 issue of *Liberation*, the same journal that had published Carl's article "Waves of the Resistance" in 1968. *Liberation* was a New Left journal edited by David Dellinger and based in New York. Many of the contributors were former SDS associates, including Todd Gitlin, Carl Oglesby, and Vernon Grizzard. Others were prominent figures from the Left, such as Paul Goodman and Noam Chomsky. Carl's former college roommate at Swarthmore and SDS member, David Gelber, was managing editor. In 1970 the attitude of the New Left toward the gay movement remained ambivalent. The Old Left, as reflected in Carl's parents, was largely opposed. The New Left recognized the oppression of gays but had trouble shaking old homophobic attitudes.[7]

Originally entitled "Refugees from Amerika: A Gay Manifesto," Carl's work put heavy emphasis on the refugee metaphor. Its opening lines have become well-known:

> San Francisco is a refugee camp for homosexuals. We have fled here from every part of the nation, and like refugees elsewhere, we came not because it is so great here, but because it was so bad there. By the tens of thousands, we fled small towns where to be ourselves we would endanger our jobs and any hope of a decent life; we have fled from blackmailing cops, from families who disowned or 'tolerated' us, we have been drummed out of the armed services, thrown out of schools, fired from jobs, beaten by punks and police-men. And we have formed a ghetto, out of self-protection.[8]

The article said that the first thing needed "is to free ourselves; that means clearing our heads of the garbage that's been poured into them." Some of Carl's claims were highly controversial. At that time and still today, two dominant and opposing positions in explaining human sexual orientation were biological essentialism and social constructionism. The essentialists claimed that the prime influence shaping sexual orientation was inherent and biological; constructionists argued that the main influence was social and cultural. Essentialists believe that a homosexual identity in some form has existed throughout history while constructionists argue that it was a development of the last century.[9] However, most essentialists and constructionists agreed that one's sexual identity was discovered rather than chosen. This was one of those complex nature-nurture debates that is unlikely ever to be resolved. The influential queer theorist Eve Kosofsky Sedgwick tried to avoid the constructionist-essentialist debate entirely by viewing gay identity in new terms.[10]

On the question of sexual orientation, Wittman anticipated later gay radicals by taking an extreme social constructionist position.[11] He wrote: "Nature leaves undefined the object of sexual desire. The gender of that object is imposed socially." Although constructionism became firmly entrenched in leftist academic circles, there was a growing tendency by many in the gay movement to understand themselves in more strictly essentialist terms, akin to an ethnic group demanding its minority rights. This created a growing tension between constructionists who operated in the realm of theory and essentialists who were trying to advance gay rights through the political process.[12]

Carl went on to say something equally uncompromising: bisexuality "is good; it is the capacity to love people of either sex, exclusive heterosexuality is fucked up. It reflects a fear of people of the same sex." This is very bold, uncompromising, even incendiary language. In the tradition of the *Communist Manifesto*, his position was less an attempt to persuade a reader through logical argument than it was a declaration of intentions and a call to action.[13] In 1966, three years before "A Gay Manifesto" was written, a "women's manifesto" had appeared under the title "Sex and Caste—A Kind of Memo from Casey Hayden and Mary King to a Number of Other Women in the Peace and Freedom Movement."[14] This is regarded as one of the first public documents of the modern women's movement and reflects a connection in the sixties between the separate liberation movements of blacks, women, and gays.

Carl's major concern in his manifesto was not to win acceptance for gays in society at large but rather to foster a healthy sense of gay identity. Once gays and lesbians were freed from feeling that their same-sex desires were evil or ugly or debasing, they could stop running away from those who voiced homophobic attitudes and who made their lives so miserable. That would free them from feeling the need to seek refuge in a gay ghetto like San Francisco. The "Gay Manifesto" expressed a "gay is good" attitude, which became part of a national movement later on; it was clearly a sixties gay counterpart of the "black is beautiful" movement.[15]

Carl's life expressed that he practiced what he preached. In the seventies and eighties, thousands of gay men were flocking to San Francisco. One estimate gives their swelling migration numbers as 9,000 between 1969 and 1973, 20,000 between 1974 and 1980, and 5,000 annually by 1980.[16] But Carl showed once again that he was in the cultural vanguard by going in the opposite direction. In 1971 he permanently moved out of San Francisco to the rural area of Wolf Creek in Oregon and later to Durham, North Carolina, in the South, areas that would not normally be regarded as being particularly sympathetic toward gays, at least in the seventies and early eighties.

The property at Wolf Creek (more precisely called Golden) consisted of almost sixty-two acres of scenic country land on a sloping hillside with a small two-story house dating from the 1940s and a barn built circa 1915–1920. In the 1870s and 1880s a vein of gold was discovered in this area and a mining town called Golden had sprung up. Thousands of people camped on the hillsides; two churches and a school opened, but the boom went bust and the area reverted to rural country. [17]

Carl first noticed this stretch of hilly country along Interstate 5 in southwestern Oregon while hitchhiking to Vancouver for a draft resistance meeting. In 1968 he and his wife were living in a commune in the house at 121 Liberty Street in San Francisco. Six of the commune members—Carl and Mimi Feingold, Lew and Amy Russell Richmond, and an unmarried couple named Cal and Kern (called by her surname)—saved some money and became interested in buying country land. On a rainy weekend in October 1968, they traveled to Grant's Pass, Oregon, where a realtor showed them the Wolf Creek property. They were struck by its beauty and bought it "cash on table." [18]

I met Lew and Amy Russell Richmond and Cal when I visited Wolf Creek in March 1969. Like Carl, they were adventuresome people. All I remember of Lew Richmond was that he had dark hair and was thin. I was told that he had studied at Harvard. Actually, he had been trained as a classical pianist and composer. [19] After leaving Wolf Creek, he became a senior priest in the San Francisco Zen Center. In 1972 he was named treasurer at the Zen Mind Temple (*Zenshinji*) at Tessajara Hot Springs, a remote 500-acre site in the Los Padres National Forest, 150 miles south of San Francisco. [20] Cal was the other male resident I met at Wolf Creek. He had gone to a Christian seminary and had a child with Kern. They later separated and are said to have returned home to Alabama.

Within months after buying the property, Carl and his wife divorced. He visited Wolf Creek periodically before moving there permanently early in 1971. He had developed a close but turbulent relationship with Stevens McClave, and they argued so bitterly over other men that they felt it would be good for them to leave the gay life in San Francisco for the peace and quiet of Wolf Creek. [21] McClave bought into the Wolf Creek property. [22] However, Carl's hope that he and McClave "would live happily ever after" in the country soon crashed because they fought constantly. Carl found refuge from their arguments in the orchard where he planted hundreds of saplings. Because of the summer drought in Oregon and the need of these fragile trees for regular watering, he had to cancel his summer travel plans. He later compared caring for those trees to raising children.

Stevens McClave (born February 1, 1945) came from Michigan and was two years younger than Carl. He was a shadowy figure whom people recall in only vague terms—not one of them could remember his last name. Physically, he was slightly shorter than Carl, but broader-shouldered and he had long dark hair. He was affable, effeminate, charming, and funny in an acerbic manner, but he also had a dark side. One acquaintance said that he looked and acted much like Zonker, a character in the Doonesbury cartoon.

Alixe Dancer (also known as Forest) had first met Carl in 1968 when she was a hippie, traveling from California to Oregon. She'd intended to spend a month but ended up staying a year. At Wolf Creek, Carl introduced her to English and Scottish country dancing which she pursued in earnest, eventually even earning a certificate as a dance therapist in New York. It was the beginning of a long and close friendship. When she returned to Wolf Creek after a year in New York, McClave was there with Carl. He was a very strange man—moody, depressed, in need of a lot of attention, and inclined to disappear whenever she was around. Although Dancer had planned on staying at Wolf Creek for a while, McClave did not want her there and Carl told her she would have to find another place to stay.

McClave suffered from ongoing depression and he became despondent after breaking up with Carl. He returned to Michigan and then visited Wolf Creek one last time. In June 1974 in Michigan he connected a hose to the exhaust pipe of his father's Buick and lay down in the back seat to die. Five days later twenty people gathered under a maple tree at Wolf Creek in the late afternoon to remember him. At the end, two of the group (one of whom was Carl's next partner, Allan Troxler) played violins as the sun went down. Shortly thereafter Carl wrote "for three years, Stevens' presence, or absence, was the overwhelming fact of my life."[23]

Later Carl indicated how intrigued he was by Stevens's suicide. He told a friend, "How easy that seemed, when he did it, and how appealing."[24] Another close friend from that period regarded McClave as a vibrant, enjoyable personality who committed suicide because of the widespread social rejection of homosexuality. Carl understood this, but he still was terribly upset. Apparently their relationship was not entirely over when the suicide occurred.

After McClave left, Wolf Creek became Carl's sole responsibility. For a while he managed on his unemployment checks from San Francisco, but when they ran out, he cut his long hair and tried to get a job at the local welfare department. He failed because, he said, "they knew I was a hippie."[25] In 1973 he enrolled at the Oregon College of Education and earned his teaching credentials in social studies. But after practice teaching at Roseburg High School, he realized he could never do that kind of work. Then a dancer-friend, Elaine Weiss, suggested he help her teach folk dancing at Rogue Valley Community College in Grant's Pass. This eventually evolved into enough classes in the seven years from 1973 to 1979 for Carl to make a living from it. When his aunt Elizabeth Freeman retired from teaching in New Jersey and joined them in 1974, she helped to secure the Oregon property financially because she and Troxler were able to buy out McClave's half of the property from McClave's parents.[26] (In the summer of 1974 as Carl and Troxler were packing his aunt's things in Paramus and driving her to Oregon, Christine and I were moving in the opposite direction from Hong Kong to Mahopac, New York, which was only fifty miles northeast of Paramus.)

Carl was also part of a small group that founded a gay-oriented, back-to-the-land magazine dedicated to serving the needs of "country faggots" and ending their isolation.[27] The magazine was issued quarterly, in accordance with the seasons: winter solstice, spring equinox, summer solstice, and autumn equinox. The postal term RFD (Rural Free Delivery) was chosen as its title because of the importance of mail in country life.[28] There was a continually evolving pun on RFD, with each issue having a different meaning for the abbreviation. The first issue was produced in the fall of 1974 in which *RFD* meant Rustic Fairy Dreams. That was followed by Reckless Fruit Delight (volume 2, winter solstice 1974), Really Feeling Divine (3, spring 1975), and Rabbits, Faggots and Dragonflies (4, summer 1973). Although the magazine was typical of the anti-intellectualism of that time in mocking "intellectual bullshit," it had a serious purpose.

In 1975 the gay rights activist Harry Hay (1912–2002) interrupted his return trip to Los Angeles from a Seattle workshop to stop off in Wolf Creek to meet Wittman.[29] Hays and Wittman became friends as Hay submitted many contributions to *RFD*, beginning in 1975 with a tribute to his mother.[30] Hay is usually credited with founding the gay spiritual movement of the Radical Faeries with a pronouncement in 1979, but clearly the publication of *RFD,* which is associated with the Radical Faeries, preceded Hay's founding pronouncement by five years. There seems to have been an overlap between the "country faggots" of *RFD* and the Radical Faeries of Hay's movement. Unfortunately, gay movement historians with the mindset of the coastal cultural establishment often fail to recognize the contributions of radicals like Wittman and others who consciously chose to work in remote, inland areas.

In fact, the first issues of *RFD* were put together by rural gay collectives in remote parts of the country, including Grinnell, Iowa; Wolf Creek, Oregon; Elwha, Washington; and Butterworth Farm, Massachusetts. But the heart of the publication lay in the gay community in Wolf Creek until 1979.[31] After the first eight issues, publication shifted from Iowa to Oregon.[32] By then, the Wolf Creek gay commune consisted of a fluctuating group, usually eight in number, who lived on different sites close to one another.[33] Even with an unpaid staff, magazine finances were tight. In the financial report of 1976, *RFD* printed 2,000 copies but had only 600 subscribers.[34] Free subscriptions were given to imprisoned gays as part of an effort to air their unique concerns.

Carl's involvement in the magazine was greatest at the beginning. The suicide of McClave in June of 1974 appears to have been a catalyzing event in transforming the idea for the magazine into a reality. The opening article in the first issue was a memorial to McClave, unsigned but clearly written by Wittman. The gay men who compiled *RFD* attempted to reach out to include lesbians who lived nearby, but lesbian separatism was very strong at the time and *RFD* remained predominantly male.[35] The *RFD* commune attracted a number of visitors, including a teenager named Scott O'Hara (1961–1998) who bicycled thirty-five miles north from his home in Grants Pass. He visited several times during his last two years in high school (1977–1979) in order to have sex with the *RFD* staff.[36] He later became a pornographic film star, wrote his memoirs, and died of AIDS.

The range of topics in *RFD* was broad, ranging from holistic health to gay politics. Many of the articles in the early issues dealt with the topic of food—growing and preparing it. The Wolf Creek community was attempting to survive as a largely self-sufficient agricultural commune and practical concerns were paramount; for example, the spring 1977 issue was devoted to rural mechanics. From the outset, the artwork in *RFD* was excellent in a way that set it apart from other publications. Carl's partner, Allan Troxler, was one of the leading graphic artists, but there were numerous others as well. It contained many poems. Numerous articles dealt with personal relationships, which were a constant concern in communal living. Some of the articles were transcriptions of taped group sessions in which daily and ongoing tensions were revealed.

Spirituality was another important topic in *RFD,* and for the first time in his life, Carl became involved in a sphere of experience that had been completely absent from his atheistic, Marxist family background. The spirituality was not only New Age but also viewed from a gay perspective with a sharp critique of heterosexist elements. Tarot card readings revived his former interest in history by providing him, for the first time, with a way of interpreting history in terms of sexuality.[37] Carl reinterpreted the twenty-two pictorial cards (the Major Arcana) as mysteries in a "pre-patriarchal" gay sense. He believed these mysteries were embedded in a "men's circle" and "women's circle" of ritual sex acts that were stripped of romantic or emotional meaning.

The spiritual thirst of that time was not merely a gay concern. The late sixties and seventies were filled with spiritual searching by a generation dissatisfied with the traditional Christianity and Judaism on which they had been raised. My own search took me to East Asian religions, and particularly to Buddhism. A minor field in my doctoral program at Berkeley had been Chinese Buddhism, which I had studied under a thoughtful Buddhologist named Lewis Lancaster. One of the most impressive things about Professor Lancaster was his tranquil demeanor, which, to me, was a sign that he was attaining the detachment Buddhism seeks to cultivate.

In contrast, my own life was filled with struggle and turbulence. Because of this search, my family and I spent the summer of 1975 at the ecumenical religious community of Koinonia, located on a former private estate on the northern outskirts of Baltimore. Its Greek name "Koinonia" meant fellowship with God or with other Christians, which reflected its Christian origins and that it had once been a training camp for missionaries. However, by the time we arrived, it was headed by a very open and syncretic Episcopalian priest named David Poist and it could no longer be characterized as orthodox Christian.

Like Wolf Creek, much of our effort was directed toward the garden. Its produce was sold to help cut the costs of feeding us residents. Soybeans in an unbelievable variety and sometimes dubious culinary form appeared in most of our meals. I taught a course in Zen that included meditation and a meatless diet.

The most outrageous article that Carl published in *RFD* was entitled "Shit." He criticized American culture's negative associations toward fecal matter that begins with toilet training. He wrote partly from a gay sensibility but also from the ecological need for recycling the nutrients for agriculture.[38] The blunt language of this essay confirms just what a radical he'd become.

Another way that the idealism of the Wolf Creek *RFD* compilers was expressed was in their attempt to fight the superficial gay meat-market mentality of urban centers by announcing that they would no longer publish height, weight, race, or age in any contact letters. Although this effort began to break down six months later when ages began to reappear in personal descriptions, still it was a noble experiment.[39]

The last issue of *RFD* to be produced at Wolf Creek was number 16 in the summer of 1978.[40] *RFD*'s move from Oregon to North Carolina coincided with Carl and Troxler's move to Durham, but their involvement with *RFD* was essentially over. The themes that *RFD* continued to explore were in large part first defined by Wittman and are a measure of his enduring influence. These include community, diverse sexuality, caring for the environment, gays in prison, poetry, prose, drawing, photography, radical faerie consciousness, nature-centered spirituality, and sharing experiences.

Carl's involvement in ecological activism came with his growing concern over the destruction of the forests around Wolf Creek. His developing spirituality was tied to the trees. In a half-serious, half-humorous scenario for a drama entitled "At the Pass—A Modern Morality Play," he linked same-sex attraction with magic and the trees.[41] He had fallen in love with the landscape and "the towering trees that inspire such awe."[42] When the trees were threatened, he protected them by organizing "a group of country faggots, lesbians and freaks against the machinery of corporate-government-bureaucracy."[43]

At one point Carl conceived of building a small house for himself in the woods at Golden, Oregon. Although there was plenty of space in the main house, he needed some distance from his partner Troxler, or as he put it, "maybe it was because of Allan and I trying to adjust our space so that we could respect each other's differences, that we needed a little bit of distance from each other, a little bit of something that was mine and his rather than ours."[44] Carl had always been fascinated by the stone house that his grandfather had built in New Jersey and there were piles of stone around Golden left over from the digging for gold using water cannons in the 1920s and 1930s. He carried these stones uphill and began to build a house, adapting its construction to whatever materials were at hand. The structure of the house reflected the evolution of his personality. For many years Carl had thought of himself as a pragmatist and the downstairs was very pragmatic and a refuge from the hot and dry Oregon summers that depressed him. But the second floor reflected his more imaginative and artistic side and was, as he said, "kind of concomitant with my increasing sense of myself as an artist rather than a politico."

NOTES

1. Steve Hogan and Lee Hudson, *Completely Queer: The Gay and Lesbian Encyclopedia* (New York: Holt, 1998), 639.

2. Richard D. Lamborn, "Radical Faeries as Excursus Religion," American Academy of Religion, Philadelphia, Pennsylvania, November 1995, 6.

3. See the invitation to the wedding of Mimi Feingold and Carl Wittman in the Miriam Feingold Papers, 1960–1967, sheet 540. The spelling of "Manifesto" with a terminal 'e' reflected the medieval theme of the wedding.

4. SDS advocated disarmament, reducing the role of private enterprise while increasing the role of both the federal government and international agencies like the United Nations, fighting poverty, promoting peaceful dissent, and transforming universities from being centers of "dull pedantic cant" into bases for assault on the status quo. Students for a Democratic Society (SDS), *The Port Huron Statement* (1962) (Chicago: Charles H. Kerr Publishing, 1990), 77.

5. Carl Wittman, "Refugees from Amerika: A Gay Manifesto," *San Francisco Free Press*, December 22, 1969–January 7, 1970, 3–5. The "Gay Manifesto" also appeared as "Refugees from Amerika: A Gay Perspective," *The Berkeley Tribe*, December 26, 1969–January 2, 1970, 12–13, 21.

6. Hogan and Hudson, *Completely Queer*, 644.

7. An editorial comment at the beginning of the February 1970 issue of *Liberation* reflects this ambivalence by noting somewhat apologetically that while gays are "one of America's most oppressed minorities," the publication of this manifesto "is, we expect, going to provoke a lot of reaction, not to mention a few of those cancel-my-subscription letters we hate to receive." "In This Issue," *Liberation* 14, no. 10 (February 1970): 3.

8. Carl Wittman, "A Gay Manifesto," *Liberation* 14, no. 10 (February 1970): 18–24.

9. Douglass Shand-Tucci, *The Crimson Letter: Harvard, Homosexuality, and the Shaping of American Culture* (New York: St. Martin's Press, 2003), 263, 287.

10. Eve Kosofsky Sedgwick, *Epistemology of the Closet* (Berkeley: University of California Press, 1990), 40–44.

11. For a recent example of this viewpoint that sees both homosexuality and heterosexuality as socially constructed, see David M. Halperin, *How to Do the History of Homosexuality* (Chicago: University of Chicago Press, 2002).

12. Steven Epstein, "Gay Politics, Ethnic Identity: The Limits of Social Constructionism," *Socialist Review* 93–94 (1987): 9–54.

13. Wittman was not the only SDS member to have applied the term "manifesto" to political statements of that time. Tom Hayden and others also referred to the *Port Huron Statement* as a manifesto. See Tom Hayden's letter to the editor, *New York Times Book Review*, January 9, 2005, 6. Robert Pardun refers to the *Port Huron Statement* as "the SDS 'manifesto'" in *Prairie Radical*, 33. Also see Gregory Nevale Calvert, *Democracy in the Heart* (Eugene, OR: Communitas Press, 1991), 1, 90.

14. "Sex and Caste" was initially circulated privately but later was published in *Liberation* (April 1966): 35–36.

15. Shand-Tucci, *The Crimson Letter,* 269.

16. Shilts, *And the Band Played On,* 15.

17. Taped interview of Carl Wittman by Marsha Emerman, Ashland, Oregon, 1980.

18. Only the two wives' names were listed on the deed (dated December 16, 1968) because both husbands were facing the prospect of jail sentences over their resistance to the draft. The Josephine County Assessor's Office in Grants Pass, Oregon, identifies the Wolf Creek property with the following map tax lot number: township 33, range 5, section 19, government lot 7. This plot dates from the mid-1950s and consists of 61.82 acres. The mailing address is 3502 Coyote Creek Road, Wolf Creek, Oregon 97497-9531.

19. Michael Downing, *Shoes Outside the Door: Desire, Devotion, and Excess at the San Francisco Zen Center* (Washington, DC: Counterpoint, 2001), 215.

20. When the abbot Richard Baker was dismissed in 1983 for financial and sexual irregularities, Richmond left the Zen Center, though he remained a lay Buddhist. Later he founded a lucrative software consulting group and pursued his dual passions—his wife and his music. Downing, *Shoes Outside the Door,* 215, 313.

21. Wittman, Emerman tape, 1980.

22. On March 8, 1971, the names on the property deed were changed from Feingold and Richmond to Wittman and McClave.

23. "Stevens McClave 1945–1974," *RFD* 1 (autumn 1974): 5.

24. Mab Segrest, *Memoirs of a Race Traitor* (Boston: South End Press, 1994), 53.

25. Wittman, Emerman tape, 1980.

26. This transfer was recorded on the property deed in January 1975, the same month that Wittman's aunt moved into the timber (post-and-beam) house Carl had built for her on the property. Within six months of arriving at Wolf Creek, she had entered into a relationship with a woman named Elena. It was her first such relationship in thirty years. Wittman, Emerman tape, 1980.

27. Wolf Creek was a stopping-off point for gays traveling between Seattle and San Francisco. This generated a steady stream of welcome visitors who not only broke the tedium of country life but also provided volunteer labor for the magazine. John Alexander, "An Interview with Faygele," *RFD* 36 (fall 1983): 10.

28. Stewart Scofield, "*RFD*'s Place in Gay Magazine History," *RFD* 34 (spring 1983): 9.

29. Harry Hay, *Radically Gay: Gay Liberation in the Words of its Founder*, ed. Will Roscoe (Boston: Beacon Press, 1996), 361.

30. Stuart Timmons, *The Trouble with Harry Hay: Founder of the Modern Gay Movement* (Boston: Alyson Publications, 1990), 253–254.

31. "Recalling Former Decades: An *RFD* Retrospective, Fall 1974 to Summer 1978, Issues 1–16," *RFD* issue 75 (vol. XX: 1) (fall 1993): 35–37.

32. "Recalling Former Decades: An *RFD* Retrospective: Part 3, Winter 1982 to Summer 1986, Issues 33–47," *RFD* 77 (vol. XX: 3) (spring 1994): 30.

33. These sites included Golden (where Wittman and Troxler lived), Lilac Ridge, Creekland, and Woodford Creek. They came together for a weekly "workday" to help one another with various projects, including *RFD*. "Golden Conversations," *RFD* 8 (summer 1976): 4–12; Webb, "Difficulty at the Beginning: A Wolf Creek Journal," *RFD* 11 (spring solstice 1977): 8–12.

34. *RFD* 8 (summer 1976): 38.

35. A survey that produced 276 reader responses indicated that most of the readers were gay men (197 out of 276) whose religious background was predominantly Christian (151 Protestant and 64 Catholic) with only 32 Jewish and 4 agnostic or atheistic respondents. Most came from urban areas and, in accordance with the times, more indicated that they used marijuana (190) than alcohol (160). The median age of respondents was 25, with the heaviest concentration between 22 and 31. Jerry, "RFD Reader Survey," *RFD* 8 (summer 1976): 39.

36. Scott O'Hara, *Autopornography* (Binghamton, MY: Harrington Park Press, 1997), 9, 85.

37. Wittman believed that these Tarot cards represented the knowledge of "various sexual-religious heretical sects of Europe" who, before being extinguished by the Inquisition, conveyed their knowledge to the Gypsies who inscribed this knowledge on the cards of the major arcana. Carl Wittman, "In Search of a Gay Tarot," *RFD* 2 (winter solstice 1974): 32–35.

38. Wittman said that terms like "shit" and "asshole" should not be used as epithets. He wrote: "If there is nothing else revolutionary about male homosexuality, at least it leads us out of this morass of tension about our assholes. Indeed, it is remarkable that anal intercourse and rimming ever become acts of love. But it is through those acts of love that I am in touch with the muscles and organs around my asshole. This now seems quite central to my consciousness as a faggot; enjoying that part of my body, not feeling so alienated or disgusted by the shit which passes through it." Carl Wittman, "Shit," *RFD* 5 (autumn 1975): 28.

39. "Recalling Former Decades: Issues 1–16," 43. In spite of their common interests in country living, acceptance of *RFD* by other alternative lifestyle publications was hard to come by. *Mother Earth News* had been founded in 1970 with articles dedicated to country living projects like organic gardening, home building, small business development, and wood-working. The articles in *Mother Earth News* had much in common with those in *RFD,* and yet three times in the years between 1974 and 1981, *Mother Earth News* rejected *RFD*'s requests to advertise in its pages on the grounds that its gay emphasis would be offensive to its readers. Allan Troxler, "A Rejection," *RFD* 1 (autumn 1974): 13–18. The third rejection letter from *Mother Earth News* was reprinted in *RFD* 26 (spring 1981).

40. After *RFD* number 16 (summer 1978), the publication was moved to Elfland in the North Carolina Piedmont where Faigele Ben Miriam led a collective effort in producing three issues (John Alexander, "An Interview with Faygele," *RFD* 36 [fall 1983]: 9–11). Faigele Ben Miriam (a.k.a. Faigele Singer) was a political activist who changed his name to reflect his sexual orientation (Faigele, literally "little bird," is Yiddish for gay man) and to honor his mother (Ben Miriam means "son of Miriam"). Faigele was an ethnic Jew who was active in the Seattle gay community in the early seventies and had helped to establish the Elwha Land Project near Seattle in 1974. The Elwha Land Project was a gay agricultural commune on sixty-eight acres west of Port Angeles, Washington, in the Lower Elwha Valley and on the Strait of Juan de Fuca (Faigele, "Elwha," *RFD* 2 [winter solstice 1974]: 5–6). Faigele had lived at the Wolf Creek commune for a time, working on *RFD*. By 1977 he had moved to his mother's farm in Efland, North Carolina, which became the home base of *RFD* for the summer of 1978 and all of 1979. Under Faigele's influence, the issues produced at Efland became more overtly political as the struggle for gay rights blended with the struggles over feminism, prison rights, and nuclear power ("Recalling Former Decades: An *RFD* Retrospective, Fall 1978 to Fall 1982, Issues 17–32," *RFD* 76 (vol. XX: 2) (winter solstice 1993): 30). Faigele survived for many years after being diagnosed as HIV-positive before dying in 2000. In the summer of 1980

RFD moved to Bakerville in the mountains of western North Carolina where it was produced by a four-man gay collective on Running Water Farm. By 1983 it had moved to Short Mountain Sanctuary in Liberty, Tennessee, and in 2009 it moved to a small collective associated with Faerie Camp Destiny in Massachusetts.

41. In this drama, Wittman draws two characters with magical meaning from the Tarot cards, Minora Arcana and Majora Arcana, who play important roles in fighting evil. These two "spiritual dykes" use their magical communion with the giant fir trees to fight the attempt of a local government building inspector ("Mr. Red Tag") to force the country inhabitants to bring their residences up to code or to evacuate them. The two Arcana get the trees to create frightening winds with their swooping and falling branches "a la the Ents in the Ring Trilogy." This causes a traffic jam on the nearby interstate highway that contributes to the victory of the country faggots allied with the magical trees over oppression by heterosexist hippies and local authorities. Carl Wittman, "At the Pass—A Modern Morality Play," *RFD* 3 (spring equinox 1975): 31–33.

42. Carl Wittman, "Letters from the Forest," *RFD* 9 (fall 1976): 19.

43. Wittman, "Letters from the Forest," 14.

44. Wittman, Emerman tape, 1980.

Chapter Fifteen

Rootless in Asia and Europe, 1973–1980

I finally found a teaching position in Hong Kong. Lingnan University was founded by American Presbyterians in 1877 at Guangzhou (Canton) as Canton Christian College. Over the years it developed a campus on the banks of the Pearl River and became one of the leading universities in China.[1] After the Chinese Communist government appropriated the Guangzhou campus in 1952, alumni revived the institution in 1967 by expanding the Lingnan Middle School on a hillside of Hong Kong Island at 15 Stubbs Road to include higher education. So when I made contact with the college in 1973, the Lingnan president, Mr. Raymond Huang, was happy to hire a Berkeley doctorate as a means of enhancing their college-level courses. He offered me a full-time position and Christine a part-time position, mainly teaching English.

Christine and I accepted with enthusiasm, but we had to find a sponsor to pay the travel expenses for a family of four. Joseph M. Smith of the East Asian Division of Overseas Ministries of the Christian Church (Disciples of Christ) invited us to Indianapolis for an interview and gave us a battery of intelligence and psychological tests. We passed and they agreed to pay our travel expenses and medical insurance. We were all set to go but lacked visas for long-term residence. Hong Kong was the last significant British crown colony and the British guarded it jealously. While it was easy to enter as tourists, the British granted long-term residence visas to non-Britons only grudgingly. So, although we had worn out our welcome in Pleasant Valley (my brother-in-law and his wife wanted to get on with their divorce), we could not yet leave for Hong Kong.

So we climbed into our aging sporty red Camaro convertible with our two children and big dog Nicholas who sat in the not-very-big back seat between our three-year-old daughter and one-year-old son. We headed to Florida where both of our parents now lived. (Where else do you go when you're broke and desperate but to your parents?) We did not have much money, but we did have an Arco gasoline station credit card, which we thought would pay for the gas to get us from Maryland to Florida.

Unfortunately, the last Arco gas station was in southern Virginia and we ran out of money in Ocala, Florida, about 200 miles from my parents. We could have called and had them telegraph money by Western Union, but that would have taken several hours and our children were getting hungry. (The only food we had left were these little marshmallows that Christine kept throwing into the back seat for the kids and dog to eat.) So we did something that neither Christine or I had ever done before: we begged.

It was a novel experience. Our little girl had left her shoes in the car and looked in her bare feet like an Okie child from the 1930s Dust Bowl. One woman looked at her and felt enough pity to give us a dollar. A young guy we begged from told us to follow him to his bank where he asked how much we needed. I will never forget the good people of Ocala. With the money we managed to collect we bought gas for the car and bananas for the children and drove on to my parents' home. After a month of sponging off our parents, we finally received our visas and took off for Hong Kong.

After arriving there, we found a flat to rent on the thirteenth (yes) floor of a new building at 58-60 Bonham Road on Hong Kong Island. In 1973 Hong Kong was a vestige of colonialism that was still dominated (that is to say, exploited) by the British. It was a place where ambitious Britons and Scots who could not make it in the home country came to find success. Their interest in Chinese culture was nonexistent and their attitude toward the Chinese was appalling. Many Chinese, especially bright, educated Chinese, resented Westerners.

The University of Hong Kong was located at the top of a long series of steps on a scenic hilltop on the island of Hong Kong. It was then an academic bastion of colonialism that was very slow to hire Chinese professors. Once at a house party on its campus thrown by the economic historian Professor Frank King and his wife Catherine, I was verbally attacked as a privileged foreigner by a young Chinese woman who knew nothing about me except that I was an American academic. For someone who had recently left the faux revolutionary trenches of graduate school at Cal Berkeley, it was a disturbing accusation that I never forgot.

In Hong Kong I may have been privileged, but I was also poor. Because two different pay scales—higher for Europeans and lower for Chinese—had been typical in colonialist enclaves, my Chinese colleagues with American doctorates on the Lingnan faculty assumed that I was being paid more than they were. But I wasn't, and my wife and I were so strapped for funds that we had to rent out the third bedroom in our flat to a fellow teacher (Jim Chapman)in order to pay the rent and to hire a part-time amah (Got Guliang) to do some cooking as well as the wash (by hand on a scrub board) and help with the children.

We loved Hong Kong. It was physically a spectacular place with wonderful views of the city and sea from its steep hills and the air was rarely as stagnant and smog-filled as in Taipei. Not only was the city beautiful, but the people were too. I never tired of looking at their handsome faces and lean bodies. (This was before growing affluence began to bloat their bodies with Western-style junk food.) As the last jewel of the British empire, Hong Kong reminded me of the past, and yet it was so vibrant and modern that it clearly was also part of the future.

At first we went to Sunday services at St. John's Cathedral on Garden Road. Founded in 1849, St. John's was a lingering bastion of Anglican colonialism attended by the British and Chinese elite. But we eventually settled into the interdenominational Union Church. We liked its congregation of bright, friendly, professional Scots (with a sprinkling of Asians). The Union Church was founded in 1844 by the famous missionary-Sinologist and translator of Chinese classics James Legge, and it retained its intellectual emphasis in the thoughtful sermons by Rev. Dennis Rogers, which were transcribed and distributed. We had our son Michael baptized there.

Hong Kong had a more tolerant sexual atmosphere than either Taiwan or the Chinese mainland. The more visible part of Hong Kong's sex life was aimed at tourists, who had more cash to spend than I did. Below that flashy disco veneer, however, I saw signs of gay life, certainly more signs than I'd seen in Taipei. Even so, during the entire year there, I made sexual contact with only one Chinese man. In Wanchai, a commercial area on the bus route to Lingnan College, there was a USO-type recreational center for British troops stationed in Hong Kong. When I used one of the stalls in the third-floor restroom there, I noticed a magazine appear on the top of the wall dividing my stall from the next one. It was a magazine filled with photos of naked men and women in soft porn poses and I realized that it was being placed there as a sexual advance by a young Chinese in the next booth. Soon after this, we got together in the same stall. Pretty tame stuff, but dangerous given the homophobic mentality of most British soldiers and the fact that we were not members of the British armed forces. But I guess love will out.

We made many good friends at Lingnan, particularly among our fellow teachers: Paul Bailey, an Englishman who later became a China historian; Lloyd Kramer, an American who later became a European historian; and his wife Sally who became a French language professor. But in a city where money was worshipped, the lack of money was a problem. Once, when our daughter was sick, Christine and I argued over whether she should use the food money to take her to a physician. I thought not, but Christine took her anyway and it turned out that she was right. Out daughter had bronchitis and needed an antibiotic. When our flat-mate Jim Chapman decided to leave at the end of the academic year, Christine and I felt that we couldn't manage another year in Hong Kong financially. I accepted an offer from Briarcliff College, a woman's school twenty-five miles north of New York City.

Briarcliff College and I were not well matched. It was a liberal arts college for women from wealthy families who were used to being catered to. There were exceptions, such as Liz Abrams (later Doyle). She arrived on campus having just buried her father, the famous Vietnam War commander General Creighton W. Abrams, and became one of my best students. For young women who are much more serious about their studies than about socializing with young men, a women's college can be an excellent choice. But for young women who are only moderately interested in academics and very interested in extracurricular life, a women's college is not where the boys are. With the advent of birth control pills and looser standards of sexuality, by the mid-seventies more and more young women were choosing coeducational schools over women's colleges. While the academically best of the women's colleges have survived, most of the others have closed or gone coed.

And so when I arrived at Briarcliff College in the fall of 1974, I did not realize at the time that I was stepping aboard a sinking ship. Loyalties toward small private colleges can be very strong and they tend to die slowly and painfully. There were heroic efforts to save the college, including the hiring of a charismatic young Vietnam veteran (and war critic), the Rhodes Scholar and novelist Josiah (Si) Bunting III. He had been on *Time* magazine's list of "200 Faces for the Future" in the July 15, 1974, issue. After leaving Briarcliff, he would eventually become the commandant at Virginia Military Institute (VMI). He was a hybrid of machismo and sensitivity who could get so emotional in addressing the troops (faculty and students) that he would weep. Unfortunately, academics are not so easily moved and they became disenchanted with him. I liked him very much but began to question whether even he could save the school.

Eventually, things became so bad that after being paid, I would rush with my check to the bank where the teller would first see if the balance in the college account was sufficient to cash it. Finally the trustees grew disenchanted with Mr. Bunting and ordered him to stay off campus, which ended all heroic efforts to save the school. The trustees then proceeded to sell the picturesque and valuable Westchester county campus to Pace University.

So after three years of teaching at Briarcliff College, I was unemployed. I celebrated the publication of my first book in October 1977 by standing in line at the unemployment office at Ossining.[2] I felt humiliated. What a comedown for a Berkeley PhD who had thought of himself as being a very valuable person—perhaps misunderstood by the world but definitely important. That winter I found out just how unimportant I was when the rejection letters poured in.

It took me several years to understand why the academic world was so unreceptive to me. There were two reasons: I was too abrasive and too creative. In academia, collegiality is the coin of the realm. Abrasive, creative personalities who do not meld well with their mentors and colleagues are shunned. Creativity inevitably brings conflict with whatever current way of thinking or doing prevails. When my mentors at Berkeley showed little interest in my use of the early Jesuit missionaries to study Chinese history, I refused to compromise and simply sought receptive collaborators in Europe and on the East Coast. Forty-one years passed before I returned to the Berkeley campus, finally doing so in 2014 to give a lecture. I doubt that I would have ever returned if I had not been invited. I did not return with a feeling of triumph, but rather with a need to put ghosts to rest. But how do you put a ghost to rest?

I was a poor judge of character, sensitive in some areas but insensitive in others. I thought my Berkeley mentors would overlook my abrasiveness and recognize my other abilities, but I failed to see that they were merely human with human feelings and that I had offended them. Since graduate school mentors play a primary role in securing the initial academic positions for former students, my rejection of them was an impolitic act. They continued to help me but only in the most perfunctory ways. As a result, I was doomed for years to be employed by liberal arts colleges who didn't want me so much as the prestige of my Berkeley PhD; and they wanted me to teach rather than do the research for which I was trained.

Meanwhile (and as usual), Christine was not as upset as I was. She had set up a pottery shop in the basement of our rented house, and she was happily throwing ceramics on her potter's wheel, firing up her kiln, and teaching ceramics to a few isolated students. In the town of Mahopac, New York, where we lived, there were a lot of nice people. Some of them were old-time residents from the days when Mahopac used to be a summer place for New Yorkers, while others were newly arrived urban refugees from the Bronx, fifty miles to the south.

It was in Mahopac that we became deeply involved with the people of the Church of the Holy Communion. I was scraping bottom both emotionally and spiritually and needed something to sustain me. Christine, a lifelong Episcopalian, had already joined the choir there when I decided to attend. I had never been baptized because Christian Science believes only in the reality of spiritual things and regards material things (such as the water used in baptism) as illusory. And so in September of 1974, at the age of thirty, I was baptized by Father Alan B. MacKillop in the wooded stream behind our rented house on East Lovell Street. It was a simple, spontaneous ceremony.

What I like most about the Episcopal Church also happens to be its greatest weakness: it is a bridge between Catholics and Protestants, very inclusive and tolerant of all sorts of believers. Episcopal parishes may be either High Church (Anglo-Catholic with an emphasis on ritual) or Low Church (less ritualized and closer to the more biblically oriented Protestants). Episcopalians can be very flaky, and the Church of the Holy Communion in the 1970s was no exception.

There was a very strong interdenominational Charismatic movement in the seventies that emphasized the use of the gifts of the spirit, such as speaking in tongues, and other very expressive forms of worship, such as lifting one's hands in the air during prayer. Instead of more high-brow instruments like the organ or violin, Charismatics favored folk music with guitars and other popular music instruments. The musical *Godspell* was practically their anthem.

Although I was deeply involved with meditation and silent prayer, I found speaking in tongues to be a bit too showy and vulnerable to exploitation. Although I felt a certain pressure to speak in tongues, I resisted. In Christian Science, prayer is intensely personal and consists of long, private meditations. Although I rejected Christian Science, an appreciation for this silent prayer was nurtured in me. For the same reason, I distrust sermons that are too dramatic because they are too much like show biz. Although High Church ritual—"bells and smells"—can certainly become theatrical, it is less personally exploitable because it must be done more or less the same way every time and with a set text.

The Charismatic movement had begun in the Catholic Church and it eased the transition of many former Catholics into the Episcopal Church. However, many of these former Catholics were actually just passing through the Episcopal Church on their way to evangelical Protestantism. At that time in Mahopac, the favored destination among evangelical churches was the Assembly of God denomination. Our priest at Holy Communion, who bounced back and forth between being Charismatic and Anglo-Catholic, went into an Anglo-Catholic mode. He purchased a carved image of the Virgin Mary from an old Catholic Church being demolished and mounted it on the back wall of the Holy Communion sanctuary. This produced a crisis among the former Catholics since nothing was more symbolic of the old-line Catholicism that they were trying to escape from than an image of the Holy Virgin.

The priest saw great promise in me, but I am afraid that his confidence was misplaced. I was psychologically and spiritually immature. At the time, he was involved in a dispute with the famously liberal Episcopal Bishop Paul Moore Jr. (1919–2003) of New York. Bishop Moore had marched for civil rights with the Reverend Martin Luther King Jr., had famously protested against the Vietnam War, had vocally demanded more aid for the poor, and had then ordained a lesbian.

Moore had what was then considered by many as a sterling background. He was a child of privilege, born into an affluent family that was only conventionally religious. After graduating from Yale, he was commissioned in the Marines and almost died from a chest wound in the South Pacific during World War II. He received both the Silver Star and the Purple Heart. After his discharge, he entered an Episcopal seminary and was ordained. In the 1960s, he gained a reputation for social activism in the Washington, D.C., diocese, and participated in the March on Washington in 1963. Although he offended many conservative Episcopalians, Moore was lionized by their liberal counterparts, and in 1970 he was consecrated as the bishop of New York. He quickly became the most controversial bishop in the US for his political and social activism (despite his conservatism in church liturgy and tradition). He married and had nine children. When his first wife died of cancer, he remarried a widow named Brenda Hughes Campbell. The great secret of his life was Moore's attraction to other men.

I met Bishop Moore in September of 1977, when he and his second wife visited Mahopac, New York. He came not only to perform the annual rite of confirmation at the Church of the Holy Communion but also to mend fences with the membership, which had been withholding its diocesan contribution out of protest over his ordination of an out lesbian named Ellen Barrett: the first ordination of an openly gay woman. Our own priest, whose own sexuality I thought somewhat ambiguous, disagreed with Bishop Moore over the ordination of gays. Church members were confused and angry over Moore's apparent violation of Scripture. That was the dispute on the surface, but there was a deeper story here, one that it took me years to piece together. I was at that time serving as the junior warden in Holy Communion, a responsibility that I was much too young and spiritually immature to handle. And I supported our priest in his opposition to Bishop Moore's ordination of Barrett.

After the service, we stood on the parsonage patio chatting, mingling with the confirmands' families, and trying to be polite to one another. None of us realized that all three of the parties in the dispute—Bishop Moore, the priest, and myself—were married and closeted bisexuals. I knew that our priest was because he had told me in vivid detail about his sexual seductions of young men in the church. The Episcopal Church has traditionally been a refuge for closeted gays, and stories of such seductions were commonplace. I was a good listener, but I was deeply closeted and I don't know if the priest had any suspicions about me. He was admittedly attracted to masculine males of Italian descent and he tended to romanticize them—and me—in ways that WASPS sometimes do. I may be wrong, but I don't think either of us knew about Bishop Moore's same-sex attraction. I didn't learn about it until thirty years later, when I read the memoir *The Bishop's Daughter* by Honor Moore.[3]

At that point in my life I was unsuccessfully trying to suppress my own same-sex feelings. On my monthly visits into Manhattan to do research at Columbia University, I was meeting guys for sex in the famous tearooms on the third and fourth floors of Butler Library. Even though I had conflicted sexual feelings, I supported the Holy Communion priest's opposition to the ordination of gays. Clearly, I too suffered from self-loathing.

I was hopelessly overwhelmed by the responsibility of the junior wardenship and was relieved when an opportunity presented itself for me to resign. What I remember most about the Church of the Holy Communion was the kindness and generosity of people like Rick and Joan Cerchiara. They housed us when we were in transition and they gave up their two-car garage for two years in order to store our car and furniture. I remember that once we had a great food fight in their kitchen.

I don't talk much about God, but that doesn't mean He isn't important to me. For me, God and sex are private things to be experienced rather than verbalized. While I talk a lot to God (I have a lot of requests), I have never found Him to be very talkative. Once in 1977 in Mahopac when I was on my knees in despair over my unemployment and how I was going to care for my family, I heard Him say, "I'll take care of you." And He did.

Out of this dismal, depressing period of unemployment came one of the great opportunities of my life. I won a postdoctoral research fellowship from the Alexander von Humboldt Foundation in Germany to study historical contacts between China and Europe. I felt like one of the enslaved Israelites being guided by a pillar of light out of my misery and into the Promised Land. On a bright spring May Day in 1978 I said goodbye to Christine and my children and left New York. I went to Göttingen, an idyllic old university town, and studied German at the Goethe Institute there. Two months later I found an apartment in Hannover for the family, who joined me.

A century ago, before the hateful, anti-intellectual, anti-Semitic, and homophobic movement of National Socialism under Adolf Hitler took hold of the German nation, Germans had distinguished themselves as the cultural and intellectual leaders of the world. After the irrational horrors of the Nazis had ended in 1945 and the German economy began to revive, there were vigorous efforts made to restore this tradition of intellectual and artistic patronage. One result of these efforts was the revival of the Alexander von Humboldt Foundation in 1953. It sponsored the research of four-hundred young foreign scholars each year in Germany, which prior to 1990 meant in West Germany.[4]

My family ties to Germany were still strong. I recall my maternal grand-father, Gustav Emil Dittmar, in his basement shop carefully packing endless C.A.R.E. packages containing food, shoes, and other needed items to send to relatives in Germany after World War II. He had financed these packages by selling his car. My family helped several German relatives immigrate to the US, although some later returned to Germany because of the generous pension benefits provided there for war widows. In 1978, I still had relatives in West Berlin, and so going to Germany for two years was a bit like going back to a former home.

In Germany I was befriended by Dr. Albert Heinekamp, a leading administrator at the Leibniz-Archiv in Hannover. He had a manner imbued with Old World gentility and loved both books and children in equal measure. In 1974 and 1977 I had briefly visited the Leibniz-Archiv to look at the manuscripts of the famous philosopher-mathematician-polyhistor G. W. Leibniz (1646–1716), who had been fascinated with China. Dr. Heinekamp had encouraged me to return, and he was instrumental in helping me to obtain the Humboldt grant.

As an academic refugee of sorts from America, I appreciated the kindness and concern he showed to me and my family. I remember numerous visits to his office on the top floor of the library with its panoramic view of the city and how patiently he would sit, listening to me struggle with new German phrases, trying to communicate. I was fascinated by his habit of smoking only part of a cigarette and then saving the butt in an ashtray on his desk for later. His help at such a pivotal time was a crucial salve for my trampled ego. I was upset when I heard that he died of a sudden heart attack in 1991.

During those two years in Hannover, I completed the research for my second book. A former professor at Berkeley, Karl Hardach, offered me the chance to teach at a German university as an adjunct professor. So in the winter semester of 1980 I traveled to the University of Düsseldorf once a week by train to give lectures in Chinese history. Professor Hardach helped me to translate my lectures into German, and I was excited and more than a little nervous about lecturing in a second language. When I lecture in English, I rarely read my lecture notes but simply use them as a guide. However, when I tried to break away from the German-language lecture notes, my syntax disintegrated. It was very frustrating, but once or twice the students liked the lectures enough to applaud (in the German academic world, that is done by drumming their fists on the table instead of clapping).

While at Hannover, my creativity resurfaced. Frustrated by the intellectual conservatism of my field, I founded a journal to foster new approaches to early modern Sino-European history. A venerable Jesuit scholar in France named Fr. Joseph Dehergne and an eminent Danish medical researcher in diabetes who had become a Sinologist (China scholar) named Prof. Dr. Knud Lundbaek contributed articles for the first issue. I produced a copy of the first issue myself on a manual typewriter in the Landesbibliothek, then had it photocopied and sent it out on a complimentary basis in an attempt to solicit subscribers. The rate of response was sufficient to sustain publication so long as I worked as an unpaid editor.[5] The lack of payment meant nothing to me since the work was so exciting.

Knud Lundbaek was a wonderful eccentric and the closest collaborator I ever had. He became a trusted colleague and friend, and—because both of us had large egos—he could be as exasperating to me as I was to him. He was born in Denmark in 1912 and was active in his youth as a surrealist poet in Paris in the 1930s. He became a physician who never had a private patient but who achieved worldwide renown as a researcher in diabetes mellitus (sugar diabetes) from 1943 to 1979 and finally became a Sinologist from 1979 until his death in 1995. He had an ascetic lifestyle, and in the last phase of his life traveled everywhere with nothing but a small backpack and two shirts (which he should have changed more often than he did). He began studying classical Chinese when he was nearly seventy years old, sitting in classes with students fifty years younger than himself.

Over the years he and I conducted an extensive correspondence, but he felt it was important for us to visit each other's homes so that we could better understand the other's work environment. During my visit to Aarhus, he pointed out the large seven-room flat where he had lived with his first wife, one daughter, and 6,000 books. Then came an unhappy divorce and the tragic death of his former wife by cancer. In 1972 he moved into a small two-room apartment in Aarhus and limited his books to 300 in number. He had a firm rule that whenever he acquired a new book, an old book had to be discarded. In the kitchen cabinets above his stove and sink, he kept books instead of dishes. He cultivated a certain degree of isolation and solitude; he had no television and he limited himself to ten minutes of radio news each day. He began each morning by reading a passage from the eleventh edition (1910) of the *Encyclopedia Britannica* and spent perhaps fifteen minutes with his favorite newspaper, *Le Monde*. Every afternoon, without fail, he had a drink of whisky.

During his youth he had lived in Paris and once when we were there together he took me to see Delacroix's *Jacob Wrestling with the Angel* in the St. Sulpice Church, which he always visited when in Paris. The painting had a personal spiritual meaning for him. We shared a dislike of pomposity and a certain ironical view of life. In 1985 when the Scandinavian Society for the Study of Diabetes established an annual Knud Lundbaek Lecture and Award, he attended the first lecture in Malmö, Sweden, and wrote, "it was a strange feeling to sit there and it occurred to me that it would have been more proper for me to be dead than to be alive at such an occasion." For a long time I thought this was just Knud's dry humor and did not fully understand what he meant, but now I do. The story of this book would be better received by readers if I were dead rather than alive.

While the two years in Germany were exciting for me and my work, they were difficult for Christine, who was suddenly thrust into a small suburb of Hannover with no knowledge of German. Our daughter, who was eight, and our son, who was six, were enrolled in the nearby local elementary school and they made German friends quickly, as children do. But it was more difficult for my wife. For her, shopping was exhausting and filled with embarrassing little mistakes and verbal blunders. In a small German suburb like Letter, English was limited to formal situations and German was the medium for daily discourse.

With her good ear and friendly personality, Christine soon learned enough German to make friends with several German women. She joined the local church choir and began teaching an evening ESL class at the Volkshochschule (a community college) in nearby Hannover. Once again, she adapted. But a lot of tension remained. She wanted to socialize more with German friends while I would come home seeking refuge from the mental exhaustion of trying to speak German all day at the library. Although we had luck in finding a very nice furnished apartment to sublet, my stipend was just barely enough to cover expenses and there was very little extra. The fellowship could not be extended beyond two years and our future was uncertain.

My daughter fell ill and became so dehydrated that she had to be hospitalized. Over the next several weeks, she was in and out of the hospital several times, but there was no specific diagnosis. During this period of worrisome uncertainty, before her problem was solved by an appendectomy, Christine was often upset. Tensions became so great that once we had a screaming argument during which she scratched my face badly. I was annoyed because the scratches were quite visible and would be noticed by others, but I did not hit her. Once long before I had hit her and she said it was wrong and I never did it again. Sometimes we unconsciously act like our fathers.

It would be nice to say that my compulsive sexual activity was behind me, but it wasn't. The attitude in Germany toward homosexuality in the late seventies was very tolerant, in part because Germans tend to have a realistic, earthy view of sex but also because of their attempt to compensate for the brutal Nazi oppression of homosexuals. When Germany was united in 1871, Prussian influence dominated over Bavarian resistance to enact a national law (Article 175 of the German Criminal Code) that made coital sex between men (but not between women) illegal.[6] Enforcement of this law intensified when the Nazis came to power, and in 1935 Article 175 was expanded to include mutual masturbation and even kissing or touching between men that might be considered indecent.[7] The Nazis added homosexuals, Romas (gypsies), and Jehovah's Witnesses to Jews on their list of undesirables to be eliminated.

In the years 1933–1944, over 50,000 males were convicted of homosexual acts by the Nazis and sent to concentration camps. Prisoners wore color-coded triangles: yellow for Jews, red for political offenders, green for criminals, pink for homosexuals, purple for Jehovah's Witnesses, and brown for gypsies.[8] In the camps, they shared with the Jews especially brutal treatment and the further indignity of having their pubic hair shaved. As many as 15,000 of them died in the camps.[9]

Article 175 was not officially abolished in West Germany until 1969. But throughout West Germany (and even more so in East Germany) there were many public places where it was easy to make contact with other men with same-sex feelings. When I first landed at the Düsseldorf Airport in 1974, I was surprised when a blond young German followed me into the restroom looking for sex.

In 1979 when I crossed into Communist East Berlin, I was amazed at all the glory holes in the first floor men's room at the Deutsche Staatsbibliothek, the main library on Unter den Linden. These holes had been carved into the wooden partitions between toilet stalls to facilitate sex. They were so obvious that the authorities must have been aware of them. When I saw them it was ten years before the Berlin Wall fell and tension was still high in this cross-roads of the Cold War. (The Staatsbibliothek was only a few blocks from the famous American crossing known as Checkpoint Charlie.) I had heard about the Soviet Communists entrapping and blackmailing gay visitors from the West with male prostitutes—most famously the conservative journalist Joe Alsop in Moscow in 1960—and I was nervous about this happening to me in East Berlin.[10] Of course, I wasn't nervous enough to stop participating, but I didn't feel safe until my subway car had passed over the border and I was back in West Berlin.

In Germany I met men for quick sex in restrooms in train stations, public squares, and universities as well as shower rooms in public swimming halls and outdoor pools. There were unheated subterranean restrooms filled with men loitering at elaborate antique porcelain urinals. When I walked down the stairs into these restrooms, it felt like I was reentering the Berlin of the 1920s and there was an excitement like a hunt in the air.[11] Most of these men were, like me, seeking a quick release on the run between trains or between home and work. The language of sex is universal. During the time that I lived in Germany, I spent hours in these places. It was pure escapism and it released tension.

One afternoon a few weeks after my daughter had recovered from her appendectomy, a policeman knocked on the door of our apartment in Letter and told me that she had been hospitalized again. My wife was not at home. After all of my daughter's previous stays at Kinderheilandstalt, a children's hospital in Hannover, I knew the way by rail and transfer to a streetcar well. One of the most difficult things about life is that it rarely allows us a rehearsal. Once we speak, we cannot take back the words. I found Lisa in bed with her arm in traction. She had been playing at a girlfriend's house and had disobeyed her mother's instruction not to get on the girl's pony. She had fallen and suffered a complicated fracture in her arm. Lisa was a terribly conscientious little girl and she knew how upsetting this would be to me.

Had it been a life-threatening condition, I would not have been angry, or at least I would not have shown it. But I knew that she would not die from the condition, though it was a difficult break and the orthopedic surgery never succeeded in restoring the full range of movement to her arm. She was in pain and already upset and I should have been understanding, but I wasn't. All I could think about was how we were going to pay for this new hospitalization. Her previous hospital stays had exhausted the limits of our health insurance policy, and there were no spare funds in my fellowship. And although I should have kept these concerns to myself rather than voice them to a ten-year-old child, I could not. I said to her in anger, "How are we going to pay for this?" She cried. I left. It is the second of my three great regrets.

NOTES

1. Kenneth Scott Latourette, *A History of Christian Missions in China* (London: 1929), 448–449, 627, 805.

2. David E. Mungello, *Leibniz and Confucianism: The Search for Accord* (Honolulu: University of Hawaii Press, 1977).

3. Honor Moore, *The Bishop's Daughter: A Memoir* (New York: Norton, 2008).

4. *Richtlinien und allgemeine Hinweise für Forschungsstipendiaten der Alexander von Humboldt-Stiftung* (Bonn-Bad Godesberg, 1977), 8.

5. Initially called the *China Mission Studies (1550–1800) Bulletin*, the journal was later renamed the *Sino-Western Cultural Relations Journal*. The thirty-seventh annual issue appeared in 2015.

6. Richard Plant, *The Pink Triangle: The Nazi War against Homosexuals* (New York: Holt, 1986), 30, 33.

7. Plant, *The Pink Triangle*, 110.

8. Heinz Heger, *The Men with the Pink Triangle*, trans. David Fernbach (Boston: Alyson, 1980), 32–33.

9. Plant, *The Pink Triangle*, 149, 154, 163. See also Pierre Seel, *I, Pierre Seel, Deported Homosexual: A Memoir of Nazi Terror*, trans. Joachim Neugroschel (New York: Basic Books, 2011).

10. Douglass Shand-Tucci, *The Crimson Letter: Harvard, Homosexuality, and the Shaping of American Culture* (New York: St. Martin's Press, 2003), 195–197.

11. A romanticized classic on gay life in Berlin of the 1920s is John Henry MacKay's novel *Der Puppenjunge* (1926), translated by Hubert Kennedy and published as *The Hustler: The Story of a Nameless Love from Friedrich Street* (Boston: Alyson, 1995).

Chapter Sixteen

Exile in Iowa, 1980–1994

Eventually, our daughter's hospital bill was covered by the emergency fund of the Humboldt Foundation, and I found a position in the history department of Coe College in Cedar Rapids, Iowa. The mental distance between Iowa and Europe was reflected in our first contact. The history department chairman Don Lisio miscalculated the seven-hour time difference between Iowa and Germany and called me in the middle of the night. When we arrived in Cedar Rapids, Iowa, at the end of June 1980, Christine and I found our positions reversed. The college was not very interested in my research, which meant another mismatch for me, but Christine thrived there. She found an ESL position at Coe College and became close friends with its director, Barbara Drexler. She joined our church choir and made friends there. She became close with our neighbors Candace and Michael Pufall who taught in the theater department and she became active in community theater musicals.

I hated my years in Iowa. I would arrive in the morning gritting my teeth and walking across campus to my office repeating the mantra: "I hate this place, I hate this place, I hate this place." In the winter, the Midwestern wind would blow with such icy ferocity that it was painful. I found it impossible to hide my unhappiness and disdain for my colleagues' lack of interest in research. They sensed my disdain and hated me back. I managed fairly well in the classroom and within a small department of congenial colleagues, but things broke down in college-wide committee meetings on which I was required to serve.

One time a colleague became so exasperated with me at an Academic Policies Committee meeting that he grabbed me by the lapels of my jacket and shook me, shouting into my face that I was a "feral child." Everyone on the committee was shocked because he had crossed a line. While intellectuals thrive on debate, it is limited to words. Physical violence is supposed to be completely alien to an academic environment. As he lost control and shook me with his shouting mouth and beard inches from my face, I became very calm, actually exhilarated because he had so totally lost. I felt completely unafraid and stared directly into his face. I could scarcely resist smiling. He somehow sensed this and it enraged him even further. Because of his loss of control, he was compelled to resign from the committee. I felt sorry for him, the kind of sorrow that one feels for a defeated foe. But it was one of the few victories I ever had at Coe College.

My father died in January 1983 at sixty-nine years of age. The call came, as those calls often do, in the middle of the night. He died in New Orleans where he had moved after separating from my mother. My younger brother Mark, who was then a Jesuit novice in New Orleans, was with him when he died. Like many men of his generation, he refused regular medical care. He had a long history of untreated high blood pressure that over the years had damaged his kidneys to the point that he could not live without dialysis. He had also become diabetic, another common side effect. But I think he died when he did because he became sexually impotent. I can understand this. Twenty-one years later something happened to me that made me see what a profound omen of physical decline impotence can be.

My father's body was shipped home to Burgettstown, Pennsylvania, for the funeral. And so I returned to the town of my childhood and youth for the first and only time since I left it in 1966. I always find it difficult to return to places where I have lived in the past. My father was a lapsed Catholic who at the age of sixty-three had been newly confirmed in the Episcopal Church; but he was irregular in attending Episcopal services and, anyway, his funeral was about family. The only natural thing to do was to have a Catholic priest conduct his funeral.

There comes that point in many lives when a son looks on the dead body of his father. I can't speak for others, but for me it was a defining moment. With his death, the bad things between us were wiped away and only the good things remained. I know that today I idealize my father in a way that makes him seem like a better man than he really was. But for me, this too is part of the obligation of a son. When he died, my father was transformed from flesh and blood into a spiritual link between me and my ancestors. My blood is from them, and for me he was a link in this sacred bond.

My mother came to the funeral, and while everyone treated her politely, it was awkward because of their divorce. Her estrangement from the family was reflected in the bright blouse she wore, in sharp contrast to the black dresses that my father's sisters wore. During the service in the funeral home, she sat apart from my father's sisters. My brother sat with her, but I sat with my father's sisters. They were my blood, and my mother had betrayed that blood by driving my father out and ending their marriage. My father's body was cremated and his ashes were buried beside the grave of his mother who had died fifty-six years before. Another circle was closed.

In 1984 I returned with my family to Germany for an entire year. We went to the wonderfully picturesque and historic small city of Wolfenbüttel where I had a postdoctoral research fellowship from the Herzog August Bibliothek. The HAB was a unique research institution built around what had been the greatest collection of books in sixteenth-century Europe. The Lower Saxony provincial government and the Volkswagen Foundation had lavished money on it in an attempt to create an international community of scholars.

Once again, I traveled to Düsseldorf every week in the spring to teach Chinese history in German. Much of my effort during that year was devoted to securing a publisher for my second book and seeing it through the press. This was an intensely frustrating period for me and it is no coincidence that sudden deafness first struck during this time. When things don't happen fast enough in my life (practically never), I fight my depression by focusing all my energy on solving the problem and circumventing the obstacle. The academic conservatism of the editors and peer reviewers of the university presses at California, Princeton, and Columbia had produced a series of prolonged and inconclusive evaluations of the manuscript without any agreement to publish it. At this point, Dr. Heinekamp stepped in and obtained an agreement to have it published by Franz Steiner Verlag, a prominent academic press in Germany.[1] I am eternally grateful to him for doing this. The reception of the book was very positive and this led to a paperback edition by an American university press where it is still in print. A quarter-century after the book appeared, it was translated and published in Chinese and Korean editions. Sometimes victory is slow in coming.

While in Wolfenbüttel, we lived in a spacious third-floor apartment in a building where the famous eighteenth-century philosopher and dramatist G. E. Lessing had once lived. Our children walked across the square to attend the nearby *Gymnasium* (college-preparatory high school) housed in an old castle with a still-preserved moat. I enjoyed looking out from our apartment onto the scene below that had changed very little in four centuries.

The scholarly atmosphere at the HAB was sparkling, with daily coffee gatherings around a large square couch for all the research fellows. These were presided over by Frau Doktor Solf, a wonderfully kind, cultivated, and attractive woman who smoked using an elegant cigarette holder and held on her lap the nastiest little dog in all of Europe. The creature was named Pom (presumably for Pomeranian) and he would growl and snap at anyone who sat near Frau Solf. She was oblivious to the discomfort her little monster caused. (It was an old tradition at European courts for ladies to keep such little dogs as companions.) There were also numerous symposia with papers delivered by both the resident fellows and by visiting scholars. Sometimes I had trouble understanding their German, but I enjoyed the challenge. Once Christine and I held a potluck dinner party for the research fellows, and the Polish scholars all brought vodka.

But as the year in Wolfenbüttel came to an end, the tension between Christine and me increased. Once we were driving back from West Berlin on the restricted access road through depressingly oppressive communist East Germany. Christine and I had such a shouting argument that I soon afterward lost most of the hearing in my right ear. I was hospitalized for *Hörstorz* (sudden deafness). It is not a well-understood phenomenon and there is no recognized treatment other than bed rest. Most (but not all) people who get it regain their hearing and so did I. But it demonstrated with frightening ferocity that the turbulence my Italian ancestors had absorbed from Vesuvius and carried to America lay buried within me. When the year was over, I really didn't want to go back to Iowa, but we had to.

The following years in Iowa passed for me in a perpetual state of frustration. We never had a third child, although I would have liked one. My struggle to advance professionally and our efforts to generate sufficient income consumed our energies. Part of the problem was due to the collapse of the previously expansive academic job market in the US. There were simply too many PhDs chasing after too few job openings, and my research and publications did not fit neatly into the established fields of history. Also there was a nationwide attempt to compensate for the earlier blatant discrimination against female academics by hiring many more women. A number of my fellow doctorates from Berkeley left the academic field in search of better opportunities. I survived, but at the expense of certain things (like a third child). Anyway, there had been only two children in Christine's family and she was content with one boy and one girl. My daughter later compensated for our restrained fertility by having five children.

My second book still didn't get me out of Coe College. At that time I was doing a lot of traveling to conferences in Europe and East Asia. In May of 1989 I disregarded the travel warnings of the US Department of State about potential political upheaval in China to make a long-planned research trip to Beijing and Hangzhou. I was in Beijing shortly before the Tiananmen Incident of June 3–4, wandering around Tiananmen Square, a massive open area in front of the old imperial palace. Here ten days later, hundreds of young Chinese demonstrators were killed by their own army units. By the time that happened, I had moved on to Hangzhou. As the violence spread from Beijing to Shanghai and Hangzhou, the foreign tourists left and the hotels emptied out. Student protesters deflated bus tires, leaving buses stranded and blocking intersections in Hangzhou. Daily life came to a standstill. I had seen similar tactics used by demonstrating students in Berkeley, but this was a foreign country and I felt less certain about what these events meant.

Although I never felt personally endangered, there was a great deal of uncertainty about whether China would once again lapse into a civil war and whether I would be stranded there. At the hostel where I was staying, the foreign students and academics sat around listening to BBC radio news reports. (The Chinese media were all state-controlled and thus unreliable.) I was unable to communicate with Christine back in Iowa who, unknown to me, had been suddenly hospitalized for food poisoning. In a scene of near-comic high drama, a local television station in Cedar Rapids interviewed her from her hospital bed while she held up to the camera my last letter, saying that she had no idea about my current situation in China but that, knowing me, she thought I would be okay. In spite of being in her nightgown, she never lost her poise and I was proud of her performance. I was fine and flew home several weeks later.

I used research material gathered from my 1989 trip to China to write my third book, which appeared in 1994, and that finally did the trick, professionally.[2] The history department at Baylor University offered me a tenure-track position, and we moved to Waco, Texas, in August of 1994. I thought it was the beginning of a new start in life and, for a while, it seemed to be.

NOTES

1. D. E. Mungello, *Curious Land: Jesuit Accommodation and the Origins of Sinology* (Stuttgart: Steiner Verlag, 1985); paperback edition by University of Hawaii Press, Honolulu, 1989.

2. D. E. Mungello, *The Forgotten Christians of Hangzhou* (Honolulu: University of Hawaii Press, 1994).

Chapter Seventeen

The Passion of the Women in My Family, 1944–1984

The Mungello daughters were filled with passion. Their men and their children meant everything to them. One of my cousins who knew them well said, "They would have killed for their children."[1] Their talents differed, but they were all aware of the value of money. Mae was the most shrewd in dealing with family property. Helen had the most acute business sense and played the stock market. She once said, "Money is my god."[2] Jeanette was the most underrated. Her siblings laughed at her naive comments, but she retained her vivid recollection of the past into her eighties and was the longest-lived survivor. Evelyn and my sister Marianne were the most vivacious and volcanic of them all.

My Aunt Evelyn was born in 1920, although she apparently later adjusted the year of her birth from 1920 to 1923 to enhance her youthfulness. At that time, this was a common practice done mainly by women who were born at home without recorded birth certificates.[3] She was prophetically named after the silent movie actress Evelyn Brent (Mary Elizabeth Riggs, 1899–1975).[4] Brent's dark hair and eyes gave her a sultry quality that combined with a brassiness that made her a favorite for being cast as the smart "bad girl" in numerous silent films. Her lesbian relationships were an open secret in Hollywood in the 1920s.[5] My Aunt Evelyn wasn't a lesbian, but her brassiness and "bad girl" qualities echoed those of her namesake.

Evelyn had been scarred by a childhood accident that had burned one of her hands and destroyed her small finger, causing her to always wear long sleeves and carry a handkerchief in her hand.[6] However, that didn't prevent her from following her dreams. After Pap's departure for California, she managed the Penn Theater and then drove Pap in his Packard out to California in 1944. She was twenty-three, and California was exciting. Although she

163

returned to Pennsylvania, she was restless, living with various relatives. Around 1951 she returned to California for good. Her relations with her older sister Mae were difficult. Since the death of their mother in 1926 when Evelyn was five years old, Mae had mothered her younger sister and was reluctant to let go, but Evelyn was headstrong.

She met Herbert (Bert) John Kelley while he was painting a house next to her father's apartment building in Los Angeles, and they were married in Las Vegas. For a while they were happy, but problems soon surfaced. Evelyn told Jeanette that Bert was a "dreamer."[7] Later Jeanette heard that Bert was violent toward her. In 1953 happiness briefly returned when Evelyn gave birth to a "bouncing boy with black hair," Herbert (Bert) Paul.[8] She had wanted a girl with red hair, but Herbie Junior was "just perfect." She had a difficult pregnancy with severe morning sickness. Herbie was born prematurely with breathing difficulties and had to remain in the hospital nursery, but he eventually recovered. My cousin Cheryl remembered Herbie as having a small round Irish face with blue eyes just like his father. He grew to be quite tall.

Evelyn's pregnancy brought temporary improvement to her marriage. She wrote, "My husband is boss. What he says goes—Boy have I changed. I think mostly because of the baby and I do love my husband—in spite of his faults."[9] His faults included a lack of ambition and success. Evelyn was ambitious, and California in the 1950s was a land of golden opportunity. Many people were finding great success there, but not Bert. Eventually this drove them apart and he left her. Jeanette said that young Bert never heard from or ever again saw his father. Evelyn was said to have had a "bad divorce" in which she was forced to give her husband part of her property.[10]

Evelyn was a stylish dresser and very conscious of her appearance. She had cosmetic surgery to reshape her nose. She sent her son to Catholic school and was active in supporting the school. She sent a newspaper clipping to relatives in Pennsylvania to show her social ascent. This picture appeared in a Los Angeles newspaper on August 15, 1963, and showed Evelyn standing beside the wife of the Los Angeles mayor Samuel W. Yorty (Elizabeth Hensel Yorty) at a luncheon in Burbank. Evelyn chaired the St. Casimir's Lithuanian School luncheon and Mrs. Yorty was the guest of honor.

In the summer of 1964, Evelyn met the powerful publisher and politician William F. Knowland (1908–1974) at the pool of the famous Ambassador Hotel in Los Angeles.[11] Unlike my Aunt Evelyn who was the daughter of illiterate immigrants and lacked a college education, Knowland was a son of wealth and privilege. His political ambitions had been stoked by his father, the publisher of the powerful *Oakland Tribune*. With the assistance of Republican friends, such as Governor (later Supreme Court Chief Justice) Earl Warren, Knowland became a US Senator in 1945. In 1953–1954, he succeeded Senator Robert Taft as Republican Majority Leader in the Senate.

However, Knowland was a rich man's son who lacked the common touch. He was a large man at six feet, one inch in height and weighed 200 pounds. He was a Methodist who did not smoke and only occasionally drank. His power was more blunt than subtle—and highly focused; he had no time for hobbies. A prominent political journalist described him as "ponderous and unfriendly."[12] His hopes for the presidency were destroyed by his own miscalculations when he resigned from the Senate and then ran and lost the California gubernatorial election of 1958 to Pat Brown. By 1964 Knowland had begun to gamble in Las Vegas and live beyond his means. At forty-three years of age, Evelyn was no longer young, but Knowland had a history of back-street affairs and a taste for dark-haired women. So this was the beginning of a turbulent ten-year relationship.

Back-street affairs of that period typically involved an older, wealthy, and powerful male with a younger female who lacked wealth and prominence. Class differences were typical in such relationships, and the man usually supported the woman financially as a "kept woman." In fact, the man's wealth and power served as a source of attraction for the woman, although the genuine love felt by the woman often prevented these relationships from being simple cases of gold digging. The woman in such a back-street relationship tended to be naive and vulnerable to exploitation and far more focused on the relationship than the man. Although exploitative, such relationships were not devoid of affection. Nevertheless they frequently stopped short of marriage because either the woman was considered unsuitable as a wife or because the man never saw the relationship as more than an extramarital affair. This is exactly the kind of back-street relationship my aunt had with Senator Knowland. Knowland had married his childhood sweetheart whom he had met in the sixth grade of school.[13] Although that marriage lasted for forty-seven years, Evelyn's romantic involvement with Knowland began long before the marriage ended in divorce in 1972.

In July of 1965 Jeanette was in California with her daughters visiting Evelyn. Evelyn was waiting to hear from a plumber and when Jeanette answered her phone, she mistook Knowland for the plumber and blurted out, "Oh, you're the plumber, we need you."[14] They all went to San Francisco as Knowland's guests. Evelyn flew there with Bert while Jeanette took the train with her daughters Cheryl and Claudia. Cheryl was just turning twenty-one and remembered staying at the Fairmont Hotel.[15] She had vivid memories of dinner at Trader Vic's where Knowland insisted that she order coconut ice cream for dessert.

Evelyn owned some very nice apartments in Los Feliz, an upscale neighborhood a few miles north of downtown Los Angeles, and she lived in one of the units. It is unclear where she would have acquired the money to buy such a valuable property. Los Feliz was an attractive area and my aunt lived well. In the late 1960s, my cousin Cheryl lived with her for a while, but she said that Evelyn's emotionally unstable and erratic behavior drove her away. Evelyn's son Bert left home at eighteen to play in a band.[16]

Cheryl was no less determined than Evelyn was. Cheryl claimed that her aunt drank too much and she may even have been an alcoholic, although none of her sisters and brothers drank much. My father never drank, although he claimed that he liked muscatel, at that time usually an abominably sweet dessert wine—a sure sign that he had never cultivated a taste for wine. Perhaps my aunt was simply trying to fit into the middle-class style of the sixties in which heavy drinking was far more socially acceptable than it is today.

My aunt's impulsiveness could be shocking. Once at a Catholic school function for her son Bert, my cousin Cheryl followed Evelyn into the church kitchen where Evelyn went through the cupboards until she found a bottle of wine under the sink.[17] She drank it straight out of the bottle. She had some quirky habits, such as taking a daily laxative. She had the volcanic Mungello temperament. Cheryl once saw her in a fit of anger hurl a large bicycle at a woman tenant.

Knowland underestimated my aunt's ambition and audaciousness. Just as her parents had gone from impoverished southern Italy to the United States to make their fortune, so their daughter went from impoverished Slovan to southern California seeking her fortune. When Knowland married a younger and more beautiful dark-haired woman named Ann Dickson (who turned out to be a destructive alcoholic), my aunt felt that he had committed an unforgiveable act of disloyalty.[18] In revenge, she went to the Los Angeles Superior Court and legally changed her surname to Knowland and sent out announcements on January 6, 1972, that read:

> Due to circumstances
> beyond "our" control
> The Honorable
> William Fife Knowland
> and
> Evelyn Mungello Kelley
> no longer have a marriage.
> However,
> In the spirit of friendship,
> along with the warmest of
> "Season's Greetings"
> may I at this time announce
> to you my name change:
> Evelyn "M" Knowland
> And
> "Let the Good Times Roll"

She continued to be an annoyance to Knowland, calling the news staff and identifying herself as "the real Mrs. Knowland."[19] She supposedly made threats to the editors and reporters of the *Oakland Tribune* as well as to Knowland's son Joe and his sister Emelyn. Early in 1971 she panicked Knowland by telling him she was pregnant. On February 23, 1974, Knowland's body was recovered by divers from the Russian River behind his summer home, seventy-five miles north of San Francisco.[20] An autopsy indicated death by a self-inflicted gunshot wound from a 32-caliber automatic pistol. A probate hearing later indicated that Knowland was insolvent at his death.[21]

After her split with Knowland, Evelyn had a turbulent affair with a Las Vegas gambler named Louis Fox. My uncle Dom Punaro was called several times in the middle of the night to help settle their arguments. One time a gun was involved.[22] It sounds like a self-destructive diversion from the love affair with Knowland that she never got over.

She and Knowland had apparently continued to have contact because as late as April 1973, ten months before his death, Knowland drew a $12,000 cashier's check for my aunt's son, Bert Kelley.[23] There is a family rumor that Knowland had agreed to pay for Bert's education, but Bert never went to college and he knows nothing of any such check. When my Aunt Jeanette wrote him about my interest in writing this book, he responded by dismissing the published account in Knowland's biography about the $12,000 check as "lies" and said that Knowland never gave him money.[24] Perhaps his mother cashed the check without his knowledge.

Not long after Knowland's suicide in February 1974, my aunt fell ill and my Uncle Dom found her in bed in her apartment, hemorrhaging from colon cancer. She died on December 13, 1974, only ten months after Knowland's suicide. My Aunt Mae arranged a funeral for her and buried her in Forest Lawn Cemetery in Glendale, near where my grandfather was buried.

The authors of Knowland's biography regarded Evelyn as a troublesome nuisance in the life of a great man and dismissed her as a "pudgy, Mediterranean-looking woman."[25] They misspelled her maiden name of Mungello as "Mugello," confusing it with the name of the Mugello Circuit (Autodromo internazionale del Mugello) in Tuscany, Italy, where Ferrari cars are tested. The authors were so oblivious of her death that over twenty years after the fact, they wrote that the phone number Senator Knowland had for her had been disconnected and their attempts to contact her were unsuccessful.[26] Such was the conventional dismissal that a back-street woman faced.

From 1960 until 1985 my sister Marianne was also involved in a back-street love affair with an older, powerful man. In fact, there was a striking symmetry to the affairs that she and my Aunt Evelyn conducted almost simultaneously at opposite ends of the continent. The similarities seem too great to be coincidental. The passion of the Mungello women was self-destructive in its intensity, and what was true of my aunt was equally true of my sister. Evelyn felt an affinity for my sister Marianne. In a letter she described Marianne at twelve years of age by saying "Marianne is such a sweet girl—Isn't she good-looking."[27]

My sister's affair began with an adolescent infatuation with an older woman. Hetty Ruth Hindman (1919–1960) was a daughter of the physician, Dr. Audley O. Hindman (1876–1965), our neighbor and the most prominent citizen of our small town. Dr. Hindman had the reputation of never turning a patient away for lack of money, although some of his medical techniques became outdated. In 1957 after fifty-seven years of medical practice, the entire town honored him with a picnic celebration, a gold watch, and a bronze plaque commemorating his "faithful and outstanding service."[28] The 81-year-old physician continued to practice medicine well into his eighties, although he was barely able to get around on his own. I remember the frequent sound of his tires spinning in the snow whenever his car was stuck in the driveway.

Hetty Ruth was the youngest of four children in this prominent family. As a child of privilege, there was a large social gap between her and my father's sisters. My Aunt Jeanette attended high school at the same time as Hetty and remembered her as a "snob." Hetty was above her because "a foreign name was dirt to Burgettstown."[29]

Hetty became a pretty, blond, and charming woman, twenty-two years older than my sister Marianne, and she lived with her husband and two small children in Haddon Township in southern New Jersey. But it was an unhappy marriage—she was married to a "crippled husband."[30] She found consolation in alcohol and a relationship with a prominent businessman in south Jersey named William G. Rohrer Jr. (1909–1989). When Hetty visited her parents' home, my sister babysat her children. She and Hetty developed an intense friendship, spending long hours together. Hetty became obsessed with her relationship to Bill Rohrer, who continued to procrastinate on his promise of divorcing his wife to marry her. My sister was a fascinated listener and Hetty poured out the details to her.[31]

In June of 1960 the unhappy Hetty suddenly died and Marianne traveled to south Jersey to attend her funeral.[32] There she met Bill Rohrer who followed-up their meeting with cards, candy, flowers, and phone calls. A remarkable generational leap occurred as romance developed in which a determined, nineteen-year-old small-town girl replaced her older friend in this relationship. In a small town like Burgettstown, this was an audacious thing for such a young woman to do, but my sister had become enraptured with this man of wealth and power. It was an unconventional romance, but also very typical of a back-street affair between a powerless, younger, attractive woman and an older, prominent businessman and politician.

Rohrer was fifty-one years old and married with four daughters, some of whom were the same age as my sister. He had inherited a Chevrolet dealership from his father in 1935 and expanded it, buying real estate and developing a bank that became the largest in southern New Jersey.[33] He became a millionaire (his wealth in 1985 was estimated at $50 million), a popular mayor, a patron of local charities, and a powerful figure. He loved to bestow gifts but was personally frugal. He was quite overweight and was called "the Fat Man" behind his back.

Rohrer used his money and power to indulge his taste for attractive women. I doubt that he initially had any intention of marrying my sister, but just as Bill Knowland had underestimated my Aunt Evelyn, so too did Bill Rohrer underestimate Marianne. He later explained his attraction to her by saying, "She was good-looking and smart. She handled me right."[34] The women in the Mungello family are not passive victims who disappear quietly into the night. But while my Aunt Evelyn failed to achieve marriage with Knowland, my sister finally succeeded after many years of effort (including an overdose of Sominex and Valium in 1972): Rohrer divorced his wife and married her in 1973.[35]

However, with her victory came tragedy. Marianne loved children but was unable to conceive. She suffered from ovarian cysts and Bill was overweight and diabetic. She turned to adoption, but Bill was reluctant. Unable to obtain a small child through adoption agencies in the United States, they flew to El Salvador early in 1975 and adopted a boy and a girl from a bankrupt orphanage.[36] Pepe (Miguelito Alvarada) was a strikingly handsome little boy, one of eleven children born to an unmarried street prostitute who had abandoned her children. Most of his life had been divided between a brothel and a women's jail. He was malnourished as a child and he was small for his age. The orphanage said he was two-and-a-half, but he was actually a year older.[37] His later behavior indicated that he probably had developmental problems. He was renamed William G. Rohrer III and called Billie. The little girl Ana Cecelia was renamed Laura. When there were difficulties with Salvadoran immigration officials, Bill Rohrer contacted Senator Clifford Chase who secured the intervention of Secretary of State Henry Kissinger's office.[38] My sister returned to the United States with the children in February of 1975. Three months later, Billie was dead.

At this time, my family and I were living in New York and we were in regular contact with my sister through telephone calls and visits to New Jersey. Visiting Marianne and Bill was always stressful as they frequently argued in public, but their stress levels increased with the adoptions. They engaged in conspicuous consumption on a grand scale that Christine and I both found unappealing. Their life was dominated by the dynamics of power and wealth, things that we had neither sought nor attained. Whereas the little girl Laura (apart from her obsession with food) was quite normal and easy to get along with, Billie was moody and withdrawn. Although my sister had done a lot of babysitting as a teenager and loved children, she was not emotionally prepared to be, in effect, a single parent. Bill provided financial support, but nothing else. He had gone along with the adoption for my sister's sake but was otherwise uninterested. Marianne had been raised in a family where Christian Science had kept her from having any experience with medical care, and she was unversed in even the most elementary ways of consulting a doctor when the children were ill.

All of this stress pushed her normally high-strung and neurotic nature over the line, and she appears at times to have lost control. A psychiatrist later hired by her defense attorney stated that she suffered from a borderline personality that went from neurotic to psychotic under stress.[39] One is reminded of the testimony of the Camorra boss Enrico Alfano (Erricone) at the 1911 trial in Viterbe when he told the jury: "We are Neapolitans. We are sons of Vesuvius. There is a strange violent tendency in our blood that comes from the climate."[40]

Other than Christine and myself, Marianne had few relatives and friends to turn to for support. What exactly happened between her and Billie is not known. The state prosecutor would later argue that she was abusive in a manner that caused his death, but Marianne claimed that, unlike his adopted sister, Billie acted in a mentally bizarre fashion. Had the bruises on his body been self-inflicted as she claimed (several witnesses supported her claim of his head-banging), or had she struck him when she was out of control? I think the pain of her experience has obliterated the memories from my sister's mind so that even she does not fully remember.

On May 28, 1975, my sister carried Billie into the kitchen and placed him in a high chair next to Bill who was eating breakfast. Billie swooned into unconsciousness, although my sister thought he was just playing one of his games. She left the room and when she returned about five minutes later, there was a trickle of blood coming from Billie's nose. She called an ambulance and Billie was rushed to the hospital where he was pronounced dead.[41] An autopsy was performed but the medical examiner could not determine whether the injuries to the head were self-inflicted or inflicted by another person, and the death was ruled accidental. Nearly four years later the case was revived and the body was exhumed and reexamined in January of 1979, but progress was slow. Some have charged that Bill Rohrer's friends in high places were stalling the case, but others attributed the delays to "agencies protecting other agencies, and some ineptness on top of that."[42] However, the case was problematic and the head of the Camden County Division of Criminal Justice said, "At any point, the Department of Criminal Justice would have been justified in closing the book on it."[43] In any case, my sister was finally indicted for second-degree murder in December 1982.

Meanwhile, as in a Greek tragedy, disaster struck across the board. Bill's previously flourishing bank, First People's Bank of New Jersey, was sued by shareholders alleging mismanagement. [44] The Federal Deposit Insurance Corporation investigated the bank because of problematic loans. Bill's friendly small-town manner of doing business and performing weddings as mayor after hours in the bank lobby lost some of its charm as he came under scrutiny for issuing risky loans with insufficient collateral. He was also accused of personally benefiting from the byzantine complexity of some of the loans. In 1983 the FDIC ordered a massive reorganization of the bank and Bill was removed as CEO, though allowed to remain as chairman of the board.

Christine and I were in Wolfenbüttel when this great crisis in my sister's life came to a head. My sister and I had always been close. Marianne was two years older than me and named after my grandmother Marianna. She had our mother's trim body but the dark coloring of an Italian. She was physically attractive, but her temperament was tainted by the intense emotional strain that ran in the family. I also had this strain, though in a more controlled and less destructive form. While my creativity was internal and intellectual, my sister's expression was theatrical. As a teenager, she'd attended drama classes at the Pittsburgh Playhouse and she'd worked in summer stock productions at the Little Lake Theater. In August 1960 she played the part of Rosemary Murphy in a summer stock favorite, the sentimental comedy, *Abie's Irish Rose*. [45] During the years she was involved in theater, she preferred the more theatrical name of Mimi over her given name of Marianne. My father was her greatest fan. While she made many demands on my parents to pursue her theater interests, I perversely did the opposite and rarely asked for anything. She was the head cheerleader who stood in front of a packed high school auditorium leading the pep rallies while I was the football drop-out. But I was merely biding my time. Both of us could be audacious, but while her life was like a meteor that burned brightest from her youth to middle age, I began to shine more slowly and steadily. Like my mother, my sister was inflexible and highly strung, with a pronounced tendency toward hysteria. In fact, my mother and sister were so much alike that they constantly clashed. All these traits contributed to this tragedy.

Marianne's trial got underway in Camden in August of 1984. The prosecutor who tried her had never lost a murder case. [46] Because of Bill Rohrer's name and the sensational nature of the charge of a pattern of child abuse leading to death, the trial received a lot of media attention, including articles in the *New York Times*. [47] If it had occurred thirty years later, it would have provided daily fodder for our national media's 24/7 news cycle. My sister made it even more sensational by one day disappearing from court and traveling to the Washington, D.C., office of Democratic vice presidential candidate Geraldine A. Ferraro to convey her suspicions that she was being railroaded by a Republican plot.[48] She also visited the Mondale-Ferraro presidential campaign headquarters and left some legal papers there. (Bill Rohrer belonged to the moderate wing of the Republican Party that included New Jersey Senator Clifford Case.)

She spent that night in a Washington area hospital where she was treated for a viral infection and severe diarrhea. The next day she returned to Philadelphia and checked into the downtown YMCA hotel under her maiden name. She was recognized by the hotel clerk who called the police. She was arrested and given a psychiatric exam, but found to be mentally competent to stand trial. From October 10 until November 30, she was jailed and brought to court each day in handcuffs. The presiding judge finally released her on bail when he felt that she was carrying on meaningful communication with her attorney.

Her relationship with her attorney was difficult and became so hostile that she petitioned the court several times, without success, to change attorneys. Originally, Raymond A. Brown of the Newark, New Jersey, law firm Brown, Brown and Furst had been retained to represent her. However, health problems caused Brown to withdraw from the case and to be replaced by his son, Raymond Brown. My sister never trusted the younger Brown. She became convinced that her defense attorney, who had been hired by her husband with a $250,000 retainer fee, had devised a defense strategy to shield him from indictment. (Brown eventually billed Rohrer $760,000 in legal fees for the trial.) In her mind, this was a form of disloyalty, the greatest of sins in my family.

My sister tried to change attorneys. She wanted Nino V. Tinari of Philadelphia for whom my brother Mark worked as a law clerk. But the judge refused to allow it because he felt that this was part of an attempt on my sister's part to disrupt the judicial process. This all makes my sister appear irrational, but it becomes more understandable as a reaction to stress. Her otherwise bizarre trip in the middle of the trial to Washington, D.C., makes sense as a form of flight and desperate attempt to take greater control of her legal defense. Also, her claim that Bill was being shielded is not totally irrational. I had seen Bill kick a bawling little Laura in the behind on the stairs (their rambling split-level house was filled with stairs). I wondered if he might have kicked Billie in a moment of annoyance with his irritating crying, causing a fall on the stairs that contributed to Billie's brain hemorrhage and death. In any case, my sister's bizarre behavior had reinforced the public perception of her rather than Bill as the possible guilty one.

In November I flew from Germany to New Jersey to testify at the trial. The sight of her walking into the courtroom in handcuffs was upsetting. I was allowed to walk up to her and hug her. Her normally vibrant eyes were semi-glazed, as if she were only partially conscious. I whispered in her ear with all the force I could muster: "Don't give up!" Inadequate words, but delivered with a feeling that I hope she sensed. In courtroom testimony I confirmed that Billie's behavior was abnormal in comparison to my own children or Billie's sister. He was stiff and unresponsive, almost catatonic, and crying almost constantly with a whining kind of cry.[49] After a four-month trial, the jury announced that it was split 10–2 in favor of acquittal and the judge declared a mistrial. The prosecutor had failed to convince the jury that my sister had acted with malice or murderous intent. The jury forewoman claimed that if she had been indicted on the lesser charge of manslaughter, she would have been found guilty because there would have been no need to prove conscious intent to kill.[50] However, the five-year statute of limitations on manslaughter had expired the day before she was indicted. The Division of Criminal Justice decided not to retry the case.

When she was released after the trial, Marianne's life was a shambles. She and Bill had separated and many people in the area of south Jersey felt that she was guilty, despite the hung jury. She obtained a divorce and a financial settlement from Bill, although she had signed a prenuptial agreement waiving certain claims as a spouse. Clearly, she had married for love, but the love was over. Bill had committed the greatest of sins in our family: he had been disloyal. My sister believed she had been a victim in a terrible tragedy. She forever relinquished her interest in theater and moved with her daughter to New York City. She began a journey of personal redemption that continues to this day.

NOTES

1. Cheryl Bidlack to the author, April 21, 2009.
2. Jeanette Boake to the author, July 7, 2002, and September 19, 2003.
3. The exact date of my Aunt Evelyn's birth is difficult to determine. The federal census of 1930, apparently taken in 1929, lists the ages of the six Mungello children as follows: Tony Mungello 18, Dominick Mungello 16, Mamie Mungello 15, Helen Mungello 13, Jennie Mungello 11, Evelyn Mungello 8. The 1940 census lists Evelyn's age as 19. Consequently, both my Aunt Jeanette's recollection that the siblings were all born at 18-month intervals as well as the 1940 census would indicate that she was born in November 1920 and not, as she later claimed, on November 22, 1923. Moreover, in his petition for naturalization of March 15, 1923, my grandfather Raffaele Mungello, listed her birth date as November 23, 1920. The fact that Evelyn later claimed to be born over eight months *after* her father had already listed her on his naturalization petition, confirms that her date of November 23, 1923, was a fabrication.
4. Roy Liebman, *From Silents to Sound* (Jefferson, NC: McFarland, 1998), 44.
5. Lillian Federman and Stuart Timmons, *Gay L.A.* (New York: Basic Books, 2006), 41.
6. Jeanette Boake to the author, March 26, 2003.
7. Jeanette Boake to the author, January 28, 2004.
8. Letter of Evelyn Mungello Kelley to Lois and Don Mungello, July 2, 1953.
9. Letter of Evelyn Mungello to Lois Mungello, March 2, 1953.
10. Jeanette Boake to the author, January 23, 2004, and September 19, 2003.
11. Gayle B. Montgomery and James W. Johnson, *One Step from the White House: The Rise and Fall of Senator William F. Knowland* (Berkeley: University of California Press, 1998), 273–274.

12. Robert D. Novak, *Prince of Darkness: Fifty Years Reporting in Washington* (New York: Crown, 2007), 83.

13. Tim Retterman, "Knowland Tributes Sent as Suicide Motive Sought," *Independent* (Long Beach, California), February 25, 1974, 15.

14. Jeanette Boake to the author, January 2, 2001.

15. Cheryl Bidlack to the author, April 24, 2009.

16. Jeanette Boake to the author, July 11, 2003, and July 16, 2003.

17. Cheryl Bidlack to the author, April 24, 2009.

18. Montgomery and Johnson, 284-297.

19. Montgomery and Johnson, 274.

20. Retterman, "Knowland Tributes Sent," 15.

21. "Knowland Reported Insolvent at Death," *Daily Independent Journal* (San Rafael, California), June 13, 1974, 6.

22. Cheryl Bidlack to the author, April 24, 2009.

23. Montgomery and Johnson, *One Step from the White House,* 274.

24. Jeanette Boake to the author, December 23, 2002.

25. Montgomery and Johnson, 274.

26. Montgomery and Johnson, 306.

27. Letter from Evelyn Mungello Kelley to Lois and Don Mungello, July 2, 1953.

28. "'Country Doctor' Is Honored in Burgettstown," *The Daily Independent* (Monessen, Pennsylvania), August 7, 1957, 1.

29. Jeanette Boake to the author, February 23, 2005.

30. Jeanette Boake to the author, February 23, 2005.

31. Saline, 171.

32. Carol Saline, "A Death in the Family," *Philadelphia Magazine* (April 1985), 171.

33. Saline, 102.

34. Saline, 171.

35. Saline, 172.

36. Saline, 173.

37. Whereas Pepe (Billie Rohrer) was said to be two-and-a-half years old at the time of the adoption, his biological parents later clarified that he was actually three-and-a-half. Ron Avery, "Hung Jury Nets a Mistrial for Mimi," *Philadelphia Daily News*, December 18, 1984, 48.

38. Saline, 173.

39. Saline, 179.

40. Dickie, 205.

41. Jane M. Von Bergen, "Rohrer Found at Phila. YMCA, Is Held as Fugitive in Murder Trial," *Philadelphia Inquirer*, October 11, 1984.

42. Saline, 176.

43. Jane M. Von Bergen, "Long Delay Undermined Rohrer Case," *Philadelphia Inquirer*, December 23, 1984, 1-B.

44. Mary Williams, "First Peoples Bank's Problems Multiply as Holder Suits Charge Mismanagement," *Wall Street Journal*, July 20, 1983, 1.

45. "Classic Comedy at Little Lake," *The Daily Notes* (Canonsburg, Pennsylvania), August 12, 1960, 3.

46. Jane M. Von Bergen, "Long Delay Undermined Rohrer Case," 1-B.

47. Donald Janson, "Wife of Jersey Mayor on Trial in '75 Death of Son," *New York Times*, October 7, 1984, 46.

48. Donald Janson, "Jersey Mayor's Wife Is Arrested; Missed Start of Her Trial in Death," *New York Times*, October 11, 1984, B2.

49. Jane M. Von Bergen, "Rohrer's Brother Says He Never Saw Her Hit Son She Is Accused of Killing," *Philadelphia Inquirer*, November 17, 1984.

50. Jane M. Von Bergen, "Rohrer Trial Ends in Hung Jury," *Philadelphia Inquirer*, December 18, 1984, 1.

Chapter Eighteen

Carl's Death, 1977–1986

Carl Wittman was one of the most charismatic voices and tragic victims of gay liberation. Both of us were loyal but to different things. He was loyal to an inner voice of gay liberation while I was loyal to my family. I don't know if he ever had pangs of remorse for not having a family, but I know that I had moments when I wondered about him and how my life would have been different if I had not left him. His life was an ongoing counter-melody to mine. It created the tension that made mine both bittersweet and meaningful.

Although Carl maintained his friendships with former SDS comrades such as Helen Garvy, his break with SDS was irreparable. In July of 1977, six former members of SDS living in the San Francisco Bay area sent out invitations to other members for a six-day (August 21–26) reunion meeting of SDS at a camp at Hell, Michigan.[1] A pre-meeting circular reproduced several responses to earlier communications about this meeting, including one from Carl that reflected the intensity of his bitterness:

> As back in the 60's, you continue to ignore what appears to me and my gay brothers and sisters as your homophobia and sexism regarding gay people. Among the profuse listings of the good work you are all doing, there continues in these letters about the gathering to be absolutely no mention of us . . . Surely you must have learned by now, revolutionaries all, that you can't really expect a group oppressed by an issue to go running after the oppressors asking to be included?[2]

The reunion organizers tried to be conciliatory, but there were few identifiably gay members of SDS who could be urged to attend. (Since the 1960s several members had come out publicly including Gregory Calvert, Carol McEldowney, Cathy Wilkerson, and Allen Young.) Still, Carl decided to

175

attend. And since Carl's partner, Allan Troxler, chose not to attend, he brought his gay friend Faigele Ben Miriam for support.

On the second day of the reunion, a workshop on gay issues was attended by two-thirds of the participants. Attendees sat in a circle, and gay and bisexual former SDS members spoke emotionally about their struggles.[3] However, Carl was angry that the discussion was soon hijacked by non-gays. He had "waited 15 years for time to talk about gay issues, and before half the allotted time was up, they had managed to get off the subject and talk about *their* hurts."[4] Moreover, sympathy toward gays among them was by no means unanimous. Others organized a competing workshop on the oppression they felt in SDS as members of working-class families and students of less elite colleges, and Carl was angered because he saw this as an intentional slight on gay oppression. Bob Ross disparaged the discussion of gay issues, saying that the issues weren't as serious as the hardships of working-class people.[5] Some members criticized Carl's behavior at the meeting.

In 2000 Helen Garvy produced a documentary on the SDS experience entitled *Rebels with a Cause*.[6] Interwoven with visual images and music from the sixties are interviews of twenty-eight leading SDS activists. The history of SDS is revealed through these differing perspectives. Several of those interviewed mention the suppression of women that personally affected them in the sixties in SDS, but not one of them raises the gay issue. One doubts that they omitted it because of conscious hostility but rather because, for them in the 1960s, it simply was not an issue of concern. In the sixties, homosexuality was commonly avoided as a topic of discussion. If the topic did come up, it was met with embarrassment or mocking derision (faggot jokes), and these attitudes continued to have a hold on SDS people's thinking.

In looking back on his own experiences with SDS in the sixties, Robert Pardun describes how oblivious he was to gay concerns. Whereas he was made aware of the oppression of blacks and women, he did not become aware of the oppression of gays because most of them "remained in the closet."[7] Pardun claims that SDS never confronted the gay issue because it remained below the surface and was never discussed. This view is shared by many former members of SDS. Although Todd Gitlin knew Carl through SDS activities, Gitlin's widely read book *The Sixties: Years of Hope and Days of Rage* (1987) makes only a single reference—a bibliographical citation in a footnote—to Wittman and only five passing references to homosexuality. By contrast, Gitlin's book gives extended treatment to the women's liberation movement. Apparently for Gitlin, as for many former SDS members, homosexuality was still a difficult topic to discuss. The reason why the gay issues were never discussed is because the atmosphere was so unsympathetic for discussion. That is also why, to this day, Carl's sexuality—and the sexuality of who knows of how many others—lingers in the history of these political radicals as a haunting ghost yet to be exorcised. For a long time, Carl had lived two separate lives, with one side of himself in the light for the movement and a second side of himself in the dark for sex. He finally tired of this schizophrenic lie, and that explains why his break with SDS was so irreparable.

But in another sense, he could *never* break from SDS. This realization struck him at the 1977 SDS reunion in Michigan: "I didn't belong in this group any more than I did back in 1966. (It was then when I quit, upset by the way leaders used women—but surely I was aware even in my closeted state that this was a bad place for me to come out in)."[8] But that fact didn't negate the emotional impact of the reunion. He compared it to a trip back to one's family or to one's high school reunion. At the 1977 reunion, Carl realized that SDS still had a power over him. The old responses were as deeply imbedded as his New Jersey accent, which only got more noticeable when he was tense. In the old settings, his new self, so carefully nurtured by gay liberation, grew thin.

Carl's criticism of SDS is reinforced by another member who believed, in retrospect, that SDS was practically an "elitist clique" and that the documentary *Rebels with a Cause* produced in 2000 comes close to hagiography. This critic saw the problem in SDS tied to a failure of leadership where the leadership structure became rapidly outdated. In this critic's view, the leaders ultimately led themselves and their friends over a cliff of self-destruction.

By 1980, Carl said that ten years of living in the country had changed his perspective on being gay. When Carl had first moved to Wolf Creek, Oregon, he had seen gay liberation as the "kingpin of everything" just as he had seen race and imperialism as the kingpins years before. His first years at Wolf Creek coincided with the growth of the women's movement and with lesbian separatism. Carl and others felt that patriarchy or sexism was the kingpin. But later on he felt that none of these issues got very far unless they were "seen in some larger context of some basic values about justice and decency."

He didn't doubt that the content of the "Gay Manifesto" was still true, but he had reservations about the uncompromising rhetorical form in which it was presented. It was "the quintessential rhetorical statement" that left no room for discussion.[9] While he felt that the condemnation of the oppression of women, gays, and blacks represented a "blinding truth" that, like the sun, you couldn't look at directly, he realized that the sun not only had the power to nurture but also to cause destruction. He realized that these political truths were such a powerful force that as a politico he had the power to "fuck up other peoples' lives." Because of this power and danger in politics, he had changed his approach. As he continued to offer dance lessons at Wolf Creek, he became aware of the power of dance to influence people. He compared dancing to the moon, reflected light; and he said, "moons don't make things grow the way the sun does and they don't cause droughts the way the sun does." That was why dancing was a medium with which Carl "could feel comfortable for decades and not just a couple summers of angry rebellion." When he said this he thought he had several decades of life left, in fact, he had less than six years.

The growing number of folk dancers at Wolf Creek led to the renovation of the barn, which was in desperate need of repair to avoid collapsing altogether. [10] Big parties were held in the barn, but there was a tension between Carl and Troxler: for the past ten years Carl had focused his efforts on the orchard, on building houses and on planting grapes at Wolf Creek. While he had been able to eke out a decent living by teaching at the college, Troxler had been unable to support himself on his artwork alone and, because of this, he decided to leave Wolf Creek and to return to his native North Carolina.

Allan Troxler was raised in Greensboro, North Carolina, along with one brother and three sisters. His father was a physician. His older brother Chris had been at Swarthmore with Carl and graduated one year after him in 1965. Allan followed his brother in going to Swarthmore and would have graduated in 1969, but he never finished his degree. He and Carl had many common friends and they first met at Troxler's brother's house in Oakland, California, early in 1972. He and Carl developed the longest-lasting romantic relationship of Carl's life.

When Troxler decided to return to North Carolina in early 1980, Carl went with him, despite his mixed feelings. [11] He loved Oregon and had created what he wanted there, but he wanted to be with Troxler. [12] In North Carolina Carl's health and dynamism both began to fade. His health began to deteriorate and his radicalism was less in sync with the times than it had been in the sixties or seventies. As a result, he was not striking as responsive a chord among potential converts and he became a more isolated figure. In one sense, his situation was the result of some degree of success of the gay liberation movement. As they gained greater acceptance from those around them, gays and lesbians felt less alienated from society and felt less called upon to challenge the system. Instead, they tried to make the system more responsive to their needs. While the culture of the sixties and seventies had fostered radicals, the culture of the eighties did not. But for Carl radicalism was not a lifestyle choice; it was part of his family background, his character, and his temperament. As a result, he was just as uncompromising during his last years as he had been in his earlier years and his charisma followed him to the end.

There were things that one woman friend did not understand about Carl's relationship with Troxler, particularly the nonmonogamous way of life. During their relationship, Carl and Troxler had other boyfriends. Conceding that having other boyfriends for sex while having a male partner was a gay men's thing, this friend nevertheless believed that Carl and Troxler loved each other.

This makes me wonder if I wasn't doing something similar with my wife. Was it a "gay men's thing" (a man's thing? an Italian-American man's thing?) that caused me to have all these other partners for casual sex while loving only Christine? Were these things that I learned or were they part of what I was? Was the loyalty I learned from my family leading me to love Christine while the liberation I learned from the sixties culture freed me to have impersonal sex with many men? Or was the blood of my family and ancestors driving me one way (toward loyalty to my wife) while the destructive force of Vesuvius was driving me in another direction (toward a thousand men)? For many years I struggled with the contradictions, but since Christine died, I just live with them. They are like my Labrador Retrievers who are with me every day, who demand something from me each day and who give me something in return. It's just the way my life is. Why try to change the way the sun rises and sets?

In 1980 Carl and Troxler bought adjacent old wood-frame houses in a poor neighborhood at 1808 and 1810 Vale Street in Durham, North Carolina. Initially theirs was a collective of lesbians and gay men, but like the collective at Golden, it soon became entirely male.[13] Carl threw himself into the project with typical enthusiasm and energy. He painted and wallpapered the inside of the house and built a greenhouse outside. He became an outspoken member of the Durham Food Co-op. He continued to fight for ecological causes by organizing opposition to toxic dumping in the neighborhood.[14]

Carl returned to Oregon in 1980 and later to participate in a dance camp in the summers of 1981, 1982, 1983, and 1984.[15] The last time people there recall him being back in Wolf Creek was in 1984. On his last visit he was intimate with a smaller group of friends than previously; people did not realize that the progression of HIV-AIDS was taking a toll on his previously abundant energy.

When Ronald Antonevich was murdered in April 1981 in Little River, North Carolina, by two men wanting "to beat up some faggots," Carl helped organize a memorial rally.[16] In 1982 after hearing stories of mistreatment of lesbians and gay men by local health care providers, he gathered friends to discuss a plan of action. He wanted to create a new 1970s-style grassroots self-help health clinic based on feminist models, but a friend and younger member of the group wanted to make already-existing health care providers more responsive to lesbian and gay needs. For a time, these two goals were blended in the creation of the North Carolina Lesbian and Gay Health Project (LGHP). But soon after the founding of the LGHP, a new illness began to absorb all of the organization's energy.

The sickness sometimes called the gay plague or gay cancer had first appeared in New York and San Francisco around 1980, and in 1982 it was named gay-related immune deficiency (GRID). This name was misleading because the illness could affect anyone who was exposed to body fluids that contained the virus: hemophiliacs, surgery patients who had received blood transfusions, infants born to infected mothers, heterosexual women with bisexual partners, and intravenous drug addicts who shared needles. Consequently, in 1982 the more neutral name acquired immune deficiency syndrome (AIDS) was adopted.[17] Isolated cases were starting to appear in North Carolina, and eventually the needs of AIDS sufferers for clinical, legal and emotional support caused the LGHP to become a service-providing organization. As this happened, Carl's original goal of organizing gays and lesbians to reject the assistance of public health institutions seemed less and less relevant. This led to his withdrawal from the LGHP. The powerful force of his will was ebbing, and fighting his illness became his last great battle.

In the 1970s and 1980s the average time from HIV infection to full-blown AIDS was commonly less than ten years. Consequently, it's probable that Carl acquired the virus in the late seventies. Based upon my sexual experience with him, I would guess that he acquired the virus through anal intercourse. I would guess, but don't know for a fact, that the virus passed from the body of an infected male into his body either through a rip in the wall of his rectum or through a sore resulting from an STD. The HIV virus is transmitted by the exchange of bodily fluids (mainly blood, semen, vaginal secretions, and breast milk).

The HIV virus effectively blocks certain types of white blood cells, mainly CD4 cells (also called helper cells or T4 cells) and monocytes/macrophages, all of which are crucial in early defense of the body from infection and cancer.[18] This results in a drastic loss of immunity and in the ability to fight off other infections. Few people die from the direct effect of HIV infection; most do so from the cumulative effect of numerous other opportunistic infections, cancers, and tumors.[19] In the eighties, these infections were barely treatable, less so than today, and included a wasting intestinal parasite, *Cryptosporidium*, that radically reduces body weight in a short period. Other common illnesses were thrush, progressive blindness, cytomegalovirus infection, cryptococcal meningitis, and, most ominously, *Pneumocystis* pneumonia (PCP). The painful itching blisters of shingles were common in the early stages, and dementia was commonplace near the end of life. The blackish-purple skin tumor called Kaposi's sarcoma (KS) was often an early disfiguring marker of AIDS.

Although the HIV virus is less contagious than the common cold, the transfer of bodily fluids through the rectum is a particularly vulnerable area because the mucous membrane lining the rectum is regularly torn during vigorous intercourse, which increases vulnerability. One of the more extreme forms of sex is S&M (sadism and masochism)—also referred to as "doing pain." Practices such as "fist fucking" (inserting the fist and arm into another male's rectum) are indicative of a particularly dangerous set of sexual practices, in terms of transmitting the HIV-AIDS virus. Carl's period of fascination with S&M bars in the summer of 1976 and 1977 might have been when he contracted the virus. However, a knowledgeable source who wishes to remain anonymous denies this and claims that he contracted the virus at another, unspecified time.

Sexual penetration is the ultimate form of intimacy. Driven by some primordial urge and intense affection, we seek to penetrate or be penetrated by someone we love or someone who simply charms us by his affection—top and bottom, lover and loved, man and wife. All the socializing of history cannot change the fundamental fact of our being. We penetrate or are penetrated. A kiss is still a kiss.

If Carl contracted AIDS through anal intercourse, then I am a survivor by fate. When I met Carl, I had no experience with anal intercourse. He and I took turns being top and bottom because ours was an equal relationship, not one based on dominance. But while he liked the experience of being a bottom, I did not. Carl was such a model for me that I not only had anal sex with him, but continued with other men over the next two months while I was following him in working as a male prostitute. After that experience ended, I stopped, but I continued to be intrigued why some guys enjoyed it so much. I was happy to be the penetrator, but I never found being penetrated to be much fun.

Who knows why we prefer certain forms of sex over others? The ancient Romans, my paternal ancestors, had nothing against anal intercourse between males, so long as the older or superior male was the top. For a male other than a boy or slave to be a bottom, and to be penetrated, was thought to be shameful.[20] Had my genes or my culture inherited this attitude? Was it a dominance syndrome? Or was it simply due to me not liking the way it felt? Many males of my generation probably attached a greater stigma to being a bottom than later generations have. It was part of a self-loathing (for being bottoms, for being effeminate, for not being attracted to girls) that many of us had internalized. The stark reality was that this simple preference probably saved me from contracting AIDS while it may have doomed Carl.

Although most friends did not learn of Carl's illness until near the end of his life, he told some friends that he had HIV-AIDS at the dance camp in June or July of 1984. Amy Beller had met Wittman in 1977 when she moved from Santa Cruz to the Wolf Creek area to live with her "sweetie" Alixe

Dancer on Cottage Lane, just up the road from Golden. It was Carl who introduced her to English and Scottish country dancing. He was one of the few men she had contact with because she was a "separatist" (believing in the separation of men and women) and she and her partner lived on lesbian land.

Beller was very fond of Carl. He taught her to see trees grow. Out on a walk one day, they came to a spot where he remembered when they planted the trees there. It was the first time Beller paid attention to trees growing. Now whenever she relocates, the first thing she does is plant trees. In Oregon, Carl had grown his hair in a long braid down his back and just before moving to North Carolina, Beller cut his hair because he was going back into the world. After Carl died, she was so affected by his death that she stopped dancing for almost six years because she could not dance without crying. Not until the early nineties did she finally begin to dance again.

Carl's cousin Marya Warshaw remembers him visiting New York in the early 1980s and complaining about feeling weak.[21] He had flu-like symptoms and skin rashes. He saw Dr. Dan Williams, one of the best-known gay physicians in New York City, who had an office on the Upper West Side, but AIDS treatment then was at a very early stage.[22] In fact, the virus that causes the illness was not even isolated and publicly identified until 1984.[23] That discovery led to the development of a blood test to determine if antibodies of the virus were present in one's body, the well-known test that categorizes one as HIV-negative or HIV-positive. However, the HTLV-III antibody test was not released for screening tests until February 15, 1985, too late to have been of much use to Carl.[24]

In his frame house at 1810 Vale Street in Durham, Carl fell visibly ill late in late 1984. His resistance to illness was low and he felt weak. In December of 1985 he came down with meningitis and suffered violent and uncontrollable vomiting. Still, the specific nature of his illness was not revealed to his friends in Durham until quite late. Mab Segrest reports learning that Carl had AIDS on December 20, 1985, only a month before he died.[25] He went into the hospital to have a catheter inserted into his chest that would enable him to be medicated at home.

In late 1985, Alixe Dancer was working in Woodstock, New York. (Ironically, Carl's sister Jane Van de Bogart lived in Woodstock, and Dancer met her there once by chance.) After dancing for Carl at the Oregon Shakespeare Festival in 1980, Alixe had seen him at the summer camps in 1981, 1982, and 1983. But she was unaware of his illness until she received the news from Troxler that he was dying of AIDS. The news came in the form of a special card designed and produced by Troxler and sent to several good friends. The card was beautiful and Dancer is not alone in her view that Troxler is a very talented artist.[26] She went to Durham and spent the last days of Carl's life with him, working on the dance book.

This dance book, entitled *Sun Assembly*, was a history and commentary on the teaching of English and Scottish country dancing.[27] It was Carl's obsession at the end, and he devoted nearly all of his waning energy to it, dictating details of the book almost until the day he died. One day Dancer decided to leave him alone and the next day he asked where she had been. It was because of her assistance in writing this dance book and because of their special friendship based on dancing that she was given more access to him than other friends during his last days. Many years after Carl's death, Troxler was still working on this dance book. It is not surprising that Carl was often impatient with Troxler's sense of time. But Dancer felt that the time lapse is understandable because of Troxler's artistry and his need for the book to be beautiful.

On Friday, January 15, 1986, Carl came home from the hospital for the last time.[28] His lungs and kidneys were failing, and the physicians were going to put him on a dialysis machine. Yet even with dialysis, the prognosis was that he had only three weeks to live. In the face of great opposition from the physicians, he refused dialysis and any further treatment. In addition to cryptococcal meningitis, he was now diagnosed with cryptococcal pneumonia. The prognosis now was that he had only three days left.

Carl's sister Jane visited him a week before he died. On Sunday the 19th Carl's parents made a last visit. There are differing views over whether his parents ever accepted his sexuality, but whether they did or not, this could not have been an easy last visit with their son. He had been their golden boy in whom they had invested so many hopes and dreams, and now he was dying young. One friend believes that the relationship between Carl and his parents was dominated not by their rejection of him but rather his rejection of them. He never reconciled himself to their manner of parenting and he was never close to them. In fact, he was closer to Troxler's parents than to his own. In his last visit with Troxler's parents, he told them how grateful he was that he had not infected their son. Troxler was not HIV-positive and this implies that the sexual part of their relationship probably had diminished several years before, a fairly typical phenomenon in long-term gay relationships.

Near the end, Carl asked Dancer, "How do you feel about me dying?" Of his own feelings, he said, "I'm not scared, I'm sad." He said to another friend: "Death, I don't mind so much. Pain, I do."[29] On Wednesday, January 22, he decided to implement the plan for ending his own life. He took things into his own hands one last time.

Nine friends gathered at 6:00 p.m. for a pot-luck dinner in the twin wood-frame house next door at 1808 Vale Street. It was a death watch. In Carl's room upstairs at 1810 Vale Street, Troxler read the last chapter of Anthony Trollope's novel *Barchester Towers* (1857). This is one of Trollope's best-known novels and it deals with the intrigues of clerical society in a nineteenth-century English cathedral town. Carl loved historical novels with an English setting. The one tangible thing that I have from him is a copy of John Barth's satirical *Sot-Weed Factor* (1960), which deals with the picaresque adventures of a character named Ebenezer Cooke who traveled from England to America in the late seventeenth century. I remember the sunny day in 1969 when he handed it to me. Finally, the two partners listened to Bach's *Goldberg Variations*. In the yard below the window the friends waited in the spring-like January night. Upstairs Carl inserted a suppository to prevent nausea, drank some of the kirsch liqueur left over from his grandmother's Christmas cookies, and then took a massive dose of sleeping pills. As he began to drowse, he took a dose of the sedative Seconal and of the painkiller Percodan. Troxler was with him when he died.

Afterward, friends entered the room. Mab Segrest writes of standing at the bottom of the bed and touching his foot, which was still warm. For the first time she noticed the gray in his beard. They placed his body in a black body bag and zipped it to his chin. Six of them then carried the body downstairs.

Carl's death certificate states that the immediate cause of death was respiratory failure due to *Pneumocystis* pneumonia (PCP) and acquired immune deficiency syndrome.[30] *Pneumocystis* pneumonia involved a yeast-like fungus that filled the air sacs of the lungs, causing the patient to suffocate. It can appear when the immune system has been suppressed, and it was in the 1980s the leading cause of death in terminal AIDS patients.[31] Other conditions listed as contributing to his death are cryptococcal pneumonia and cryptococcal meningitis. *Cryptococcus* is a parasite commonly found in bird droppings and it is normally prevented from infecting humans by healthy immune systems.[32] However, because AIDS suppresses the human immune system, cryptococcal pneumonia and cryptococcal meningitis were commonly found in terminal AIDS suffers during the 1980s. These conditions were very painful.

Today not only is *Pneumocystis carinii* pneumonia usually controllable by drugs, but the onset of full-blown AIDS can also be delayed indefinitely through the use of a cocktail of new, inhibitory drugs. Although AIDS remains an incurable illness, it is increasingly treated as a chronic illness like diabetes rather than a fatal one. But these medical advances came more than a decade after Carl's death. Aware that there was no cure, he refused to prolong a hopeless situation and become dependent upon professional health care. His rejection of that care in 1986 in the face of strong objections from numerous physicians and his decision to commit suicide was characteristic of his entire life. It was a personal decision, but it was also a defiant political act in which the personal was political. His death was recorded as one of 9,714 men who died of AIDS in 1986 in the United States.[33]

The time of Carl's death is given as 10:20 p.m. on January 22, 1986, one month before his forty-third birthday. The next day his body was cremated by the Duke University Medical Center. The death certificate lists his occupation as "teacher of dance," but for me, he was much more.

NOTES

1. The organizers were Jane Adams, Helen Garvy, Alan Haber, Barbara Haber, Ken McElldowney, and Terry Roberts.

2. A copy of communique #3 (July 10, 1977) is preserved in the Miriam Feingold Papers, 1960–1967, sheets 544–554. Wittman's mailing address given at the end of this quotation, 2503 Coyote Creek Road, is incorrect. It appears that someone mistakenly inverted the 2 and 3 in the street number. The Josephine County Assessor's Office in Grants Pass, Oregon, gives the street address of the Wolf Creek property as 3502 Coyote Creek Road.

3. Gregory Nevala Calvert, "Democracy and Rebirth: The New Left and Its Legacy," doctoral dissertation, University of California at Santa Cruz, 1989, 562.

4. Carl Wittman, "Us and the New Left," *Fag Rag* (Boston), Fall 1978, 23.

5. Calvert, "Democracy and Rebirth," 562–563.

6. *Rebels with a Cause*, produced and directed by Helen Garvy (New York: Shire Films, distributed by Zeitgeist Films, 2000).

7. Robert Pardun, *Prairie Radical: A Journey through the Sixties* (Los Gatos, CA: Shire, 2001), 183.

8. Wittman, "Us and the New Left," 23.

9. Taped interview of Carl Wittman by Marsha Emerman, Ashland, Oregon, 1980.

10. Dancing in the living room of the main house was impeded by a prominent pole, so the barn was repaired and the main hall of the barn was converted to a dance floor. Wittman, Emerman tape, 1980. One participant recalls Wittman and Troxler dancing together in plaid Scottish kilts, which Wittman enjoyed wearing.

11. With the decision to move to North Carolina, there was an attempt to sell the Oregon property; however, two sales (in 1981 and 1984) both later had to be foreclosed, presumably for lack of payment. By 1984 the flourishing gay and lesbian community at Wolf Creek had disintegrated. From a group that once numbered over thirty-five, it was reduced to a handful who had little contact with one another. Len Richardson, "Look Who's Coming Home," *RFD* 40 (fall 1984): 29. The residents of communal property in the seventies tended to be free spirits and not the most financially stable people. By the time of the second foreclosure in May 1986, Wittman was dead and his share of the property went to Troxler. In September 1990 Troxler ceded his share of the Wolf Creek property to Freeman by a warranty deed, and it was finally sold in April 1991. Information drawn from an old tax lot card in Josephine County Assessor's Office, November 13, 2001. Sometime in the early 1990s the main house at Wolf Creek had a tragic ending when it burned, killing two people in it.

12. Carl compared leaving the Oregon orchard he had planted to an enlightened parent who leaves his adolescent children alone when they are able to take care of themselves. He felt a tremendous relief about letting go of the responsibility of caring for the land and trees at Wolf Creek. He expressed it this way: "For more than ten years most of my work, my work-life has been built around Golden. . . . I do feel like this is a turning point. It is like graduation from country skills 101, 201, 301, 401 or something. . . . As for the objects themselves, I don't feel real attached. I feel like . . . it's all right if somebody else is enjoying those buildings or that fruit or whatever. Sometimes I get little qualms, you know, how discouraging to have to go start that all over again somewhere else. But mostly I don't look back. I feel good about, about the work there." Wittman, Emerman tape, 1980.

13. Mab Segrest, *Memoir of a Race Traitor* (Boston: South End Press, 1994), 43, 63.

14. As a leader of the Citizens for a Safer East Durham, Wittman collected signatures from the mainly black residents of the neighborhood. This led to the passage of Durham's toxic waste ordinance and the closing of the Armageddon Chemical Company. However, opposing

interests fought back and had this ordinance pre-empted by the North Carolina state legislature. When the pro-growth interests of Durham sought to build a civic center, Wittman opposed it and coauthored a study called "Durham's Convention Center: In Whose Interest?" Cited in the obituary "Carl Peter Wittman, 43, Community Leader," *Durham Morning Herald,* January 24, 1986, 14A.

15. When the regular choreographer of the Oregon Shakespearean Festival in Ashland took a leave of absence, Carl agreed to fill in for her. He returned to Oregon in February of 1980 and remained there until September or October. He assembled a group of ten dancers who ranged in age from Amy Beller at twenty-five to Alixe Dancer at forty. Carl's efforts in Oregon later evolved into a statewide organization called the Heather in the Rose dance group that had formed after Wittman's departure in 1980. This group attempted to remove gender distinctions from English and Scottish country dance. Carl returned to Oregon for several summers to participate in the dance camp organized by Heather in the Rose. It took place on a summer weekend at Camp Low Echo, a Girl Scout camp in the Oregon mountains.

16. The information in this paragraph on Wittman's activity in North Carolina in the early 1980s is taken from Ian K. Lekus, "Health Care, the AIDS Crisis, and the Politics of Community: The North Carolina Lesbian and Gay Health Project, 1982–1996," in *Modern American Queer History,* ed. Allida M. Black (Philadelphia: Temple University Press, 2001), 227–252.

17. Randy Shilts, *And the Band Played On* (New York: St. Martin's Press, 1987), 121, 171.

18. Paul Harding Douglas and Laura Pinsky, *The Essential AIDS Fact Book,* rev. ed. (New York: Pocket Books, 1996), 2.

19. *Merck Manual of Medical Information, Home Edition,* ed. Robert Berkow, M.D., et al. (New York: Pocket Books, 1997), 926–930.

20. See Craig A. Williams, *Roman Homosexuality: Ideologies of Masculinity in Classical Antiquity* (New York: Oxford University Press, 1999), 160–197.

21. Marya Warshaw interview, October 5, 2001.

22. Shilts, *And the Band Played On,* 11, 12, 18–10, 50, 152–154.

23. The sad story of the impediments and delays created by competition between not only the Pasteur Institute of Paris and Robert Gallo of the National Cancer Institute (NCI) but also within the U.S. government between the NCI in Bethesda, Maryland and the Centers for Disease Control (CDC) in Atlanta has been well told in Randy Shilts's book *And the Band Played On.*

24. Shilts, *And the Band Played On,* 514.

25. Segrest, *Memoir of a Race Traitor,* 52.

26. Dancer interview, November 28, 2001.

27. John Alexander, "Remembering Carl Wittman," *RFD* 46 (spring 1986): 7.

28. Most of the dates and details in the following description are from Segrest, *Memoir of a Race Traitor,* 59–63.

29. Segrest, *Memoir of a Race Traitor,* 60.

30. Certificate of death 001363, Carl Peter Wittman, Vital Records Branch, Division of Health Services, North Carolina Department of Human Resources, signed by Thomas R. Monk, MD, January 22, 1986.

31. Shilts, *And the Band Played On,* 34–35.

32. Shilts, *And the Band Played On,* 36, 59–60, 99–100.

33. US Bureau of the Census, *Statistical Abstract of the United States: 1990,* 110th ed., (Washington, DC: US Government Printing Office, 1990), p. 83, table no. 119. Over 90 percent of the 10,620 people recorded as dying from AIDS in 1986 were men; 906 were women.

Chapter Nineteen

The Horse Was Already Out of the Barn, 1996

Ten years after Carl's death I was sitting in an oncologist's office. One minute I was feeling hope and the next minute there wasn't enough air in the room to breathe. It was 3:00 in the afternoon on April 30, 1996. The oncologist had just told us that Christine's breast cancer had metastasized to her bones and that her condition was incurable. That was when we began our long descent into hell.

There was a lot of longevity in Christine's family and very little history of cancer on either side of her family tree. She had had regular mammograms, including one only three months before this diagnosis. Unfortunately, not all breast tumors can be detected by mammograms or by the radiologist reading them.[1] Although she had been called back for more X-rays, the radiologist had concluded that things were okay and that she need not come back for another year. (Later her oncologist at MD Anderson in Houston conceded that one of their radiologists probably could have detected the tumor in her X-rays.) However, she had questions about a pain in her right hip. Her gastroenterologist thought it was a referred pain from the gastrointestinal upset that she had been suffering from since January. But when her left nipple inverted, she decided that she needed to see a gynecologist.

The gynecologist didn't seem terribly concerned, but he referred her to a surgeon; an appointment took three weeks to schedule. The surgeon did an immediate needle biopsy that confirmed that she did have a malignant tumor and then scheduled a modified mastectomy. When we asked to see an oncologist, he said that normally that sort of consultation came after the surgery, but he did arrange an appointment. When we saw the oncologist, we asked for a bone scan. This was done the following day and at 3:00 p.m. we received the news that the breast tumor had metastasized. The mastectomy was canceled because, as her MD Anderson oncologist later put it, "the horse was already out of the barn."

Sometime (probably) in the early 1990s a tumor in Christine's left breast was activated. Much is unknown about cancer, but many physicians believe in a two-hit theory that combines genetic and environmental factors. According to this theory, some cells in one's body are genetically askew, altered from birth and made more susceptible to cancer. However, they still need to be activated by a carcinogen (a chemical, virus, radiation, or UV rays).[2] Who knows exactly? We didn't know, but we both believed that the tumor was activated by the estrogen skin patch that she began wearing at the time of her hysterectomy in 1991. Recent studies have confirmed that estrogen therapy not only can stimulate breast tumor growth but can also cause changes in breast tissue that make it harder for tumors to be detected with mammograms.[3]

Her hysterectomy in 1991 was elective; Christine decided to have it done together with some other surgery she needed to repair a minor problem involving bladder control. Although her ovaries were not removed, she was worried about preventing osteoporosis, a serious bone-deteriorating condition that was common in the women on her father's side of the family. Statistically she knew there was a small chance that the estrogen patch might cause cancer, but she regarded medicine as a rainbow of options. And so she opted for estrogen replacement therapy. I thought it was a bad idea and I felt the same way about her elective hysterectomy.

One reason for that is that I have a minimalist view of the powers of medicine. My view was shaped by my mother's belief in Christian Science. Although I did not practice this religion, I was influenced by it. I followed the suggestion of a physician for a particular therapy only if it was said to be absolutely necessary. That didn't keep me from taking (all too many) pills, including a beta blocker for high blood pressure. But both sides of my family tended to be short-lived, whereas her family, especially her father's family, was long-lived. Even her mother, a long-time smoker and emphysema sufferer, lived into her eighties.

We both assumed that Christine would inherit her family's longevity and that I would predecease her. She had the strong body of a natural athlete, but she had abused it. She'd begun smoking as a teenager and she did not give up cigarettes until she was thirty—it was not an easy task, but she had a lot of willpower. For a time she had a routine of throwing her cigarettes into the trash in the morning, only to be sifting through the trash in the evening trying to find one to smoke. She was among the first generation of women to use oral contraceptives, another risk factor for cancer. She had been raised in an English family for whom no vegetable was spared culinary destruction through overcooking. When we were raising our children, she would often cook a vegetable for the rest of us but not eat it herself, except for frozen green peas and canned corn. We joked about how much we differed in our taste for foods. She ate Twinkies and I ate granola.

Christine liked fatty junk foods and she often indulged herself. She would gain a few pounds and then go on a diet to take them off, again counting on her willpower. One time at a restaurant, we argued about some particularly greasy food she had ordered. She angrily told me that she would eat what she wanted. After that, the subject became taboo. Unfortunately, a diet high in fat increases one's risk of developing breast cancer. Later, after she had been diagnosed with metastatic breast cancer, she admitted that she had been "overconfident" and had abused her body, but by then it was too late. And I was too distraught by her condition to claim having been right. Anyway, one of the things that made our marriage long-lived (although far from perfect) was that we both gave the other person room to choose.

In her initial reaction to the devastating news, Christine lay on the floor in the den and was tearful, depressed, angry and defiant—all at the same time. She was bitter about missing out on one of her greatest desires—enjoying grandchildren. She was full of fight, but her fighting spirit would weaken as her body deteriorated over the next nineteen months. She also mentioned the possibility of taking her own life, but I told her I would not help her with that and we never discussed suicide again.

After the diagnosis of Christine's cancer, friends and contacts at Baylor helped us to get an appointment within days at the MD Anderson Cancer Center in Houston, one of the world's leading treatment centers for cancer. In our first meeting with the oncologist, Dr. Daniel Booser, he made it very clear that although there was no known cure available at that time, a number of aggressive treatments were available that could prolong life. Moreover, there was always the hope that there would be a breakthrough with a new and more effective treatment. Much to our regret, we would learn over the next few months that most of the advances in dealing with cancer over the past few decades had been in the area of diagnosis and prevention rather than cure. And so we began. None of the treatments that we pursued over the next nineteen and a half months were very effective, and yet, in retrospect, I doubt that we would have been satisfied without trying them all.

The first good news came with the estrogen receptor test on which Christine's cancer had a nearly 100 percent positive reading. This was an important indicator that the cancer might be responsive to hormonal therapy that could block or slow the growth of cancer cells. This could allow Christine to avoid an immediate, traumatic treatment like chemotherapy. The treatment that the oncologist recommended at first surprised us. The day her breast cancer was diagnosed in Waco, Christine had removed the estrogen skin patch. The oncologist at MD Anderson recommended no treatment other than "watchful waiting" for the time being (although Christine had her doubts).

At the time of the initial diagnosis I had felt that Christine was dying and would not live through the summer. She was in constant pain; she could barely get up from a seated position without help; she could not bend over to pet the dog; her sleep was very restless; and as a husband sleeping beside her, I was very aware of her moaning from the pain every time she turned at night in bed.

But then things began to improve. The tumor in her breast became smaller and more diffuse. The areas of bone (in the hips and back) where the cancer had metastasized and damaged the bone showed signs of reossification. And another positive sign: the oncologist did not want to see her again until September 1996—nearly three months away. For a while, she was much better; her energy level was higher, she could get up from a chair without help, she could bend over to pet the dog, and she did not moan in her sleep when she turned.

The day we received the diagnosis of metastatic breast cancer, Christine, by some cruel irony, received the offer to become director of the new ESL program at Baylor. She had to turn it down although she had negotiated for it for months. By good fortune, it was offered to another woman who could do it only for the summer and so the offer came back to her again, and by that point, she was feeling well enough to accept. She loved this kind of work (the students, teaching, and administration) and her life now had something very positive to focus on.

How close can we get to another person? Even when that other person is someone we love, there is a distance. Four years after Christine died, I found a journal that she had kept during the first six months of her illness. Although I remember her saying that several people had suggested she keep a journal, I never realized that she had done so. At the beginning, her entries were hopeful. On May 4, 1996 she wrote:

> More time has gone by and now I've been to MD Anderson, which has at least given us some hope. I've always thought I was courageous, but lately have been doubting my resolve. Or rather, waffling and wavering again. My bones are hurting more and I feel like it's spreading to more spots. The other part of me resists this. I try to picture nasty cancer cells being killed from lack of estrogen. I picture them crying out for estrogen and then dying. I'm going to learn how to meditate too. I think anything I can use to marshal my mental energies will help. I also picture God's love as a warm force enveloping me and supporting and curing me.
>
> . . . I'm not crying so much any more—wonder if this means I've moved to another phase—stage (hate that word).
>
> Tomorrow we go back to MD Anderson for more tests—Lisa will take me. I just glory in being with her, basking in her glow. . . . I look at David and can't believe that I took our love for granted recently. The tie between a man and a woman who've been together 30 years is an amazing thing. We're so connected, but I never cherished the connection as I do today. I'd cherished the

children, but taken D for granted. I find myself wanting to touch and hold him, to feel his strength and lean on it.

However, over the next six months, the changed tone soon reflected her discouragement until she wrote:

kind of a down day. We've had a good time with the . . . I can't read my own writing anymore. I'm going to have to swear to write larger and more carefully.

Her writing in the entry dated November 2, 1996, had become so illegible that even she could not read it. Although she would live for another thirteen months, she made no further entries in her journal.

An unfavorable comparison that Christine made in her journal between her lack of self-discipline and my obsessive sense of discipline was a standing joke. She had a normal sense of personal discipline. My greater discipline was part of a driven personality that enabled me to focus on a project for months or even years at a time. It had both positive and negative sides and tended to create both good and bad habits. It enabled me to achieve what I set out to do, but there was also a compulsive aspect that would drive me in ways that were not particularly admirable. I was frequently restless. Things never moved fast enough for me. My compulsiveness was part of my sexuality and what drove me into sexual encounters with a thousand men. But it was also part of my commitment to my wife that sustained my part of the relationship through good and bad times. It helped get me through those days when the morning began with despair at 5:00 a.m. and I knew that things were going nowhere but down.

While Christine was beginning her treatment for cancer, my mother's health was failing. She had fallen ill at her home in Florida the previous year and her second husband was both unwilling and unable to care for her. So she moved to an apartment near my brother Mark in New Jersey. My brother had left the Jesuit order and was a practicing attorney. He had married a warm and attractive woman named Ann Marie (Anna Maria) from an Italian-American family in south Philadelphia, and they cared for my mother during the last year of her life. My mother was a very spiritual woman who lived her religion on a daily basis, and I am astounded that she lived through the cancer that killed her without painkillers. She suffered with great dignity until November of 1996. Only at the end when the necrosis was invading her body did she allow my brother to take her to a hospital. She received a morphine injection and stopped breathing. She was eighty-two.

I did not go to her funeral, although by not going I felt I had failed to perform one of my duties as a son. But my feelings toward my mother were deeply conflicted, and at the time I lacked the energy to fight any other battle beyond what Christine and I were engaged in. I knew there was no set structure to the funeral of a Christian Scientist and so there would be no ritual to get me through the process. Funerals are not very important in Christian Science because the religion denies the reality of material things like the human body. Death is a non-event; only spiritual things are real. My mother believed that her soul was far more important than her body, and she was absolutely convinced that her soul would live on after her body had perished. For her, it was a good thing to be released from her body and Christian Science sees very little to mourn in death. It is a viewpoint without passion and it is alien to my soul.

Although Christine's estrogen receptor test had been very positive, hormonal therapy (part of a clinical study in which she received either a new drug Droloxifene or the standard drug Tamoxifen) had limited effectiveness. And so in early December 1996 she began chemotherapy using a combination of an experimental drug Taxol with Adriamycin, administered once every three weeks on an outpatient basis in Houston.

During her trips to Houston for treatment, I would ask friends or relatives (her brother or our daughter or son) to make the 180-mile-plus drive with her instead of going myself. Christine preferred me to go with her, but I felt unable to constantly face the hopelessness of our situation. I had a lot to learn about dealing with medical emergencies, and at first I was not up to the challenge. Late one night Christine began experiencing intense intestinal pain due to gasses created by her treatments. I was tired and intimidated by the prospect of taking her to the hospital, a place that since moving to Waco I had never visited. So although she wanted me to take her, I hesitated and the pain eventually receded. A week or so later I had to take her to the hospital to deal with her nausea and I learned the procedure. Over the next year, I would check her into the Hillcrest Baptist Medical Center numerous times, at any and all hours of the day and night.

Going to the hospital was always unpleasant. The emergency room was always jammed with people suffering from all kinds of maladies, from broken bones to gunshot wounds. When we were finally called into a curtained cubicle, we answered questions that had been asked many times previously by medical personnel who had never seen us before and who probably never would again. Some of them were not used to dealing with patients with advanced cancer. I recall one young intern looking at me with almost terror in his eyes when I explained my wife's condition. He asked me (it was 1:00 a.m. in the morning), "Do you realize how sick your wife is?" I sensed that he somehow hoped we would go elsewhere.

Eventually I learned how to ask our private physician to admit Christine directly so that we could avoid the emergency room. She would be admitted straight to the hospital's eighth floor, which was reserved for cancer patients and was decorated with paintings and comfortable furniture. The best moment of every trip there was checking her out. The trip home always gave us a brief moment of happiness.

NOTES

1. *Merck Manual of Medical Information, Home Edition,* ed. Robert Berkow, M.D., et al. (New York: Pocket Books, 1997), 1097.

2. *Merck Manual of Medical Information,* 789–791.

3. Denise Grady, "New Evidence of Cancer Risk in Hormone Therapy Study," *New York Times,* February 13, 2002, and "Study Finds New Risks in Hormone Therapy," *New York Times,* June 25, 2003.

Chapter Twenty

Memento Mori, 1996–1997

Watching someone we love die is one of the most painful experiences in life. When I read Paul Monette's moving account of his partner's sickness and death from AIDS in 1985–1986, I was struck by the time between his lover's diagnosis and death: nineteen months and ten days.[1] For Christine it was nineteen months and nineteen days. There were amazing parallels between the two illnesses, even though one was AIDS and the other was cancer. But while the parallels are striking, I have never understood why I have survived and Carl and Christine did not.

For 598 days we battled Christine's cancer until we were in a state of exhaustion. Our life became an emotional roller coaster. Christine and I never thought this would happen to us. These sorts of horrible things only happen to other people, don't they? One of the worst things was her vomiting, which became chronic. None of the drugs (Compazine, Metoclopramide, and Phenergan) would stop the vomiting and so it continued until the last day of her life. Her breast cancer continued to metastasize into her bones, mainly her hips and vertebrae. I am told that this is one of the most painful cancer conditions to bear. She would ask me to drive slowly over bumps in the road because of the pain.

December of 1996 was the last Christmas that Christine sang with the church choir. She wore a decorative cap to cover the loss of her hair, her beautiful blond hair that I had been helping in the last few years to lighten with one of those hair-tinting kits requiring a rubber cap and holes. I would pull patches of her hair through the holes with something like a knitting needle. She looked ridiculous wearing that cap with her hair sticking out in tufts and we got almost hysterical laughing about it, but the resulting blond highlights always looked nice and reminded me of the beauty of her youth. She also had a very good facial bone structure. By December of 1996 she was using a cane to ease the pain in her hips. But she sang with the choir at St. Paul's Episcopal Church that Christmas Eve midnight mass. At the end of the mass, everyone sang "Silent Night." Christine came to the back of the church where our family and I were sitting and we all sang it together as the lights in the church were dimmed. It was one of those moments I will always remember because of the symbolism: the light was beginning to dim in her own life as well. She was leaving me.

Beginning the day after Christmas in 1996, Christine underwent ten days of emergency radiation treatments in Houston. The treatment involved such massive doses of radiation that it could only be done once. This experience devastated my daughter Elise, who spent those ten days with her mother in Houston. Ever since her childhood, my daughter was filled with a sense of doing the right thing. She could become indignant when she saw someone doing the wrong thing, but she was saved from self-righteousness by always making the greatest demands on herself. She is one of the most dependable people I know and later she became a totally devoted mother. Elise is a problem-solver and at the time of her mother's final illness she had difficulty dealing with a problem that could not be solved. The very deep bond in their relationship was being reversed too quickly for her to adjust. At the time she was also confronting those flaws in her husband that would lead eventually to the destruction of her own marriage—she no longer felt able to turn to her mother for help. Something in her was crushed by these experiences and she began to withdraw emotionally.

By contrast, my son Michael was one of the most undependable people I had ever known. He had attended Sewanee (the University of the South), a very traditional, Episcopalian liberal arts college in southern Tennessee. Its 10,000-acre campus, called "the Domain," sits atop a beautiful and remote forest-covered mountain in the Cumberland Plateau. It is a wonderful college and full of opportunities that he studiously avoided in passive-aggressive style while using recreational drugs, which would eventually lead to his addiction. His mother and I bought plane tickets to attend his graduation not once but twice, and each time had to cancel the reservations at the last minute when the dean of students called to say that Michael would not be graduating. He finally did graduate and applied his degree to delivering pizzas.

And yet this unmotivated, unreliable son, whom his mother and I had been forced to ask to move out of our house, began to do things that no one else wanted to do. He changed the catheter dressing on his mother's arm (used for chemotherapy) with regularity and without the slightest murmur. Just a few days before Christine died, we had one of the spring-like days that intersperse the winters in central Texas. He took his mother out for a ride in her wheelchair. I remember looking through the window and seeing him briskly roll her down the street.

The radiation of Christine's lower back devastated her digestive system, giving her chronic and violent diarrhea that debilitated her further and from which she never fully recovered. The massive doses of corticosteroids changed her personality dramatically. She became so nervous that she could not sit still for more than a few minutes. And yet she was too feeble to walk about on her own and, if she tried, she would fall on the floor. This continued day and night while she was on the steroids. Once I was so exhausted by her calls in the middle of the night to help her get up (she would beg me to help her) that I simply covered her with a blanket and left her on the living room rug where she had fallen.

After the radiation treatment, chemotherapy with Adriamycin and Taxol at MD Anderson continued at three-week intervals throughout most of 1997. The infusions lasted three hours and were usually administered to her in the evening after an exhausting day of consultations and tests. There is a wonderful hotel called Rotary House, run by the Rotary Club, just across the street from MD Anderson and linked to it by a skywalk. That skywalk made it easier to bring Christine back to our room in a wheelchair. The hotel kept wheelchairs everywhere so that they were at hand whenever we needed one.

Almost all of the guests at Rotary House were cancer patients or relatives and friends, and everything was arranged to ease their strain. I remember the women guests in particular with their gaunt bodies and creative hair coverings over their bald heads. They were like a sisterhood. (Now I can often identify women who are undergoing chemotherapy and I want to go up to them and tell them how sorry I am for what they are going through; but of course, I don't.) Although tests indicated that Christine's cancer markers were down and that she fell into the 60 percent response rate for that particular chemotherapy, she never attained remission and continued to lose height as well as weight.

In September of 1997 we made a difficult decision. In order to avoid her losing bladder control and the ability to walk, she underwent an eight-hour surgical operation in Houston to fuse some collapsed vertebrae. The surgery was successful but she never fully recovered. As the cancer progressed, her vomiting became even more chronic, and in November a food tube was inserted into her intestines (jejunum) in order to prevent her from starving. During 1997 she was hospitalized almost monthly at a local hospital in Waco in order to stabilize her condition. When the veins in her arms became exhausted from having been poked with needles, an infusion port was implanted into her chest to receive injections. She needed Phenergan shots every few hours to ease the nausea. I remember her patting my hand in relief as I emptied the syringe into the catheter.

In the spring of 1966, before Christine and I were married, we had visited her grandmother and maiden aunts (Auntie Kittie and Auntie Norah) in Hempstead, Long Island. The elderly Mrs. McKegg was ninety years old and a tiny, shrunken little old lady who spoke with a very British accent and who was somewhat imperious in manner, although kind to me. In 1997, thirty-one years later, Christine's cancer had ravaged her body to the extent that she looked very much like her ninety-year-old grandmother had, although she was only fifty-one. The cancerous deterioration of her vertebrae had caused her to lose inches in her height. Her chronic vomiting and inability to eat caused her muscles to atrophy, so much that the skin hung loosely on her body and legs. The wasting of muscle and other tissue due to malnutrition is called cachexia, and she acquired the haunting look of a Holocaust prisoner. Her aging was so pronounced that an embarrassing event happened on one of our many trips to the local hospital to stabilize her vomiting. After I wheeled Christine into her room, the young nurse turned to me and asked if I would like to wait outside while she undressed my mother. It was the sort of remark that one lets pass as gently as possible.

I had never been very teary-eyed, but now I cried a lot. I almost always cried alone, but once when Christine was still asleep, I sat at my desk in our bedroom watching her and started quietly to cry. Suddenly her eyes opened and she saw me; and our roles were reversed as she began to comfort me and said, "I never realized how much you loved me." That was soon after her diagnosis in the spring of 1996. Later, about a month before she died in December of 1997, a good friend, Shari Hoech, was visiting from Iowa and helping care for Christine. At one point I was so overcome by grief over the inevitable that I asked Shari if she could leave us alone for a little while. I knelt down by Christine's side of the bed and I buried my face in her lap. My tears were uncontrollable. As sick as she was, lying there sustained by a tube of liquid food running into her digestive tract, she patted my head and once again comforted me. I didn't plan it that way, but I think it was good for her to feel, at least for just a moment, that she was still needed. That's what love is, isn't it?

After Christine died, there was a tendency for some people to praise me in caring for her, but I knew that I was repaying a debt. At times, I could not hide my despair over the hopelessness of her condition. I had always tended to walk faster than her and we had joked about it, but once when she was well into her illness we were walking from the parking lot to the hospital entrance, I intentionally walked ahead of her. She was even slower than before due to her need for a cane. It was very cruel of me and she made some comment, which made me feel ashamed.

Numerous generous people helped us: Christine had always bonded well with other women and these women were very loyal. I have a photo of a gathering of three of these friends (Ann Karaffa, Wanda LeMaster, and Dottie Mathews) with her. Christine was wearing a hat because she had lost her hair due to the chemotherapy, and so they all wore hats to match hers. Visitors are often afraid to touch sick people, but Dottie climbed onto the bed and lay down beside Christine and that's exactly what she needed. Sick people need to be touched, like the rest of us. Her friends from Iowa, Barbara Drexler and Shari Hoech, visited more than once and drove her to Houston for her chemotherapy. Christine's brother, Al, also came and drove her to Houston. A woman from our church named Donna Ragland, who Christine felt comfortable with, once drove her to Houston for treatment.

Some people felt unable to visit in person and sent flowers instead. This became a problem because our cat liked to eat flowers and they had to be put out of the cat's reach. At one point our mantel was loaded with them while I was cursing the cat. Much more appreciated was the food that was sent by people like B.J. Smith, a woman in the church choir with her own physical problems. Toward the end, the illness and the pain had so ravaged Christine's attention span that she could not even follow a television program, much less read a book. The one thing that she really enjoyed was visits by friends. Some friends, mostly women, were very loyal in this. But most people, for very understandable reasons, were not capable of dealing with such a situation. They felt awkward, they did not know what to say, some felt they were impinging on Christine's privacy, or they were upset at the prospect of looking death straight in the face.

In the early 1980s I had developed a working relationship with a genial Jesuit priest named Edward J. Malatesta, SJ. Our ancestors came from the same region of Italy. His family came from Caserta, the site of the grand palace built by the king of Naples in the eighteenth century, only a few miles northwest of my ancestral village of Roccarainola. After immigrating to the United States, the Malatestas finally settled in Los Gatos, California. Initially trained with a doctorate in Scripture from the Pontifical Gregorian University in Rome, Father Ed began studying Chinese in 1979 and became deeply involved with Chinese Catholics in mainland China. In the fall of 1989 he became the first Western professor in almost forty years to teach a theology course at the Sheshan Catholic seminary near Shanghai. We collaborated in organizing international symposiums on China and Christianity in 1992 in San Francisco and in 1996 in Hong Kong.

In November of 1997 Father Ed underwent prostate surgery. The following month he flew to Dallas to meet with a corporate head in the hopes of putting the University of San Francisco Ricci Institute on an endowed financial footing. In spite of the fact that he was still visibly suffering from the effects of his prostate surgery, on the afternoon of December 15 he drove a hundred miles south to Waco to say goodbye to Christine. He sat by her side of our bed and said a simple celebration of the Eucharist with the three of us sharing the bread and the wine.

Father Ed died in Hong Kong just a short while later, on January 27. He had returned on his thirty-second trip to China in order to make contact with the Catholic seminarians to whom he felt so committed. In Shanghai he developed a bad cold that aggravated his asthma, and he was flown to Hong Kong where he died of a pulmonary embolism, a common postoperative problem with prostate surgery.

The day after Father Ed's visit, I returned from work to find my wife smiling. Seated beside her bed was my colleague from the history department, Jim Vardaman. I have never met a more powerful combination of tough Texan, learned Anglophile, and gentle soul than Jim Vardaman. Earlier in the spring, he had brought the Anglican theologian Michael Mayne and his wife from England to visit. It had been springtime and we all talked on the back patio beneath two giant elms filled with fresh green leaves and chirping birds. And for a moment, Christine was happy again. Now it was now six months later and Vardaman had come again, this time to say goodbye. He later told someone that he visited Christine because "his soul had to touch her soul." He brought a small, bright moment of happiness to her last days.

There is much that I would like to forget about my wife's suffering, but one image I will never forget is coming home to see her smile, one of the last times. Three days later she was dead.

NOTES

Memento mori refers to the ancient practice of meditating on one's inevitable death and contrasting the passing and vain nature of earthly rewards with eternal verities and the immortality of the soul.

1. Paul Monette, *Borrowed Time: An AIDS Memoir* (San Diego: Harcourt Brace, 1988).

Chapter Twenty-One

Christine's Death, 1997

Guilt shadowed me and caused me to wonder if I had been the cause of my wife's cancer. Could I have contracted some bacteria or virus from one of my casual encounters with men? The detection of hepatitis B antibodies in my blood in 1988 had indicated that I had contracted hepatitis B (possibly through sexual contact in Germany in 1984). Hepatitis B has recently been added to the list of known carcinogens. The papillomavirus that causes genital warts is thought to be a cause of cervical cancer in women. I never had genital warts (although I might have been an asymptomatic carrier), and my wife did not have cervical cancer. After a brief period of exposure in 1969, I had avoided anal sex. Even so, I wondered.

It is difficult for those unfamiliar with same-sex relations among men in the 1960s and 1970s to comprehend the significance of sexual contacts. For many men like me, a sexual contact was made as casually as taking a drink of water. Nevertheless, I had absorbed an attitude from my father's Italian background. The family was sacred, and so a man was loyal to his family. A man did not desert his wife. For me, it was an absolute if flawed loyalty. The casual sex I had with males never threatened my marriage. Carl was the only one who threatened my relationship with Christine because he was the only man I loved. But had the casual sex caused me to introduce an alien bacteria or virus into my wife's body? Was I loyal or disloyal or both? I don't know the answer, and my guilt would not let the question go away.

I hated Christine's cancer. It was an enemy and even if I wanted to, I could not escape it. But I did not want to escape it; I wanted to fight it. From the very beginning, we never hid the fact that she had untreatable cancer: we confronted it head on. Sometimes I was too brutal, as when I took her to see the cemetery plots I had bought for our burials. She cried, of course, since for me it was a prospect far in the future, but for her it was imminent. As much as I confronted her cancer directly, I can't kid myself into thinking that I always faced reality. I was so intent on fighting her cancer that I failed to see the signs that we had lost. In the fall of 1997 Betsy Oates, a friend from our church who regularly visited Christine, asked me if I realized that Christine was going to die. She was, of course, right. Christine was going to die and we needed to prepare for it. I tried, but Christine was much better at accepting her approaching death than I was. I fought it so much that when she did die, I was only a few feet away and didn't realize that she was gone.

On December 17, 1997, two days before her death, we sent out our last Christmas card. At the end, we conveyed the inevitable with the following words.

> Our physical horizons have shrunk to the confines of our bedroom and adjoining bathroom where most of our time is spent. We hold hands lying in bed, we laugh at our bad jokes, Christine leans her head on my shoulder as I help her walk. Her head falls much lower on my shoulder than it used to, my hands feel the bones poking through her back and we march on together to the end. For 31 years we have sent out a Christmas card and this will be the last time that we join together in wishing each of you the joy of Christmas and the blessing of a new year filled with happiness.

When we gave up all hope for treatment, we turned to a hospice for help and the angels of death arrived to care for Christine. They included a very efficient nurse who visited almost daily to deal with her medical needs and a very gentle large black woman who came every weekday to bathe her. She would never see a physician again. I didn't realize how close to death she was and thought she would live through Christmas and into January.

I did not want her to give up, although there was very little left for her to enjoy in life. She could no longer eat without vomiting and she was surviving only because of the liquid nourishment called Sustecal that flowed through a tube into her digestive tract. And even so, she still continued to suffer from nausea and vomiting. My son-in-law had installed a television above her side of our bed with earphones so that she could watch when I was sleeping, but she no longer had the concentration (or interest) to watch anything very long. I recall lying on my side of the bed in the middle of the night with the patterns of light and shadow from the television screen flickering on the wall as she channel surfed continuously . . . click, click, click.

In order to qualify for hospice care, Christine's local physician had written a letter indicating his prognosis and he'd sent it by fax to my office. When I read it, I was astounded by his statement that she had only one or two months to live. Logically, I knew that was true, but emotionally I was not ready to see it stated so starkly. Still, I could not let her go. I prided myself on being able to take of her. I fought against using the portable toilet at the side of the bed: I could not let her give up making the short trip of a few feet from her side of the bed to the bathroom. I would help her. We would refuse to give up. Now that I look back, I see that she was going along only to please me. She was giving up hope because she knew the end was near, and all my willfulness and help could not stop the inevitable degeneration of her body that would make her one of 41,943 women who died of breast cancer in 1997 in the United States.[1]

I wondered if I denied Christine the freedom to take her own life in the way that Carl did. When she once raised the possibility of suicide, it was on the day of her diagnosis, and whether she said it out of anger and despair or as a serious option, I don't know. I do know that I refused to have any part in a suicide attempt at that time and I would have refused if she had raised the matter later. Toward the end, she was not capable of ending her life without help. Christine always had a way of finding joy in small things and even on the last day of her life, she was waiting to hear from our daughter about the results of a test on the twins she was carrying. Elise's first sonogram indicated that one of the twins was a boy, but it took a second sonogram to determine the sex of the other child. She was waiting to hear the news on the day she died and it gave her one good thing to focus on in the midst of her despair.

It was decided that a catheter would be inserted into her bladder so that she would not have to move to and from the toilet. This was to be done on the morning of December 19, 1997, a Friday. But I would continue to help her move to the bathroom until then. As I helped her rise from the bed that morning, she suddenly lost control of her bladder and collapsed on the floor. Her death certificate would list the immediate cause of death as pulmonary edema, a form of congestive heart failure.[2] Her heart, weakened by malnutrition and hindered by blood leaking into surrounding tissue (edema), could no longer supply her body with enough blood and she passed out. Her bones seemed to give way as she crumpled on the floor. Her body looked like a puddle of flesh lying on the carpet.

We were alone. There was no one else in the house to help me, and in that silent moment, I was overwhelmed by grace. This may sound overly dramatic, but unless you have been alone with someone who died, then you will not understand what I am saying. If someone were to ask me the high point of my life, I would answer with that moment. For in that moment I had been given the chance to redeem myself for the hurt that I had caused her to feel twenty-eight years before when I left her pregnant during the week of her twenty-third birthday to go off with Carl. I lifted her (she had become so light) and lay her on the bed on her side. I kissed her. Had I known she was leaving me, I would have kissed her again.

As a boy I had seen so many movies at my father's theaters that I always wondered about deathbed scenes. Did the lover really gaze into the eyes of his beloved as she returned his loving look, breathing her last and closed her eyes? For us, it was not like that. After collapsing on the floor, Christine never opened her eyes again. Did her body suffer some violent trauma that took her, even as I needed to believe that I was helping her? Perhaps, but I hope that she lost consciousness less suddenly. I thought she was still with me until a few minutes later, when the hospice nurse arrived and took her pulse. She turned to me and said, "Dr. Mungello, she's gone."

The first time I saw Puccini's opera *La Bohème* performed was at the Rock Creek Park outdoor summer theatre in Washington, D.C., I was nineteen years old and had not yet met Christine. The tragic love affair of Mimì and Rudolfo ends with Mimì's death by consumption. The emotional crescendos of the music are not for everyone, but it stirred something in me. It's as if my soul were anticipating my fate but, of course, that's impossible, isn't it? Little did I realize that Christine and I would one day act out the parts of Mimì and Rudolfo when Christine died alone with me in our bedroom. At the end Rudolfo thought Mimì was merely sleeping, but she was really dead. I thought the same thing about Christine. The only difference was that when Christine died, there was no music. It was absolutely quiet.

When I lifted her from the floor and laid her on the bed, I believed that in some way she would have sensed that she had been lifted and kissed. I need to believe that, although I knew that kiss could never wipe away all the hurt of twenty-eight years before. Grace is something we do not earn. We don't deserve it.

The month after my wife died, my anger and grief were so intense that I drove around aimlessly every night (as I've said, I am compulsive). I have never liked bars and so was out sitting in my parked car late one evening in a park. It also happened to be a park frequented by local gays. Two guys started talking to me. Both of them were redneck types in their thirties, one blond and overweight with a large beer belly and the other dark and thin. If I had met them in other circumstances, I would have had nothing to say to them, but here I was late at night, killing time, walking around with them. As we walked around, I could not understand why they kept patting my jacket. Only later did I realize they were queer bashers and were checking to see whether I was carrying a gun (concealed handguns are legal in Texas).

They wanted me to walk to the edge of a spillway where water flowed in a fast current down from a reservoir above. There was a railing around the spillway to keep people from falling in and drowning. I must have sensed a danger in going that close to the water and some sort of self-preservation instinct led me to refuse. Then they asked if I wanted to sit in their car. One sat at the wheel, I sat on the right side of the front seat and the other one sat in the back. Suddenly I felt a sharp thud (something like a tire tool) hit the back of my head. And then a second time. The blows must have been audible because a car parked on the other side of the road quickly drove away. I became very calm, maybe more focused than calm and yet (this will sound strange) exhilarated. My adrenal glands were pumping like mad. I got out of their car, got into my car, while they sped off, put my cap on backwards to slow the blood flow and drove to the hospital emergency room. I didn't know how deep the wounds were, but I knew that I had to get to the emergency room soon because there was a good bit of blood flowing down my neck and I didn't know if I was going to pass out.

I didn't pass out. Superficial scalp wounds bleed a lot and all that blood makes them look more serious than they really are. But while I was waiting in the emergency room, among all these sick and wounded people (everyone has to wait his turn), the memories of all the times I had sat in that same room waiting with Christine flooded back. The blood I had shed was nothing compared with what she had gone through. When the physician who stapled my head shut asked if I had been assaulted, I told him that a stored lawn mower had fallen on my head. I don't think he believed me. I guess I was lucky to be alive, but I really didn't care very much at that point. In the months after Christine died, I would sometimes see a woman who from behind looked so much like her that I would rush forward to see. Of course, it wasn't her. At other times I would look around and wonder how so many women could continue to live, while she was gone.

The hospice nurse once said to Christine that she worried that I did not show my grief more visibly. After Christine died, hospice kept sending me invitations to share my grief with others at these group sessions. They were well intentioned, but my love for Christine had been intensely private. Now that she was gone, there was no one to share it with. Love does not end when we say goodbye. Love continues for as long as we feel it in our heart. Several months after she died, Christine appeared to me in a dream. Her features were swollen and puffy, as if decomposing in the grave, and she could not talk, but she had an urgent message for me that our daughter, who was standing beside her in the dream, delivered. She was okay. What did that mean? Was it just a dream or was it her love reaching from beyond the grave? It was both upsetting and comforting.

In terms of after-death experiences, my dream followed the pattern of a classic dream visitation. It was an attempt to communicate coming from something outside of myself.[3] While ordinary dreams usually require inter-pretation, the classic visitation-dream conveys a simple and direct message. My dream of Christine fit these characteristics. Of course, since the contents of my dream are not verifiable, it is possible to dismiss it as a product of my imagination. And yet, just as Christine used to squeeze my hand when some-one was singing off-key while I was oblivious, spiritual experiences are often apparent only to one with the sensitivity to feel them. Can someone with an atonal ear dismiss tonal variations as unreal, even if he can't hear them? Was Christine singing to me? She appeared only once in an after-death dream. This, too, is characteristic of the classic dream visitation. When I visited

Christine's grave, I spoke to her many times. Of course, she didn't answer me because she was dead. And yet, I felt she was listening.

NOTES

1. US Census Bureau, *Statistical Abstract of the United States: 2001*, 121st ed. (Washington, DC: US Census Bureau, 2001), p. 79, table no. 105, records a total of 42,300 deaths from breast cancer in 1997 in the United States. World Health Organization Statistics clarify that 41,943 of these were women. See http://www3.who.int/whosis/whsa/whsa_table1.

2. Certificate of death 61314, Christine Mungello, Bureau of Vital Statistics, Waco-McLennan County Public Health District, signed by Keith Horner, MD, December 22, 1997. See Shermin B. Nuland, *How We Die* (New York: Knopf, 1994), 27–28, 34.

3. Joel Martin and Patricia Rowanowski, *Love beyond Life: The Healing Power of After-Death Communications* (New York: HarperCollins, 1997), 35–45.

Chapter Twenty-Two

Lies, 1998–2015

Life moves on. I ordered a granite angel copied from an original in Venice for Christine's grave. It was sculpted in China and took six months to arrive. The angel is carrying flowers and reminds me of how Christine looked on our wedding day. Every Saturday for eight years I visited her grave and left a red rose. My grief dissipated slowly, but it left an emptiness in my heart. And as irrational as this may sound, I was angry with her for leaving me alone.

Our twin grandsons were born in April 1998, four months after Christine died. One (Jordan David Pflum) weighed almost six pounds and was fine, but the other (Dylan George Pflum) weighed only three and a half pounds and had to stay in the hospital for two weeks more. He looked incredibly tiny and my daughter became frantic, rushing back and forth between the one twin at home and the other in intensive care, trying to satisfy the hospital's calls for more breast milk. Despite that, both grew and are healthy. They have since been joined by two younger brothers and a sister.

One day I heard from my brother-in-law. He had just attended the sixtieth birthday party of Dinah (née Grey, formerly Prentice) Wiley who years ago had sung with Christine and her brother in the Al McKegg Trio. The party was given by a younger woman named Lynn (and here it gets a bit complicated). Patrick, the best man at my wedding, had left Dinah years before for Lynn. But more recently, Patrick had left Lynn for a still younger woman. Dinah had become Lynn's consoler and confidant and, in return, Lynn gave her a birthday party. In some ways, the years had not changed Patrick and Dinah at all.

I did not become aware of Carl's death until ten years after he was gone. When Christine fell ill and began her slow descent to the end, I did begin to wonder what had happened to him and I looked for any reference to his name in the gay media. Eventually, I read that he had died of AIDS in 1986. As I learned more about his death, I was struck by the striking symmetry in how Carl's and Christine's lives have intersected with my own. The only two people I had ever loved outside of my family both died from two of the most terrible illnesses of the twentieth century. I hadn't caused their deaths, but I had been close to each of them in the most physical and sensual ways. And the reason one relationship lasted less than three months and the other thirty-two years is because the only way I could love two people with such intensity was that one of them had to become a secret of my heart.

In the spring of 2004 I learned that God has a sense of humor: I was diagnosed with prostate cancer. A routine PSA test led to a second test eight months later and indicated that my PSA score had doubled (a bad sign). A biopsy followed. Since I had not known of any prostate cancer in my family, I was surprised. I had always thought that I would die, like so many members of my family, of heart problems.

The prostate is a puzzling thing. How could such a little gland (normally the size and shape of a chestnut) that performed no essential function cause such major problems? Like most men having routine physicals, I had bent over and gritted my teeth during the routine digital examination of my pros-tate. It was an uncomfortable experience and I always found it puzzling when men who liked being bottoms in anal sex told me just what a source of ecstasy the prostate was. Although I never experienced that ecstasy, I did find out just how troublesome this little gland was.

Something called a Gleason Scale (1–10) is used to rate the rising serious-ness of the malignancy in tissue samples from a biopsied prostate. Mine was a 7 (intermediate), which called for prompt treatment. The options were surgery, external beam radiation, or radioactive seed implants. At first I shied away from surgery because of the danger it carried of sexual impotence. Although nerve-sparing techniques had been developed, my reading of testi-mony from men who had undergone the surgery indicated that erectile dys-function was chronic. In addition, I was appalled to learn that shrinkage of the penis was a common postsurgical problem. (There are not many greater horrors for a man than having his penis shrink.) Some urologists claim that the shrinkage is a myth, and, anyway, they tend to be so focused on dealing with the cancer, that they usually avoid mentioning these problems in ad-vance.

Although very worried about impotence, I was oddly detached about the cancer itself. Consequently, I was able to see that for my age and condition, surgery was the best option. In order to find an experienced surgeon, I re-turned to the site of Christine's cancer treatments, MD Anderson Cancer Center in Houston, even though its halls were haunted for me with memories of her suffering.

I had a bilateral nerve-sparing radical prostatectomy early on the morning of July 9, 2004. Surprisingly detached, I took off all of my clothes, put them in the plastic bag provided, got onto the gurney, and was wheeled away. I don't remember anything about the surgery. The two-day postsurgical stay in the hospital was memorable only for the fact that my three grandsons were allowed to visit me. They climbed onto my bed and played so much with my automatic bed that I felt like a pretzel when they left. The real problems began when I returned home to Waco.

I have often thought how fitting it is that the most serious illness of my life should wound me in that particular area of my body. Had someone somewhere in heaven written a script to fit me? Sex had been the driving force in my life. It was as if all the good and bad of my life had been concentrated in the physical core of my sex drive and then I was stricken with this particular possibly life-threatening illness.

For those unfamiliar with the side effects of a radical prostatectomy, they are considerable. Because the seminal vesicles are also normally removed in this surgery, orgasms thereafter are strangely dry and infertility results. The idea that I still had the power to conceive a child was stripped away. Urinary incontinence also typically follows surgery and it recedes only gradually (and sometimes never). I wondered how I could lecture to a class of students if their concentration was diverted by the growing wet stain on my pants? I had to wear the male version of female sanitary napkins. I had to laugh while changing my diaper.

Still, all of this I could deal with, as well as the lack of strength. Ten weeks after surgery I was back in the exercise room lifting weights and using the running machine. The one thing I could not deal with was the lack of erections. Erectile dysfunction (ED)—sometimes temporary, sometimes permanent—is an almost inevitable result of this surgery. The lack of erections during convalescence produces a fibrosis that, even if it doesn't cause the penis to shrink, certainly can cause it to acquire a permanent bend (Peyronie's disease). In order to combat this, I was given an EVD (erection vacuum device) that I used faithfully every day. The artificial erections created by the EVD were about as erotic as trying to have sex while cleaning the black wax out of one of my Labrador Retriever's ears. In addition, I was to take mega (100 mg) doses of Viagra either once a week or every other day, depending on whether I was listening to the male urologist or the female ED consultant at MD Anderson. After a year, things began to return to normal. Well, almost normal, but I survived.

I once asked a philosophy professor in a college where I once taught if they still tried, like the ancient Greeks, to search for the True, the Good, and the Beautiful. He replied, "Of course not." How sad. The search for Truth, Goodness, and Beauty has been what my life has been about. The reader may laugh: how could this guy who had sex with a thousand partners have been searching for anything but a quick thrill? Good question. I didn't find Truth,

Goodness, and Beauty with any of those thousand partners. I found it with Christine and Carl.

And yet what I just wrote is not completely honest because there is more. My search eventually led me to a less admirable truth. While I was searching my past and discovered the extent of my father's dishonesty, I was being forced by my son's drug addiction to confront his dishonesty. Ever since he had been a little boy, Michael had told minor fibs, but he never grew out of telling them. They just became more serious as he grew older.

It was not until after Christine died that I realized the full extent of his dishonesty. When he wanted to buy a small house, I helped by giving him the down payment. A year later he began having car accidents and was fired from his job at the local newspaper. It took me several more months to realize that he had become addicted to crack cocaine. Late one night while I was lying in bed worrying about him, I called him and he admitted that he was addicted. That very night at 2:00 a.m., I drove to his house and brought him home. I thought I could help him, but in fact he was the only one who could help himself.

At about the same time I realized that he had been stealing from me—money and tools that could be pawned to buy drugs. I was devastated. He lost his house because he could no longer make the mortgage payments. After a few months, when I pressed him about the need to find a job and he indicated an interest in becoming a chef, I paid his fees and living expenses at a culinary institute in Austin. But he was still using drugs and developed a staph infection that required hospitalization and an infusion of a special antibiotic. He dropped out after one semester and returned to Waco. He entered my locked house through a window and made himself dinner. The drugs caused a wild fluctuation in his appetite. I refused to let him live with me again. When his auto loan financer threatened to repossess his car, I made payments on it. I learned that his car had been confiscated from some local drug dealers. Michael owed them money for drugs and he had loaned them his car to make drug deliveries as a form of repayment. He became paranoid and said these dealers were after him. One Saturday night when he was arrested on an outstanding warrant for an unpaid speeding ticket, I went to the jail and paid the fine so he could be released. I remember waiting at 3:00 a.m. in this ugly neon-lit room at the county jail for him to be released. A cockroach crawled out of the wall and across the cheap institutional-blue vinyl tile floor. I stepped on it.

Bill collectors and drug dealers called continually for Michael. I had my will rewritten so that his share of my estate would go into a testamentary trust that he would not control. I paid and paid what amounted to thousands of dollars, but my greatest concern wasn't the money. I worried endlessly about what would happen to him and would wake up in the middle of the night feeling frustrated and helpless. My greatest fear was that one day I would meet him on the street as a homeless man asking for money. Eventually, he got off the drugs (for a while) and found a respectable job, but then he backslid. His life totally collapsed and he came close to suicide. Once again, I took him in. I didn't understand my son because he was so rarely truthful to me in matters of the heart. I don't see how he can be happy if he doesn't have someone to love. He loved drugs.

I encouraged Michael to leave Waco to get away from all his drug contacts. In 2011 he moved to Dallas and worked for some Latino soccer organizers called the Tex-Mex Sports Federation. (He was good at picking up foreign languages and he was able to speak a lot of street Spanish through refereeing Latino soccer matches.) But that didn't last because he lacked the focus and motivation to become an effective salesman. He ended up refereeing soccer and falling into debt and taking more drugs. I sold him my car, which he never finished paying for. He proceeded to trash it through repeated fender-benders because of the drugs he was taking. He was arrested several times on minor misdemeanor charges involving unpaid traffic violation fines and inspection violations. He failed to stop in a hit-and-run accident.

In August of 2014 he was arrested for the possession of enough crystal meth in his car to constitute a third-degree felony. I refused to help him post bail because I felt he deserved to be in jail. At least I knew he would have a hard time getting drugs there. He was released from the Tarrant County jail after two months into probation. When I made the mistake of sending him a birthday check, he used it to buy drugs and violated the terms of his probation. At the urging of my brother Mark, an attorney in New Jersey who dealt with minor criminals, he turned himself in and was sent to a Texas Department of Corrections prison. I have to face the possibility that my son's self-destruction is a trait that, as in other Mungellos, runs in his blood and that he lacks the strength and willpower to overcome it.

I was struck by how this family trait of lying had resurfaced in my son (from my grand-uncle Filippo to my father to my son), but I thought it had skipped a generation (me). However, one day while I was fretting over my son's lies, I realized that I too had lied, not about money or drugs but about sexual fidelity. Did I have honor? Honor has two dimensions—an inner aspect (integrity) and an outer aspect (reputation). I can't defend my lies of infidelity to Christine. The fact that I felt guilt over them indicated that I felt they were indefensible. All I can say is that I tried to redeem myself when she was dying, and I believe I was given the gift of grace in doing so, that I was forgiven. But I had cheated her out of a having a more faithful husband.

Sexually I was a split person. The fluidity of my sexuality was not infinitely malleable. I could make love to my wife in order to fulfill my marriage vow and to conceive children, but my greatest passion was destined for men. Whether or not I had honor is an ongoing debate I will carry on until my death. What I learned of myself may not be admirable, but it is the truth to the best of my knowledge. It is the story of my life and of my family. I am responsible for what I have done and what I have done is to have found in my own measure and in my own time Truth, Goodness, and Beauty.

Chapter Twenty-Three

My Third Regret, 1972–2015

This is a dog story, and if you're not into dogs, it might not mean much to you. It is my third and final regret. When my family and I returned to Berkeley from our stay in Taipei in 1971, we were living on a second-floor apartment with a balcony on Ellsworth Street, near the Cal campus. Our good friend Jason Bishop found a stray puppy, a sweet little black Labrador Retriever-German Shepherd mix who wandered into his office and sat under his desk. He couldn't keep it and offered it to us. I love dogs and had grown up with them. I had always wanted a Lab, and so I jumped at the chance.

Of course, living in an apartment is not the best way to raise a Lab puppy because not only do they have tremendous amounts of energy that need to be worked off, but they also eat and defecate a great deal. I walked the pup twice a day and kept him on the porch where he proceeded to disgust us all by eating his poop. But we all have bad habits and nothing could have kept me from loving this dog. I named him Nicholas. Christine liked him, but she wasn't really passionate about dogs and so he was really more my dog than hers. I spent a lot of time with him and he responded well to my training. He was smart.

When I finally passed my oral comprehensives, we moved to my brother-in-law's place in the Maryland countryside and took the dog with us on the plane. He loved the countryside and he especially liked the walks we would take every day to the pond in the center of the village. In the summer he would retrieve sticks out of the water and in the winter, he would retrieve balls, sliding across the frozen ice. He loved the cold weather. When we left Maryland to go to Hong Kong for a year, my brother-in-law kept him. When we returned, I was overjoyed to see Nicholas again and we took him off with us to Mahopac, New York. We had big yard in Mahopac, although it was not the Maryland countryside and sometimes Nicholas would wander. I was very strict with him about leaving the yard and we butted heads over it.

Then after three years in Mahopac, Briarcliff College closed and I went through this difficult period of unemployment. I had a lot of free time and sometimes when I was caring for my little boy Michael, we would take our lunch into the woods not far from our house for an adventure. It was just the three of us—my son, Nicholas, and me. But when the opportunity to go to Germany came, I had to make a decision about Nicholas. Giving him away (which some people euphemistically call "finding a good home for the dog") was out of the question because I wanted him back when we returned in one or two years. But it is not easy finding someone to care for your dog for that long: either they don't really bond with dogs like my brother-in-law (and I couldn't possibly ask him to take the dog again, particularly since he had broken up with his wife), or someone does like dogs and bonds in a way that makes them reluctant to then eventually give the dog up. Debbie Sayre, the wife of my boyhood friend Blaine, loved dogs and was willing to take Nicholas. She and Blaine, who was a pediatrician, lived on a large farm in central Missouri, and this was perfect for Nicholas. Perhaps too perfect. I drove him to LaGuardia Airport and shipped him to St. Louis.

When we returned from Germany in the summer of 1980 and bought a house in Cedar Rapids, Iowa, our realtor gave us a pure-bred black Labrador female who was six months old and too hyperactive for his wife. I liked Miss Shadow, but never bonded with her the way I had with Nicholas. In the fall of 1980, my family and I made the trip to Missouri to visit Blaine and Debbie on their farm and ostensibly to retrieve Nicholas. It was—and you may not understand this unless you're a dog lover—one of the most poignant moments in my life: Would he remember me? He did! But he was so happy on that farm and Debbie was so attached to him that I decided not to bring him back to Cedar Rapids where we already had one large dog and a small backyard.

Christine was happy with my decision because she really did not want two large dogs, but it was a decision I have always regretted. Nicholas was my dog and I had betrayed a trust. No matter how good his new home was, I had abandoned him.

Later Debbie and Blaine divorced and Debbie went off to veterinarian school. She and their children moved to a suburban area in Oklahoma that was too confining for Nicholas. He kept escaping through the fence and wandering and one day he did not come back. She never knew what happened to him. Debbie was one of the sweetest people I have ever known and she loved that dog, and so I couldn't blame her for what happened; but I did blame myself. I felt that I had betrayed Nicholas. When we love something that lives and breathes, something that we can bond to, whether a human being or animal, what we love depends on us and trusts us. I sometimes wonder what Nicholas thought about me leaving him. I know that he was only a dog, but he was very smart and he did recognize me after being separated for two and a half years, so I'm sure he didn't forget me. It's not that he had a bad life, but still I felt that I had betrayed a trust and been disloyal.

When my family and I moved to Texas in 1994, we took Miss Shadow with us, but she was fourteen years old and feeling her age. When I saw an ad in the paper for Lab pups, I called. I guess I was looking for another Nicholas. They had one black male left. Christine and I went and wanted him as soon as we saw him. When we brought him home, Christine drove and the pup sat on my lap. She said he was full of fleas and wanted to bathe him right away, but that didn't matter much to me. I named him Herzog (German for "Duke") after the Herzog August Bibliothek in Wolfenbüttel, Germany, where I had been a research fellow in 1984.

Little Herzog's father had been a field champ and he trained beautifully. He had what Christine called a "work ethic" and he began bringing in the morning newspaper. I took him for walks every afternoon after work in a big intramural field nearby. I taught him to wait on one side of the street until I went over to the other side and called him. He never moved, even when cars passed between us. I also took him to a nearby marina, especially in the hot Texas summers, where he leaped high off a dock into the water to fetch tennis balls.

Herzog was so special that after Christine died and my grandsons were born, I decided to breed him so that my grandsons would have a special puppy. When the potential breeding dame owners were reluctant to give me the pick of the litter, I bought a female, a chocolate Lab whom I named Daisy. Five minutes alone with this dog will tell you why I named her Daisy. She was a beautiful airhead. Daisy and Herzog eventually bred (I think I looked out the kitchen window to see the moment of conception) and she gave birth to a litter of eight pups on January 15, 2000, her second birthday.

Watching Daisy birth those pups was a moving experience. As each one came out, she would lick it into consciousness and swallow the placenta. A ninth pup was not completely formed and when it did not respond to her licking, she swallowed the whole pup and placenta together. She produced four blacks, two chocolates, and two yellows. Only two of the eight were females. I gave my daughter her pick of the litter and she chose one of the yellows, the lightest-colored one. I decided to keep the other yellow. Daisy was a superb mother and nursed and licked her pups diligently, and when weening time came, I took over. At eight weeks I began to sell them, but I had difficulty saying goodbye. After one negligent buyer caused one of the pups to be killed, I decided against dropping the price for the last one for fear of attracting another negligent owner. So although I originally wanted to keep only one pup, I kept two. I wouldn't abandon another dog.

Later my son, overwhelmed by drugs and unemployment and lies, dumped his dog on me. It was a stray Lab mix without papers. She was cute (though not beautiful), sweet, and timid. She would cringe whenever I walked by her, and I guess that she had been mistreated as a puppy. Michael named it after his mother, Christine. I was not too happy about caring for a fifth dog and when someone reliable asked to take her, I thought about doing it. But I finally decided that I just didn't feel right about giving her away. She wasn't a cute little puppy anymore and at eight months of age, she would not bond as well as she had earlier. I can't betray a trust to an animal again, and that's how I ended up with five Labrador Retrievers.

I loved them all, but there was one favorite. He was a big brute of a Lab, a yellow who was both an alpha male (who sometimes growled at even me) but also the most affectionate of all five. His name was Koenig (German for "king"). He had his daddy's work ethic and wanted to please. He fetched the ball with enormous enthusiasm, and his big square build made him look like a tank racing across the grass. He was always eager to be petted. I looked into his golden-colored eyes and felt warm all over. As he aged, I made plans to continue the line. I bought a female (small and fast to counter Koenig's cumbersomeness) whom I named Lady. I bred her with Koenig, and Lady gave birth to six yellow Labs. I kept one who grew into a beautiful and strong—if a bit hyperactive—dog named Bruno who watched and followed my every move. He became my new alpha dog and my loyal companion.

Bruno was a little smaller than his father Koenig, but faster and certainly more energetic. Bruno's temperament was sweeter and I can never imagine him growling at me. He always lies at my feet. But he and his father were too much alike in their alpha tendencies. At first Koenig dominated Bruno, but as they aged, the dominance shifted. At thirteen years of age Koenig developed hip dysplasia and had increasing difficulty getting up. Eventually I had to lift him from behind to help him and he was no small dog. Defecating became a problem for him.

Putting a dog down has been one of the most wrenching decisions of my life. The process involves two injections, administered by a veterinarian. The first is a tranquilizer and the second causes the dog to stop breathing. The decision of when to do this is rarely clear-cut. One hopes for clear indications that it is time. I got them clearly with Koenig's mother and brother when they stopped eating, but Koenig did not stop eating. He wanted to live and he wanted to eat on the very last day of his life. I started crying the moment I raised the back door of my hatchback and lifted him in for his last ride to the vet. His weight had fallen from 100 to 80 pounds. He was a shrunken form of his previous self except for his head, which retained the original large and noble shape. It was a trip to the vet's that I don't want to remember, but I do remember the last hug I gave him as he lay on the vet's table. I still get upset thinking about it. Koenig's death was more difficult than my wife's death in one way because I did not make the decision of when Christine died. But I had to decide when to end Koenig's life. I hate playing God.

I often wonder if Vesuvius will erupt again in my lifetime. But whether it does or doesn't, it will continue to smolder beneath the surface, if not in my blood then in the blood of my grandchildren and their sons and daughters, firing their passions, loyalties, lies, and dreams. On July 4, 2015, I held my newest grandson, Holden Charles Howard, in my arms. Blood of my blood, we flow on.

Index

41808519R00159

Made in the USA
Middletown, DE
23 March 2017